He Hath Not Let Me Die!

From Ashes to Life

Sam Domb

"The Lord has chastised me severely;
but He hath not let me die."
Psalms 118: 18

Sam Domb

He Hath Not Let Me Die!

From Ashes to Life

Researched and Written By:
Gershon Stav

Hebrew Language/ Text Editor:
Yehudit Schwartz

Translated into English By:
Nachama Kanner

English Editor:
Yael Unterman

Sam Domb

He Hath Not Let Me Die!

Jacket Design: Yariv Stav

Graphic Design: Diza Noyman

Production: Hauser Printing Ltd.

Printed in Israel, 2012

ISBN: 978-965-91838-1-4

ACKNOWLEDGEMENTS

Writing this book was no easy task. Reconstructing the difficult times I experienced made it even harder. With the work completed, I wish to thank all those who lent their assistance in overcoming this challenge:

First and foremost, my sister Zipporah, whose unflagging support helped me survive childhood, and who sustained me as I embarked on a new life in the United States. Zipporah refreshed my memory and added many important details throughout the writing of the book. I thank her from the bottom of my heart for all her sage advice.

I am indebted to my friend Gershon Stav, who researched and wrote this book from a place of profound identification with its contents. With dedication and endless patience, he heard my tale, made my words come alive with credibility and professionalism, and checked sources and testimonies which completed the puzzle. For this I am deeply grateful to him.

My compliments to Mrs. Yehudit Schwartz, language and text editor of the Hebrew book, whose professional wisdom, sensitivity, thoughtful comments and discerning eye contributed to the content and special nature of the book.

Special thanks to Mrs. Marta Goren, author and Holocaust researcher, who devoted time and provided much assistance in the initial stages of writing the book. We thank her for sharing her extensive knowledge, the fruit of her many years of researching the Holocaust.

I appreciate the help of Mr. Oded Yedaya, headmaster of the "Minshar for Art" college, in obtaining critical information for the chapter "Hanitah."

I am very grateful to the Hanitah Wall and Tower Museum and its director, Mr. Yoel Gozlan, for welcoming us to the museum and permitting us the use of its archives.

Special thanks to the translator, Nachama Kanner, whose professional talent helped convey the content and spirit of the Hebrew text in its English version. I also thank the English editor, Yael Unterman, whose cooperation and skillful editing helped complete this work.

My sincerest thanks and appreciation to my family: my children Ron, Jay, and Michelle, and my grandchildren Morielle, Tomer, Adam and Sara, and to my late wife's family, the Siri family, in Israel and around the world.

In conclusion, I wish to express my deepest gratitude to Orly Gal, my life partner, who contributed to the efforts involved in preparing this book, for her insightful wisdom and, not least, for her years of patience and support.

May they all be blessed.

Sam Domb
Kislev 5773

Monument in Bat Yam cemetery in memory of the Pultusk martyrs killed in the Holocaust

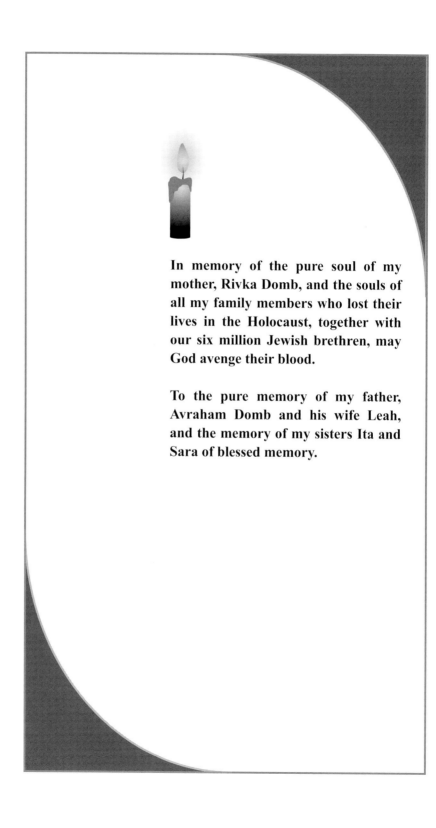

In memory of the pure soul of my mother, Rivka Domb, and the souls of all my family members who lost their lives in the Holocaust, together with our six million Jewish brethren, may God avenge their blood.

To the pure memory of my father, Avraham Domb and his wife Leah, and the memory of my sisters Ita and Sara of blessed memory.

Table of Contents

Yona Metzger

Chief Rabbi of Israel
President of The Chief Rabbinic Council

יונה מצגר

הרב הראשי לישראל
נשיא מועצת הרבנות הראשית

בס"ד, ג' סיון, תשע"א
5 יוני, 2011
ספח/-777.עא

<u>מכתב ברכה</u>

לרגל הוצאת ספרו המרתק "ולמות לא נתנני" של ידידי הדגול מר **סם** שלום **דומב** הי"ו הנני לבוא בזה בדברים מועטים, לתפארת המחבר הנכבד, ולכבוד סיפור חייו המיוחד.

חשתי התרגשות רבה בקראי את הספר. שכן, מאורעות חייו של סם היקר, הם בבואה נאמנה של הנאמר **באיוב** [ח', ז'] "והיה ראשיתך מצער ואחריתך יִשְׂגֶּה מאד". צער ויגון ליוו את ראשית חיי המחבר כאשר כבר בילדותו חש על גופו באכזריות את זוועות מלחמת העולם השניה. סם טעם מלא חפניים מנחת זרועה של "ההיה הנאצית" הארורה, הוצרך לברוח ולהטלטל בדרכים לא דרכים, ברעב ובצמא, להסתתר במרתפים ובנקיקי סלעים, ביערות ובחולות, מתחת לגשרים ובין עשבי התירס, במצור במצוק ובחוסר כל, שתה את כוס התרעלה עד תומה, כאשר אמו ע"ה הי"ד נורתה בראשה כשהוא אחוז בזרועותיה, רגע אשר הותיר את חותמו המר על נפשו הרכה וצרב ככויית אש את אישיותו החזקה, כל ימי חייו.

כל שנות הזעם כאשר חרון אף ה' שלט בעולם, מחוץ תשכל חרב ובחדרים אימה, הכל בוער בדם ואש, ותמרות עשן, קיים הקב"ה במחבר את דברי הנביא **יחזקאל** [ט"ז, ו']: "ואעבור עליך וארך מתבוססת בדמיך ואומר לך בדמיך חיי". לאורך כל התקופה הקשה, ה' עמו להצילו בדרכים מופלאות על ידי שליחי ההשגחה. נתקיים בו הפסוק **בתהילים** [כ"ג, ד']: "גם כי אלך בגיא צלמות לא אירא רע כי עתה עמדי". אכן לאחר המלחמה, זכה להיפגש שוב עם אביו ואחיותיו. כאוד מוצל מאש זכה לצאת משואה לתקומה, לעלות לארץ ישראל, לגור בה תקופה, להקים משפחה ולתרום לבניין הארץ ולדאוג לביטחונה אף בחו"ל.

כל זה הוא סיפור ראשית המצער. בארבעים השנה האחרונות סם גר בניו יורק, ה' הטוב אשר היה עמו להצילו בעת צרה, שגשג אחריתו מאוד. שם ראה ברכה בעמלו ועשה חייל באופן מופלא. "ויגדל האיש מאוד וכל אשר הוא עושה ה' מצליח בידו".

אף הוא השיב אהבה אל בוראו מטובו, ומשתמש באונו ובהונו להיות מעמודי התווך של הקהילה היהודית בארה"ב, לקרב בפעולות שונות וייחודיות את צעירי יהודי אמריקה אל נועם אור היהדות. בתבונתו ובנועם הליכותיו השכיל לקשור קשרים אמיצים עם ראשי השלטון בישראל ובאמריקה, ולהעמיד קשרים אלו לטובת מדינת ישראל ולכל יהודי באשר הוא.

עתה רחש לבו דבר טוב, להעלות עלי ספר את תולדות חייו. בספר חשוב זה אשר בשם "ולמוות לא נתנני" ייקרא, ברצותו לפתוח שערי שערי צדק, לבוא בם, להודות לה' על חסדו עמו לאורך כל שנות חייו.

על כן הנני לברכו ולאמצו מעומק ליבי, כי יוסיף ה' חיילו לשנות חיים ארוכים מתוך בריאות איתנה, למען יוכל להרבות עוד פעלים לתורת ישראל, עם ישראל וארץ ישראל. ויהי רצון שיקויימו בו דברי דוד הנעימים בתהילים: "עוד ינובון בשיבה דשנים ורעננים יהיו להגיד כי ישר ה' צורי ולא עוולתה בו", וכן "והיה כעץ שתול על פלגי מים... וכל אשר יעשה יצליח", אמן כן יהי רצון.

מוקירו בכל לב בברכה בהערכה ובידידות רבה,

יונה מצגר
הרב הראשי לישראל

הכנסת
THE KNESSET

Dr. UZI LANDAU

Member of Knesset

ד"ר עוזי לנדאו

חבר הכנסת

יקומו ויספרו לבניהם

המעלעל בפרקי הספר, בעיקר בשערו הראשון, יתרשם ממודעותו ההיסטורית העמוקה של המחבר, ומהצורך לספר ולתעד בעיני נער דרך חווייתו האישית את הטרגדיה הנוראה שפקדה את עמנו, השואה, "למען יידע דור אחרון", כמצוטט בהקדמה לספר.

הזיכרונות שעולים ומציפים את עולמו של שלום סם דומב, גם לאחר יותר מיובל שנים של הדחקה ושכחה, מביאים בפנינו את סיפורו האישי המרתק. סיפור זה הוא גם סיפורם הטרגי של משפחתי, של קהילתו ושל עמו.

עוד חיים בקרבנו שורדים מימי התופת ההם, וכבר קמים לנו מכחישי שואה, ובהם "מנהיגים" ידועי שם ו"אנשי אקדמיה". את כזיביהם האנטישמיים הם משמיעים בשם חופש הדיבור, מעל במות של המתורבתות במדינות, ומאמריהם מתפרסמים במוסדות אקדמיים ובאינטרנט חובק העולם.

סם דומב, כמי שחווה על בשרו את מוראות השואה, מתייחס בספרו לתופעה זו ומתריע בפניה. בסיפורו חייו כאן, נחשפים לראשונה פרטים על חוויות האימים שחווה במהלך מלחמת העולם השנייה, האימה שבמלחמות, חוויות שהשפיעו ללא ספק על עיצוב דמותו ועל השקפת עולמו של סם הילד.

מבין דפי הספר עולים זיכרונותיו מעולם יהודי תוסס ויצירתי שנמוג בעשן המלחמה. שליש של עם נכחד, ברוע ובשנאה שטרם נודעו כמותם בהיסטוריה האנושית. הוא הושמד באש המלחמה, בכדורים ובקתות רובה, בעשן כבשני אושוויץ, טרבלינקה, מיידנק ובוכנוולד, ביערות אירופה ובבורות המוות.

סיפורו הפרטי של סם מקפל בתוכו את ההיסטוריה של עמנו, בדור השואה והתקומה. הוא עלה ארצה מאירופה בתום המלחמה כנער ניצול שואה וגדל בה, תחילה בקיבוץ חניתה שעל גבול הלבנון, ואחר כך ברעננה שבשרון, התגייס לצה"ל והשתתף במלחמת "סדאי". נסיבות הימים ההם הביאו אותו לארה"ב, שם חי כיום. הוא אינו רק איש עסקים מצליח, אלא גם אחד ממנהיגיה הבולטים והפעילים של הקהילה היהודית בניו יורק.

סם חברי לעולם אינו שוקט על השמרים. הוא מקדיש חלק ניכר מזמנו, ממרצו וממממונו להנצחת זיכרון השואה, לתמיכה בפעולות חינוך יהודי ולשימור מורשת ישראל. כציוני גאה הוא שוקד בכל הזדמנות על טיפוח התמיכה בישראל בארה"ב ובעולם, ונאבק ללא פשרות בכל המנסים לערער על זכות קיומה של מדינת ישראל, כמולדת העם היהודי.

הישרדותו כנגד כל הסיכויים של סם הנער, כמו גם אישיותו הייחודית, והישגיו הנכבדים האישיים כיהודי-ישראלי בוגר, הם תשובה לצורר הנאצי של אז, ולצוררי ישראל דהיום. המאבק נגד על חיינו ועל חירותנו נמשך גם בדורנו זה. הספר שלפנינו הוא העדות לכך, לנו ולדורות הבאים אחרינו. על זאת, ועל פועלו למען העם היהודי ומדינת ישראל – תבוא עליו הברכה.

Introduction

And You Should Tell Your Son

"That the generation to come might know them,
the children who should be born;
who should arise and tell them to their children."

Psalms 78:6

Every Jewish boy and girl is familiar, from an early age, with the story of
the Exodus from Egypt. This wonderful story from our heritage, telling
of Jewish redemption, is perpetuated through the holiday of Passover,
which has been celebrated for many generations. The story is recounted
in the *Haggadah*, which is read each year in family gatherings on Seder
night in accordance with the instruction: "And you should tell your
son."

Among the prominent Jewish holidays symbolizing important
historical events in the Jewish people's life and preserving them
throughout the generations are Passover, *Hannukah*, *Purim*, and recently
Israel Independence Day; as well as, in contrast, the Fast of *Av*. But it
seems that another historical event, one of traumatic upheaval for our
people and for all of human history, which occurred over fifty years ago
and saw the destruction of over one third of the world's Jews, has not yet
been properly incorporated into our nation's legacy. Although official
Holocaust memorial days exist in Israel and worldwide, an accepted
"Haggadah" relating what transpired and permanently inscribed in
our nation's heritage has not yet been written. Such a commemoration
exists historically in the *Eichah* lamentations of the Fast of *Av*, or even
in the brief pledge every groom makes in memory of the destruction of
the Holy Temple when he breaks the glass under the wedding canopy:

"If I forget Thee O Jerusalem, may my right hand wither."

Of particular urgency in an era when renewed Holocaust denial exists even in democratic and "cultured" countries, everything must be done to maintain the enduring memory of the Holocaust, both for our people and for the world at large. This obligation of perpetuation rests, first and foremost, upon those who experienced the horror – the dwindling number of Holocaust survivors – and, of course, on the Israeli authorities, on the heads of Diaspora Jewish communities and on international organizations.

Post-Holocaust works of testimony and memorial, such as this book of mine, are the most effective response to those who wish to blur the scope of our people's destruction. Remembering the past is important if we, indeed, can successfully learn its lessons for the future.

Over the generations, our life in exile was filled with religious persecution and deportation, humiliation, and hatred towards our people, its religion and its heritage. Today, this hatred is expressed in increasing anti-Semitism, anti-Israel resolutions, anti-Zionism and racism on the international stage. This situation teaches us, the generation of Holocaust and Rebirth, that we must jealously guard our Hebrew state. We must do everything to ensure that "Never again" is an oath that is honored, and not just an empty slogan.

Two fundamental days of destruction stand out in our history: The destruction of the first Temple in 586 B.C.E. and that of the second, in 70 C.E. The establishment of the State of Israel, the memory and lessons of the Holocaust – in the sense of "Remember what *Amalek* did unto thee, thou shalt not forget" (Deuteronomy 25:17) – the striving for internal unity, and the development of Jewish defense forces, will guarantee that a third destruction will not occur.

The story of my life unfolding in the pages of this book is but one narrative in an ocean of events experienced by survivors like myself. This is my personal story, told in accordance with the instruction, "And you should tell your son." May this book stand as a tribute to the memory of the soul of my mother (May God avenge her blood), and the souls of members of my family and community who, pure in life and holy in death, were exterminated; as well as a monument for my children and grandchildren, who should know what happened to our people in the hell of the Holocaust. I also present here the account of my personal rebirth, interwoven with that of the Jewish people who achieved liberation of their homeland and established a Hebrew state and Hebrew army after two thousand years of wandering and suffering.

In post-war Germany, survivors and refugees were referred to as "the surviving remnant of the nation." I do not know who coined this phrase. In Israel I first heard the expression "Holocaust survivor" in the kibbutz and in the new immigrant camps; it eventually became widely used. On the radio and in the print media, it was used in its plural form: "Holocaust survivors." The more I matured and reflected on it, the more discomfort I felt upon hearing how common it had become. If those who used the phrase only knew what lies behind it – fear, cold, suffering, wandering, helplessness, acts of courage, martyrdom, the battle to survive, orphanhood, humiliation, face-to-face encounters with death – then the attitude toward the phrase itself, the survivors and the entire topic of the Holocaust would certainly change. Perhaps this might lead to a better understanding of the subject, to greater consideration, and possibly even to a sense of holiness.

Even now, after more than fifty years, I do not find the words to express my feelings and describe the traumatic experiences of those days. I am trying to convey the intensity of the word "fear," but it is impossible. I've perused dictionaries in various languages, searching for a sentence or phrase that could portray the concept of "fear" as I felt it then – but to no avail.

For many years, I've had the feeling of being inside a hazy

bubble, unable to pinpoint the events I experienced on an exact timeline. The images float up from an indefinable reservoir, and, along with them, a storm of emotions, a legacy of the Nazis' unfathomable acts of horror. I attempted to focus my thoughts on those days. Pictures and details arose as out of a fog, as if they were etched onto my brain cells, like a hard disk that had to be reactivated.

In writing these lines, I tried to dredge up names, facts and numbers from the depths of my memory, which has certainly faded over the years. This was no easy task. Childhood images and events emerged, but I do not know to what extent they are realistic or how much they might be the result of the vivid imagination of a boy who underwent such terrible experiences. This is a boy whose mother was murdered in cold blood by Nazi troops – in front of his very eyes.

The story presented in this book relating to the period of the Holocaust and World War Two, is based primarily on my memory of my ordeals from age five until age thirteen, as well as testimony I heard from my father, sisters and others. In my attempt to reconstruct the events and create as true a picture as possible, I created a chronological analysis of what had transpired. I also cross-checked the information at my disposal with various sources and with testimony I had heard or read about.

After seventy years, perhaps the wounds on my hands, feet and other exposed parts of my body have healed, but the wound in my heart continues to bleed and will never heal, it seems. Many changes have occurred in the world since those days of horrible devastation befell our people and all humankind. New issues are at the forefront, and new dangers are looming. Life in our time is completely different from what it was during World War Two. The weaponry of that terrible war pales in comparison to nuclear developments and their deadly power. These new destructive capabilities are being directed into the hands of those who hate Israel and who pose an existential danger to the State of Israel and the entire world. It seems that our current concerns have drawn the veil of history over that period. Therefore, the memory of the Holocaust and its lessons are an important reminder to our people and to all the nations of the world about the future dangers on our doorstep.

My book is divided into three main sections: The first section includes the period of World War Two and the Holocaust, until my aliyah to Israel. The second details my life in Israel: on the kibbutz, in Ra'anana, my service in the Israel Defense Forces and for the State. The last section reviews my life in the United States – my family, my business dealings, my activities on behalf of the State of Israel and in the service of the Jewish community, in the United States and worldwide.

My wish is that this story of mine, together with tens of thousands stories, poems and essays that have been recorded, as well as those that have yet to be written, would lead to the birth of that very Haggadah – that of the generation of the Holocaust and Rebirth – whose time has come. And if this were to be embedded deeply in our nation's heritage and be retold from one generation to the next, perhaps its lessons would bring us to the final redemption.

Never Again!

Section I

Destruction

1939-1949

"...I said to you when you were in your blood, Live!
I said to you when you were in your blood, Live!"

Ezekiel 16: 6

Chapter 1

An Inferno of Explosions

"For God called up the slaughter and the spring together,
the slayer slew, the blossom burst, and it was sunny weather!"

"Be'Ir ha-Haregah" ("The City of Slaughter"), H.N. Bialik

I will remember that particular day, September 5, 1939, as long as I live. I was a little boy. The non-stop German shelling of my native city, Pultusk, Poland, had been going on for days. I sat trembling in fear with my sisters, huddled under a blanket in a corner of the room in my parents' home, trying to close my ears and shut my eyes to the noises and the flashes of the explosions. This is how we spent the entire day, with exploding bombs and the roar of planes in the background. My parents' and sisters' eyes spoke volumes; they radiated fear and desperation. Shells went off one after another, shaking the walls of the house. The screams and cries of both children and adults came from every direction.

On September 7, 1939, I heard the tank tracks and engines of the Nazi occupying forces' vehicles moving along the roads of Pultusk unimpeded. The Polish resistance collapsed and the Nazis took control of the whole city. No one guessed that the life of a vibrant Jewish community was about to be extinguished on that day. Within nineteen days, every trace of the existence of a city on the banks of the Narew River, steeped in green tranquility, was eradicated. One thousand years of Jewish life in Europe and the unique Jewish enterprise on that continent likewise ended.

The noise of the cars and trucks was deafening. I stood on my tiptoes, moved the curtain aside a tiny crack to see what was going on outside; and then, for the first time in my life, saw the face of *Ashmedai* (king of the demons), a round helmet on his head, wearing an SS uniform with a swastika on his arm. I also managed to see a little of the destruction sown by the bombings of the previous horrible day.

On that day, with the discerning eye of a boy who suddenly discovers a new reality, laden with fear of what was to follow, my battle for survival began. This battle was to accompany me for long years in forests and cities, camps and villages, winding roads and dirt tunnels. This struggle to survive encompassed the world's continents and has never ceased, even as these lines are being written. While it was my own personal struggle, it was also that of a member of the Jewish people.

It all began on September 1, 1939. Hitler ordered German forces to attack Poland without declaring war, thus, in effect, sparking the beginning of World War Two.

In those days of pre-war Poland, a considerable number of Germans lived in the towns and villages surrounding Pultusk. The provocative behavior of these Germans already signaled what was about to transpire. Hitler viewed Poland as a worthy *lebensraum* (living space) in which to advance his goals; as part of the plans he devised, his foreign minister Joachim von Ribbentrop was sent to Moscow to meet with his Soviet counterpart Vyacheslav Molotov. The meeting led to a non-aggression pact known as the Molotov-Ribbentrop Pact. The secret clauses of the agreement determined that in the event of war, Poland would be partitioned between the two sides. The ten-year pact was signed on August 23, 1938.

Although Germans were not seen in Pultusk until September 7, 1939, we already inferred their might from the heavy bombardment of the town. The Jewish community grew increasingly apprehensive, and its fears were, indeed, confirmed. The Nazi atrocities against the Jewish community commenced immediately upon the occupation of the city, hours after the invasion. The oppressors brutally crushed all civilized human values. It is beyond human comprehension to grasp why all the evils in the world suddenly descended, of all places, on Pultusk, a beautiful and enchanting town. How could a place so blessed by God with ancient splendor, where the Narew River flows and its many gushing tributaries criss-cross the city, now resonate with the cries of fear and disaster? How does a town adorned with surrounding pine forests, steeped in abundant green meadows, become a center of hell and terror overnight? In place of beauty and serenity, the Nazi monsters generated ugliness and evil. The air was filled with the shouts of the invaders and the noise of their vehicles:

"*Raus! Raus!*", "*Jude raus!*", "*Juden! Auf arbeit!*" (Out! Out! Jews, get out! Jews, go to work!)

Confused and frightened, we cowered inside our house. For where could we go? With every knock on the door, our pulses became more rapid, as if our hearts were being torn from our chests. The door burst open and Germans stormed into the house holding bayoneted rifles pointed in our direction. They shouted:

"*Raus! Jude raus!*" (Out! Jews, get out!)

They ordered us outside. I clung to my mother's dress, and our whole family was dragged into the courtyard in front of the house. We stood there for hours. Every minute that passed seemed like eternity. Along the street where we lived, Warszawska Street, we saw many Jews, old and young, standing in front of their buildings. Everyone was there: pregnant women, babies loudly crying, respected rabbis, elderly people who could barely stand on their feet. The wailing cries of babies and mothers intermingled with the shouts of the Nazis, who ordered the men to step out of the lines and be taken into forced labor. They took Father, too – we did not know to where. We returned home weeping in fear.

With the arrival of the Nazis in the city, the lives of the local Jews became untenable. Jewish property was torn from its owners. Without any consideration whatsoever, people young and old were cruelly snatched from their daily routine and conscripted by the

Germans for round-the-clock difficult, dangerous work. Decrees and edicts against the Jews were publicized: Bank savings were confiscated; Jews were forbidden to walk on the sidewalks; a strict nighttime curfew was declared.

As if the evils of the Nazis were not enough, many Poles, who had been considered long-time "friends of the Jews," joined the Nazis and lent their assistance to the discriminatory policy against the Jews. On more than one occasion, they even spread libelous rumors and created provocations that resulted in the murder of Jewish residents. The bodies were dragged into the courtyard of the Great Synagogue on Kotlerska Street and the Jews were commanded to bury them at once.

The regular patrols of the Gestapo in the city instilled sheer terror in the Jewish community. Every man they encountered was immediately seized for various types of forced labor, without pay of course, and he did not know when – or if – he would return home. Objections were not tolerated; refusing an order meant death. Every command was accompanied by merciless, bloody beatings. Rumors circulating in the city about the murder of one neighbor and the disappearance of another raised the level of fear and the sense of helplessness. The victims' names were spread by word of mouth.

They made Father report to work every day. He would leave early in the morning and return at nightfall, exhausted, crushed and depressed. Upon his return he would update us on what had transpired in town and the new Nazi decrees. He reported that the Germans had demanded of the rabbi of Pultusk, Rabbi Lowenthal of blessed memory, to immediately gather 20,000 eggs and 500 pairs of socks. This, after first torturing him, viciously beating and humiliating him. They also ordered him to sweep the streets in front of the community. It was a chilling scene that caused outbursts of weeping among the townspeople.

We spent the first weeks of occupation in this atmosphere of humiliation and terror, with our lives and property easy prey for the Nazi beast. Until the terrible day, Tuesday, September 26, 1939, the day before the eve of *Succot* (Tabernacles).

Father returned very agitated one evening, after one of those days of back-breaking work. He described the growing Nazi atrocities, which included beatings, debasement and cold-blooded murder. He told us about surprise searches of Jewish homes and the confiscation of money and property. Every day we heard additional names of Jews who had been shot to death.

Father also spoke about Jewish refugees who had arrived in Pultusk after being expelled from Nazi-occupied villages. They hid in the surrounding forests and in the courtyards and houses of Jews. The Germans appeared to have set about their conquests with a detailed and organized plan, repeated in every city and village they occupied. The refugees reported what had transpired in their villages, which was identical to what had taken place in Pultusk. The occupiers scurried about the city with precise lists and knew everything about the Jewish community. High on their lists were the names of prominent Jews in the town: rabbis, businessmen, lawyers, doctors, etc. These were the first to be arrested. The Nazis aimed to undermine the morale of the city's Jews by removing these key people. They compiled the lists with the aid of local collaborators and Germans who lived in the occupied areas.

Jews who innocently wanted to close their window shutters or courtyard gate in the evening were considered to have violated the curfew and were shot to death on the spot. The tales and rumors aroused terrible fear in us. Mother was strict about our not walking around the streets. She forbade us from leaving the house unless it was absolutely necessary.

One day, Father came home from his day of hard work, tired and perspiring, with news he had heard about England and France declaring war against Germany. On September 17th, there was a report on the radio that the Russians had gone to war and invaded Poland from the east. At the same time, rumors spread about the advance of German forces eastward and the atrocities of the Nazi soldiers against the Jews in every city and village that fell into their hands.

This was during the *Tishrei* (first month of Jewish calendar) holiday season. We had already celebrated *Rosh Hashanah* and *Yom Kippur*, and *Succot* was to begin in two days. An atmosphere of gloom pervaded our home and town, and there were no signs of holiday preparations. Everyone hid in their houses, frightened and terrified, waiting for what would come next. In ordinary times, the town was vibrant and full of life. Jews were busy with holiday purchases and everyone built a *succah* (holiday booth); people walked around with *lulavs* (palm fronds) and *etrogs* (citrons) in their hands, joyous with the approaching holiday; pleasant songs of prayer emanated from the synagogues. But now, under the Nazi axe wielded with such cruelty, these songs had been exchanged for heart-wrenching cries. A somber gloom settled on the city. Not a soul was visible in the streets. The town was dead. Here and there, a Jew was spotted running across the street, scared to death and pale as a ghost. Mother stood guard at the window, checking to see if SS men were approaching the house.

In this fashion we welcomed the *Succot* holiday in 5700/1939.

Chapter 2

Mother

"And no language of poetry exists that can articulate our tragedy on the written page"

Uri Zvi Greenberg

On the night of September 25, 1939, we waited for Father, who was late in coming home. None of us knew where he had been taken or for what purpose or when he would return. Night fell. My mother was gripped in fear and she took me into her arms. I was the youngest of the siblings. My oldest sister, Ita, aged twelve, tried to instill calm, embracing her two younger sisters, Sara and Zipporah. With tears in their eyes, they huddled together in the center of the bed near my mother. We awaited the unknown.

Heavy gunfire shattered the quiet of the night. Shots were heard at increasingly shorter intervals. Suddenly, the door opened and Father entered, exhausted and perspiring, a look of desperation on his face.

"The accursed Germans are slaughtering us mercilessly, cruelly and without cause," I heard him whisper to my mother.

Father went into the kitchen, seeking to satisfy his hunger. Afterwards, he joined us in bed. We lay in tense anticipation of the next day. The volleys of gunfire that echoed in the air were constant, not ceasing for a minute. Not one of us fell asleep during that night. We lay in each other's arms, drifting between sleep and wakefulness. Every attempt to close our eyes and sleep was interrupted by the sound of bullets and the roar of cars and tanks. It seemed as if everything was aimed at our house. With every burst of fire, my mother would embrace me more tightly. In the background, I heard my sisters' wails of fear.

Father tried unsuccessfully to soothe them.

The night dragged on. Every minute that passed seemed like eternity. Machine guns spat out fire in every direction and the noise was unbearable. Father occasionally opened the window a crack to let some fresh air into the room, taking deep breaths of air into his lungs, like a hospital patient desperate for oxygen.

A temporary lull prevailed for a moment, within the house and outside. It seemed as if we had fallen asleep when heavy blows struck our door, breaking the silence. Rifle butts banged heavily on the door and I burst out crying. My mother and sisters also cried. Father stood and covered us with his body. The door flew open and five armed Germans stormed into the room. With hate-filled looks, they dragged us from the bed calling "Out! Out!" We were pushed outside with their bayoneted rifles. The roars "Jew, get out! Jew, get out!" grew louder. Father wanted to take some items from the house, but was forbidden to do so. Prodded by the Nazi's bayonet, he was forced to leave empty-handed. Thus began our day – Tuesday, 13 *Tishrei* 5700; September 26, 1939.

They ordered us to march to the main street. We went up Warszawa Street with everyone, and from there joined the mass processions along Elaikes Avenue toward the park around the District House. The sight that greeted our eyes was shocking. Hundreds of Jews marched along the street, one family after another, all surrounded by armed German soldiers. Our family also joined the march to an unknown destination and an unknown fate.

The Germans pushed us into the line of marchers. Mother carried me in her arms, breathing heavily. Father was behind her, holding Sara's and Zipporah's hands. Ita walked to our right, her arm around Zipporah. Entire families continued to join the marchers along the way and the line grew longer. It now already included old and young, the ailing and the handicapped, pregnant women and children, babies and middle-aged men, rich and poor. Everyone marched. This strange procession was accompanied by the curses and shouts of the Germans. They beat the marchers without let-up.

The Jews were banished from their homes in the early morning hours. Most did not have time to get dressed or prepare anything to take along. Some were still in pajamas and robes; some were barefoot. The line of people grew longer and longer. Hundreds turned into thousands. Wails and shouts from babies and mothers were heard from all sides. Armed and threatening Germans marched along the sides of the road. They were careful to let no Jew escape. Whoever tried to leave the line was shot and killed. We passed several people whom we knew, lying dead. Their bodies were dragged to the side, their blood still flowing down the street. Nobody dared disobey the Germans. The crying mingled with the fear and became a din that the soldiers tried to silence, but to no avail.

Terrified, I buried my head in my mother's chest and tried to close my eyes. My mother's breathing became increasingly ragged from one minute to the next. It was hard for her to walk while carrying me. Her exhaustion was taking its toll. The march of terror reached the park at the foot of the ancient castle, not far from the Wishkov Bridge.

Upon reaching the park, we were ordered to relinquish all our valuables, including rings and jewelry. A thorough and embarrassing search was carried out on each and every Jew. All were forced to undress and anyone found hiding something of value was flogged in front of everyone and shot to death. The Germans did not overlook a single one of the thousands gathered there. For some reason, I clearly remember, as a boy, that there was a soccer field in this park. In any case, it was now crowded with humiliated Jews.

The Nazis' goal quickly became clear. They wanted Pultusk to be *Judenrein*, free of Jews. The entire Jewish population of the town was ultimately shoved into the park. The tumult was awful: the cries of babies mingled with the shouts of Jews being beaten and the groans of the sick and the elderly.

Toward evening, an order was given and the line of marchers was pushed out of the park with blows and shouts. It looked like a herd of animals being driven forward. We were to march toward the Wishkov Bridge, the wooden bridge that connected the two banks of the Narew River. Mother still carried me in her arms. My father and sisters dragged on from behind, and five Germans urged us along, beating us and stabbing at us with their bayonets. Amidst all the haste, the uproar and the fear, Mother tripped and fell on her face, with me in her arms. Father paused to help her get up, but was hit viciously by a Nazi who yelled at him like a madman. I couldn't understand what was being shouted in German. In the end, the Nazi aimed his weapon at Mother and shot her while she was still holding me. Her screams were bloodcurdling. My sisters and I set up a deafening wail. In a split-second decision, Father pulled me from Mother's arms, though I sobbed bitterly and held my arms out toward her, vehemently refusing to part from her.

Mother was shot to death by a Nazi monster, without reason and with absolutely no hesitation.

There are moments in one's life that can never be forgotten. They are engraved on the walls of your heart and become an inseparable part of your being. I went through many periods of suffering, depression and battles of survival in my life, but this one moment is buried deep in my heart and will never be erased from my memory. It is written in my mother's blood, on my arms still outstretched toward her, as in those terrible moments. Her heart-wrenching cries as she bled at the foot of the wooden bridge still reverberate in my ears. Not only did I hear her cries, I also *saw* her screaming voice.

It is written of the Revelation at Mount Sinai: "And the entire people saw the thunder" (Exodus 20:15). In the course of my life, I never understood how it was possible to see sounds; I was not present at the Revelation at Mount Sinai. But this time – I saw the sound, the sounds of my mother's screams. This is what remained with me of her. Not a photograph, nor a souvenir, only the sound of a heart-rending cry. And this I hear and see even now, many years after her murder. These are the sights and sounds that have accompanied me for my whole life, and it is they which have determined my character and my path in life.

We were forced to continue on our way, while being pushed and beaten by our "escorts." We traversed the bridge crying and broken-hearted, leaving Mother behind wallowing in her blood. Father plucked me from Mother's arms, lifted me up, and we continued to tramp along the bridge, together with my sisters. This was a journey of unadulterated suffering. Not satisfied with murdering Mother, the Germans continued to beat and snipe at us, while laughing derisively. Father covered me with his strong arms and pushed my sisters forward, as far away as possible from the whips and bayonets.

The Germans knocked off the hats of the Jews who passed in front of them, and threw them in the Narew River. Their shouts of glee were drowned out by the cries and wails of the marchers. A German officer standing on a jeep driving on the bridge called out to the Jews on a megaphone to hurry up and cross over. Those who couldn't maintain the necessary pace were shot and dumped into the stormy waters of the river. The first leg of the march of terror and the humiliation on the bridge had come to an end. We reached the other side of the river, and here were confronted by beastly shouted commands and beatings.

"Run to the Russians, your allies!" called out one of the Nazis, and another roared: "Jump into the water, filthy Jews!"

There was no time to look back. Night fell on the area and thousands of terrified Jews, who had been chased out of their homes, made their way into the unknown, beaten and degraded.

Starved, broken and exhausted, we reached a crossroads. Where should we go? The night's chill began to make itself felt. My whole body was trembling in fear, and now from cold too. My body craved food and water. It had been many hours since any food had entered our mouths. Along the way, we encountered families as unfortunate as we were, going nowhere.

Little by little, thousands of Jews gathered on the other side of the river. From everywhere came the calls of children looking for their parents and parents seeking their children. Women sought their husbands and vice versa. All were searching for acquaintances and relatives. People stumbled around amidst the confusion, clamor and sobbing, without knowing where they were going. And we, too, marched over there, to the pandemonium on the other side of the bridge.

It is impossible to put the sights we saw during those hours into words. As stated, dozens of Jews were thrown from the bridge into the river. Many were beaten and tortured for no reason. Others were shot to death in cold blood. Our senses urged us to flee as far away as possible from the fear and the horror. Many escaped to surrounding villages, to Avrita, Delogoshadla, Wishkov and other hiding places, in the hopes of eluding the Angel of Death.

Our family, however, had already suffered the Angel of Death's visit; we were horrified at having witnessed Mother's murder right in front of our eyes. Father decided that I, his only son, a small child, had to be saved at any cost. Thinking aloud, he decided that my sisters were sufficiently "mature and independent" to survive this period together with him. He deliberated about what could be done so that I, little Sholom, would remain alive. An idea occurred to him. He would hide me with his Polish friend, with whom he had business ties. The friend lived in one of the villages en route to Wishkov. Father decided to hide me there until the danger passed. He asked Ita to remain with my sisters in a hidden spot on the side of the road until he would return. He promised to come back as soon as he had delivered me to the Polish friend.

We endured several moments of terrible fear. My sisters cried bitter tears of utter anguish, wrapped their arms around me and refused to give me up to Father. Father had to forcibly remove me from their warm embrace. I choked on my sobs and my arms remained outstretched toward them for a long moment. For the second time on that same terrible day, I was torn from someone who loved me, from the human warmth and feminine love of the family.

Father was determined to save my life. The further we went, the more the sounds of my sisters' cries faded. Father disappeared into the darkness, with me in his arms. Along the way, we saw hundreds of families going eastward. Father left the main road where the masses were walking and started his hike through the plowed fields, toward his Polish friend's village.

Chapter 3

The Angel

*"For He will order His angels
to guard you wherever you go"*

Psalms 91:11

Father carried me in his arms and strode through the fields in the dark that led to the Pole's house. On the way he tried to reassure me, explaining that the Pole was his good friend and would watch over me. In the meantime, he and my sisters would search for a safe place to live. Father promised to come and get me as soon as matters were straightened out. The few garments I wore were not sufficient to keep me warm in the chill of the night. My legs were frozen stiff and I was barefoot, as the Germans had not given my mother time to put shoes on my feet. The path was filled with potholes and Father stumbled every few steps, and I too with him. The silent night and freezing cold were of no help in forgetting the shocking sights of the day, least of all that of my mother, murdered and left behind. I burst out crying again.

Father hugged me and whispered:

"Calm down, child, everything will be okay; behave like a big boy and be strong. My friend will watch over you. In the meantime, I'll search for a new place to live; and I promise to come and get you. Don't worry."

Father's voice cracked, tears choked him and he was deeply pained. German planes flew above and from all around came sounds of explosions. Father resumed walking and increased his pace.

The Pole's house was isolated and stood at the edge of plowed fields. Apparently, this was an agricultural area where various crops were grown. After hours of strenuous walking at night, through mud and furrowed fields, we arrived at the Pole's house. Father knocked on the door. The Pole, a tall man with a roundish face, dressed in work clothes, peered through the crack in the door and then opened it. They exchanged a few words and Father handed me over to him, though not before hugging and kissing me. In a voice choked with tears, he whispered into my ears:

"Don't be afraid, child, he will watch over you. I'll return for you very soon. Be strong and act like a big boy."

Father embraced me again and disappeared into the darkness. The Pole took me to a shed in his yard and told me that I would spend the night there. The door of the shed was open and I went inside. The Pole directed me to a staircase that led to a cellar where potatoes were stored, left me there and returned to his house.

I walked hesitantly to the corner of the cellar. There were other Jews there who had apparently also found haven with the Pole. Among those hiding was a young boy whom I estimated to be five or six years older than me. His face was visible in the dim light that penetrated the shed. He gestured to me, and in a calm voice invited me to sit next to him. I walked confidently over to him and did not hesitate to sit down there, as if we were old friends. He did not ask my name, just put his arm around my shoulders and said:

"Come closer, don't be afraid."

For some reason I felt safe. I tried to keep myself from crying, to control myself and not exhibit any signs of distress. The cold seeped in through my bare feet and caused my body to tremble. My new friend hugged me, brought a bit of straw and a rag he found there and covered my feet. To this day I do not know his real name and what happened to him. For ease of reference, I'll refer to him here as Michael. In any case, it seemed to me that the two of us were the only children in the cellar.

I tried to fall asleep, but do not recall if I succeeded. We sat this way, wordless in the darkness, that entire night. At first light, we heard from afar the noise of motorcycles and other vehicles approaching the Pole's house. It was a group of armed Germans. Through a crack in the shed, we saw Father's Polish friend speak with them and point to the shed in which we were hiding. Michael, who had apparently developed a special survivor's instinct, heard what was transpiring and whispered in my ears:

"The Pole is giving us up to the Germans."

I clung to him. He hugged me and grasped my hand tightly.

"It looks like they're about to take us away," he mumbled.

"Where to?" I asked. Before he managed to respond, we heard the screech of car wheels in front of the shed. Armed German soldiers jumped out and surrounded it. The Jews hiding there panicked and sounds of crying were audible. I did not cry, but was afraid. Now I discovered that other children were there, together with their parents. The horrible images of Pultusk resurfaced. Shouts of *"Juden raus! Juden raus!"* (Jews out! Jews out!) came from all sides.

The armed Germans burst into the shed. Roaring and poking us with bayonets, they seized everyone who had taken refuge and loaded all of us like animals onto a truck parked at the entrance. The military truck was too high for me to climb onto. One of the Nazi soldiers grabbed me by the waist and threw me into the truck as if I were an object, not a human being. I suffered a painful blow to my body. Michael came over to me and pulled me to his side. The Germans combed every corner of the shed and threatened to kill all of us if they found anyone who had not surrendered himself to them.

"I hope you weren't injured," I heard my friend whisper in my ears.

"My knees hurt a bit," I answered.

"Where are they taking us?" sobbed a woman standing next to me, holding her little daughter by the hand. The German soldier shouted at her, silencing all of us.

The Germans demanded that we crowd together and stay

close to each other. At the order of the officer in charge, the convoy of vehicles started moving to another house in the area, not far from that of the Pole, where they also searched for hidden Jews. Dozens more Jews were loaded onto our truck, among them men, women with babies and some elderly people. We traveled like this for several hours, transported like animals in trucks. The scene repeated itself at each and every stop along the way: searching for Jews and loading them onto the trucks.

The convoy was surrounded by jeeps with machine guns. The cruel armed guards did not hesitate to shoot and kill anyone who violated an order. After traveling a distance of several kilometers, the convoy stopped at the edge of a forest bordering an expansive corn field. The Germans commanded us to get off the trucks and form a line.

Surrounded by a guard of armed Nazis, we marched into the forest. Our blood froze from fear and cold, but on we went. Michael was in front of me and his hand did not let go of mine. When he thought I was about to fall, he pulled me toward him and steadied me. The shouts of the Germans in the forest mingled with the sounds of crying and the wails of the marchers. I wanted to ask my friend where they were taking us, but my tongue stuck to the roof of my mouth and I did not have the strength to move my lips. The Germans urged us on, poking us with their bayonets and hitting us with the butts of their rifles.

After about an hour of walking, we reached a clearing in the forest. The officer at the head gave a signal and the line of marchers was ordered to stop. Two jeeps with machine guns were positioned in one corner. The Germans arranged us in groups of ten. Michael and I were in the second group. The Nazis commanded the first ten to line up in the center of the clearing, dozens of meters in front of the jeeps. Suddenly, the German officer gave an order and the machine guns began to reap their harvest of death. Those shot at crumpled and dropped like felled trees, while their comrades screamed and howled. The cries tore through the forest. Those left knew that their turn would come.

I stood with my friend in the second group, ready to be

slaughtered. I was shocked by the scene. The blood froze in my veins. A mere thirty meters separated me from death. The German yelled at us to move forward to the shooting area. The wails of the women and cries of the children were heart-rending. While preparing to move, I felt a strong tug on my arm, accompanied by a whisper:

"Run after me quickly!"

Michael forcefully pulled me out of the line that was forming the next group and broke into flight in the direction of the forest's edge, the corn fields. He did not let go of me for even a moment. With his cleverness and agility, my friend managed to exploit the murderers' momentary delay while they stilled the Jews and positioned the jeeps at a better angle for shooting.

My friend ran, with me following, straight into the long, twisted rows of corn, far from the eyes of the Germans. I clung to him as to a magnet; the strength of our connection was amazing. I could not understand from where Michael drew such powerful strength. His palm gripped mine as if we were born attached. I was in a panic and an inner voice propelled me forward: "Run, lad, run!"

One of the German soldiers had noticed our escape. He chased us and tried to locate us, but the corn stalks were sufficiently tall to conceal us fully. The German fired several rounds at us. The bullets passed over our heads. My friend made me lie down among the corn stalks, bent over me and hid me with his body. For a moment it seemed as if Michael was sent to me as an angel from heaven in order to watch over me.

Eventually, the firing stopped and we saw the German retreating back into the forest. That day I began to believe in angels.

We were lucky that the corn stalks were taller than we were and afforded a safe hiding place from our pursuers. This was a very large corn field; most of its crop had been picked but not harvested, apparently due to the events of the war. Michael seized hold of my hand again and continued to run endlessly. Suddenly, he switched directions and went into the heart of the corn fields, to the forest's other edge.

While still running, we heard machine gun fire from the direction of the forest clearing. We understood that another group had been shot to death by the bloodthirsty Nazis. The barrages were accompanied by cries and heart-wrenching wails and, at the same time, a measured shout of men and women burst from the background:

"Shma Yisrael, Adonai Elohenu, Adonai Ehad!" ("Hear O Israel, the Lord is Our God, the Lord is One!")

Once again, we heard a barrage of machine gun fire, followed by another. The shooting stopped eventually. From then on we only heard the sound of voices repeating the *Shma* prayer, voices which rose and were swallowed by the darkened skies. I wondered about the meaning of these heart-breaking words that accompanied the persecuted Jews to their deaths….

The human slaughter was now completed. I felt as if my legs were moving while I remained glued in place. My bare feet began to bleed. I tried to slow my pace, but Michael persisted in running forward, pulling me after him into the rows of corn stalks without letting go of my hand. Sharp as razors, the branches sliced through our skin, tearing it to shreds. Our clothes were ripped into pieces, as if in mourning for our world that had been destroyed. My friend stopped for a moment, looked back and saw from afar that the convoy of German vehicles was leaving the area. Michael sat down on the ground, took a deep breath and announced:

"We are saved!"

He sat down next to me, his face lit up like that of an angel. He hardly spoke. His firm grip on my hand infused me with a feeling of security.

"We are saved!" he repeated, and did not let go of my hand.

Here, sitting on the ground in the midst of corn fields, I, the boy Shalom son of Avraham Domb, began for the first time to develop a survivor's instinct, with the assistance of my young friend – like a wild beast abandoned to its fate by its parents. Slowly, the realization that crying and wailing were of no value began to penetrate my awareness, and I realized that I would have to constantly seek means of survival, and to persevere.

With a sure hand, "my angel" led me to a hiding place at the other end of the forest, near the corn fields. Here we hid, in the shade of the trees of the thick grove. I lay down on my back and excruciating pains began to shoot through the soles of my feet. I looked at them; they were red with blood. While running in the corn fields and in the forest, I had apparently stepped on objects and thorns that broke through the skin of my feet. Only now did I begin to feel the pain that spread through my bleeding soles. Strangely enough, I did not cry and was not frightened, for "the angel" was watching over me.

The exhaustion and the events of the terror-filled days took their toll. I felt as if I was at the edge of an abyss. The horrors I had experienced were too unbearable. I lay down and fell into a deep sleep. I do not know how long I slept. When I opened my eyes, I saw Michael sitting next to me, his hand in mine. I tried to get up, but sharp pains radiated throughout my body. The hunger, thirst and pains did not ease up.

"You slept soundly," noted Michael. "It seems that you had many dreams. What is your name?" he asked for the first time.

"Shalom Domb," I responded and looked upward toward the tops of the surrounding trees. It was twilight, several minutes before sunset.

"Where are we?" I asked.

"In the forest, far from the Germans. Have no fear. I am with you and watching over you," he reassured me.

"I'm hungry," I said. "I want a drink."

"Me too," answered my friend, and gave me a big hug.

We sat huddled together in the forest for several long minutes, looking at the growing darkness enveloping us. Suddenly, Michael perked up his ears and whispered:

"I hear the sound of automobiles."

He stood up and lifted his head, strained his eagle eye and called: "Germans!"

The frantic run resumed, this time into the depths of the forest. To nowhere and to the unknown. Like a big boy, I rose to my feet. It was as if the pain had disappeared. I did as I was told by my older brother. I trusted him implicitly: he knew where he was taking me. To nowhere, but far from the accursed Germans who were chasing Jews like animals after their prey. We ran in the forest for hours. Darkness blanketed the area. We paused to catch our breath. Our ears finally caught the sound of trickling water.

"Water, do you hear? Water! We've reached the river," Michael whispered to me.

"Yes," I answered. My eyes lit up and my heart beat in joy, as if I was about to receive a long-anticipated gift.

I walked behind Michael in the direction of the flowing water. His hand was still in mine. It seemed as if our hands were glued to each other with some mysterious substance. This hand did not leave mine from the moment we met in the Pole's shed. Feeling our way in the dark, we reached the river bank and excitedly fell upon the water. We drank and drank without stopping. This was the first time water had entered my mouth since we had been expelled from our home in Pultusk.

We lay down on the river bank, apparently a tributary of the Narew, and looked up at the sky. My friend drew a little water with the palms of his hands and washed my bleeding feet. Sharp stabs pierced my feet. I gathered my courage and did not utter one groan of pain.

Strange sounds haunt the forest at night. Jackals howl, frogs croak, birds of the night call out to each other. I do not know how long we remained in the forest, but I became immune to the fear. I stopped being frightened. Only the thought of my father and sisters brought me back to the bloody visions in the public park near the bridge and to the image of my mother wallowing in her own blood. The brutal scene of rows of Jews being mowed down by the murderous Nazis' machine guns also kept coming back to me over and over. The sounds of *Shma Yisrael* repeatedly reverberated in my ears.... When such thoughts arose, I tried to distract myself by focusing on my immediate surroundings – the flowing water, nesting birds, the tall trees enveloped in fog and humidity.

The night sounds were interrupted by the thunder of explosions and shooting heard from afar, from the other side of the river. We walked in the dark along the river bank until we reached the bridge. Michael said that it was best for us to stop and look for a place to sleep under the bridge. Once again, his strong instinct did not disappoint. He led me to a narrow area between the bridge's pillars. We found refuge for the night in a corner that provided a feeling of having a kind of roof over us. We lay down on a pile of leaves we had gathered and tried to fall asleep to the sound of the flowing water. The bridge seemed deserted. No one crossed it at such hours of the night. Here we slept for a few hours – hungry, but at least not thirsty.

The bridge did not remain empty for long. We awoke to an increasingly loud noise, a familiar one that I had already heard in Pultusk: the sound of tank tracks on the move.

"German tanks," murmured my friend in a weak voice.

"I know," I answered.

A terrifying sight unfolded before us. With an ear-splitting din, the iron monsters crossed the bridge one by one and advanced toward the road that wound along the length of the river. Covering our ears, we lay in our hiding place under the bridge, but kept our eyes peeled on what was transpiring.

Several hours of nerve-wracking tension passed. The convoy of vehicles continued to stream along the bridge, in parallel with the flowing water beneath them. Above our heads were tanks and trucks packed with soldiers, jeeps carrying machine guns, vehicles towing artillery and a company of SS soldiers on foot. The German officer at the head of the company stopped directly over our heads. From our position we were able to see his face and uniform clearly. He directed the traffic with muffled shouts. Two officers standing next to him gazed out toward the river, filling their lungs with fresh air. Again we clung to each other, afraid of being discovered by the Germans. A jeep with several antennas attached to it came to a halt on the bridge. The officers got into it and disappeared.

Once again, that same silence of the forest and the sound of flowing water enveloped the area in unexplained mystery. The bridge was again deserted and we lay under it, starving and frozen, with the thought gnawing at my brain: "Now what, where to?"

"I think the Germans are gone. We're lucky, they didn't find us," murmured the boy.

"Where were they going?" I asked.

"I don't know," replied my friend and continued: "It's about to rain. I can smell the drops."

"Tell me," I asked, "why are the Germans chasing and murdering us? What did we do to them?"

My question hung in the air and dissolved into the rain that began to fall. He muttered something unintelligible and finally stated:

"Because we're Jews!"

I asked nothing further, just mentioned that I was hungry. My friend said he was also hungry and would try to "think of something."

It was noontime. The cloudy sky peeked out between the treetops. The sun was entirely hidden and rain began to wash over the whole area. We sat silently under the bridge and looked out at the streaming water. My friend looked pensive and suddenly called out:

"I have a plan!"

Looking at the flowing water, he explained:

"When the Germans brought us by truck from house to house, gathering Jews who had hidden among the Poles, we passed a lone farm, the home of a Pole who was my father's friend and business partner. I visited the house many times and know the family well. Now that the Germans have collected all the Jews who had been in hiding, perhaps he'll agree to host us and we will find food and refuge there. I heard from my father that the Germans threatened to kill any Pole caught hiding Jews, so we'll have to be careful that they don't see us entering his house. Do what I tell you and stick to me the whole time." Thus Michael summed up his "rescue plan," giving me the warm embrace of a loving brother.

"Okay," I agreed obediently.

Thanks to Michael, my life was given to me as a gift. A miracle had happened to me. An angel had descended from the sky and watched over me. Maybe Mother sent him "from that place"?

Even now, more than fifty years after these events, I cannot find the words to properly express my feelings and describe the traumatic experiences of those days. I have tried to convey the intensity of the word "fear," but it is impossible. I have perused dictionaries in various languages, searching for a sentence or phrase that could portray what I felt during those moments of terror – but to no avail. Many years later, I still have the sensation of living inside a hazy bubble, unable to pinpoint the events I experienced on an exact timetable. The images float up from an indefinable reservoir inside me. I don't know how to explain this. It is possible that everything got mixed up in the imagination of a little boy who experienced unfathomable horrors and a terrible reality, resulting in an uncontrollable mix of emotions. The wounds on my hands, feet and every exposed part of my body may have healed, but the deep wound in my heart still bleeds today and will apparently never heal.

Michael interrupted my thoughts: "We'll wait for evening and leave when it becomes dark. But we must be very careful."

"Okay," I again responded obediently.

The hours until dark seemed like eternity. There was no movement on the bridge. It stopped raining and my friend explained to me repeatedly that we had to avoid the Germans by any means possible. We particularly had to be careful of those in green uniform bearing the skull and bones symbol. Those, he said, "are the SS, the military arm of the Nazis. They are extremely cruel and it was they who slaughtered us in the forest clearing." He also cautioned me against the Gestapo, the Nazi secret police, who wore black uniforms with the skull, bones and swastika depicted on red armbands. I reminded him that I had seen many wearing such uniforms in Pultusk and en route. To illustrate his explanation, Michael drew the shape of a swastika on a piece of sand. He emphasized that I must walk behind him and not to let go of his hand under any circumstances.

I nodded in understanding and agreement. When he finished, Michael gripped my hand tightly as usual, just as he had done ever since we were taken from the Pole's shed. Daylight dimmed and darkness began to take over the forest. Michael rose suddenly and said:

"The time has come. We have to be on our way. Remember what I told you. Be brave!"

He gripped my hand and, with measured steps, we began to walk – at first along the length of the river and then into the forest. I was not afraid. He walked as if a hidden compass determined his direction. It seemed to me as if we were returning along the route we had taken to the bridge. It was totally dark by the time we neared the edge of the forest. He stood and looked around. In front of us was the vague outline of the corn fields; a sea of corn stalks, once again taller than we were.

"We'll enter the rows of corn and head this way," whispered my friend, pointing in a direction that seemed to me to lead nowhere. But I trusted him. He was my angel, delivering me from all that was evil, and would surely bring me to a safe place. After all, he had kept his word until now.

Walking in the corn field was difficult. The rain had made the ground muddy and the corn stalks wet; their leaves were razor-sharp and tore at our flesh. The "angel" sensed my distress, stopped walking and sat down. He tore off an ear of corn forgotten by the pickers, removed its husk and said:

"Time for supper!"

I had never eaten corn this way before. He took a bite of the ear and said:

"It tastes heavenly. Like manna in the desert."

I, too, started to bite into the corn, and its taste was delightful. This was the first time food entered my mouth since I had left home. We ate the ear together. My friend searched for another and found one, and we ate that, too. The corn was dry, but very good. If there had been a way to carry them, I would have taken more for an emergency. But my friend said this would not be wise, as it would be harder to walk; if we were forced to flee the Nazis, the weight would hinder us. He asked if I was full and I said yes.

Michael rose to his feet and looked at the sky, again pointing in a certain direction and saying that we had to resume walking. We were still in the corn fields. All we saw in front of us was – again – corn stalks all around with a partly cloudy sky above. The break we had taken and the food that had passed our lips lifted our spirits. We continued making our way through the stalks. The walk in the mud and in darkness was slow going.

Eventually we reached the edge of the corn field, where we heard dogs barking in the distance. We found a path leading to an isolated house. My friend said that we had to skirt the house from the right, as far from it as possible, to avoid getting close to the dogs and arousing the suspicion of hostile Poles in the area. He reassured me, saying:

"Now I know exactly where we are. I know the way to the house of my father's Polish friend. I've taken it many times when we visited in the past."

Michael noted that we still had a long way to go. Although the shorter route was the road that wound its way not far from the forest and lay adjacent to the field, my friend decided to stay as far away from it as possible so as not to be discovered by the Germans.

We strode in this fashion for several hours without pause. Luckily, we did not encounter any Germans or Poles. The navigation skills exhibited by "my angel" were impeccable. Eventually, Michael whispered to me:

"We've arrived at the Pole's house; here it is on the left."

He pointed to a house several hundred meters from where we had stopped. He scanned the area and said:

"It is best that we leave the path and approach the house via the fields. We need to step carefully, because this road is full of bumps."

He pulled my hand that attached to his and trod onward.

The closer we got to the Pole's house, the more rapidly my heart beat. The house was lit by an oil lamp that stood on the window sill. It was isolated, just like those of many farmers in the area. This isolation made it easier for us. We entered the yard and hid behind a hay-filled wagon near the stable. I was told to remain in place, behind the wagon of hay.

"Stay here and don't move. I am leaving you for a few minutes to go speak with the Pole and I hope that he will agree to hide both of us. In any case, don't be afraid. I won't leave you on your own. Until now you've proven yourself to be a big, brave boy. Wait for me here, I promise to return," declared Michael.

He removed his hand from mine, gave me his usual warm embrace, and confidently walked to the door of the house.

It was after midnight. It looked as if the Pole was awake because the oil lamp was lit. For a moment, I worried about being alone. This was the first time I had been separated from my friend. My heart pounded more and more powerfully. I heard Michael knocking on the door. No one opened it at first. Eventually, the voice of a woman emerged from inside the house:

"Someone's knocking on the door!"

Then: "Who's there?" her voice thundered again.

My friend knocked on the door once more and it opened. The Pole stood in the doorway, the oil lamp in his hand lighting up his face, looking surprised. The Pole took the guest into the house and the sound of the door being locked and bolted split the air. There are no words to describe my feelings during these terrifying moments. Every passing minute seemed like an eternity. Michael remained in the house for a long time. I trembled in fear and worried that the man was evil and would kill my "angel." I could not understand what was taking so long. My heart continued to beat wildly, as if about to break out of my chest. In the background, my father's voice reverberated in my head:

"Be strong, child. Behave like a big boy!"

I remembered my friend's request and did not move from my spot. He had promised to return. The sound of dogs barking could be heard from the other side of the house. My eyes did not leave the entrance door. At last, a woman's silhouette appeared in the window. The door suddenly opened and I heard Michael call me:

"Shulem! Shulem! Come, don't be afraid."

I left my hiding place drenched in a cold sweat, my legs barely carrying me to the door. My friend sensed my distress and came toward me, grasping my hand again. At that moment, a spark of life passed from him through our hands, into my body. I made a quick recovery and walked in with him, to the surprised faces of the Pole and his wife.

Seeing me barefoot and bleeding all over my body, the Polish woman resolved to take care of me. She bathed my wounds in water she had heated, and removed the thorns embedded in my body and in the soles of my feet. Then she applied a stinging ointment to my wounds. I, however, did not utter a sound. The farmer's wife also treated my friend. Afterwards, she went to the kitchen and brought us two large baked potatoes, which we devoured as if they were a feast fit for a king. This was my first warm meal since being deported from Pultusk.

Michael told the couple everything that had transpired since we were handed over by my father's Polish friend. His account moved them very much, and they hung on every word. He looked at the two of us and said:

"You know that the Germans are everywhere. They expelled all the Jews from here. We're also aware of their acts of horror and murder. They patrol this area daily and send special squads to locate Jews hiding in Polish homes and the surrounding forests. I am surprised they didn't catch you until now. In any case, you should know that any Pole caught hiding Jews is put to death. I'm very sorry to say that there are also local Poles who inform the Germans who is hiding Jews, so my wife and I are greatly endangering ourselves. If you're discovered here, neither you nor we will be spared. I hope that no one saw you enter my house."

"We detoured around the main roads on our way here. We walked only when it was dark so that we wouldn't be spotted. That's why we arrived at such a late hour," answered my friend.

The Pole nodded his head and said:

"We must work out how we can rescue you without being caught. We'll look for a way to bring you safely to the borderline where the Germans were halted, and try to smuggle you to the Russian side. Rumor has it that all local refugees who were saved from the Germans crossed over there en route to Bialystok. Near the border crossing is a town which you must reach where you will surely find your parents or other relatives. Now, I suggest that you go up to the attic where there is a place to hide. My wife will give you blankets and you can sleep until morning. The main thing is to get you away from the area where the Germans are. You'll be able to manage better on the Russian side and move around freely. There you won't need to hide."

The Pole continued to describe the situation. He told us that according to rumors, the Polish resistance had collapsed on all fronts, the Polish army had surrendered in Warsaw and Hitler had held an impressive victory parade in the city. Poland was currently divided between the Russian and German armies. He explained that, in his opinion, the situation was complex and unclear, and no one knew what would happen.

The Pole's wife apparently felt tremendous pity for us. She gave us two blankets; and, under the cover of darkness, our host led us to the barn at the end of the yard. He pointed to an attic above the barn door and whispered:

"This is a safe hiding place. Find yourself a spot among the things stored there and go to sleep. A hard day awaits us tomorrow," he concluded. My friend thanked him profusely for his hospitality and we were left alone. We went up to the attic and fell asleep. At long last we had a safe place to rest for the meantime, without worrying about beasts of prey or Nazis. However, who knew what tomorrow would bring....

Chapter 4
By Roundabout Paths

"And wayfarers went
by roundabout paths"

Judges 5:6

The Pole's extra belongings were piled up in the barn's attic. We located a comfortable corner behind a piece of furniture. At last we had a hiding place inside a building.

"Let's take advantage of the opportunity and sleep a little," my friend whispered to me. "I understood from the Pole that a difficult day lies ahead. I don't know what will happen tomorrow, but I believe what he said. I hope he'll take us to a safe place and not hand us over to the Germans as your father's friend did. He and his wife seem to be decent, sympathetic people."

We stretched out in the corner we had set up for ourselves. I do not know how long I slept. The sound of the Pole clearing his throat woke me. I found Michael sitting next to me.

"The Pole asked me to wake you. We're leaving in a little while," he said.

"Where to?" I asked.

"I don't know. He said that he'll take us to a place where there are no Germans."

I rose to my feet and felt my whole body ache. The attic ceiling was low and we had to walk bent over.

"The Pole asked that we wait here until he calls us. He's concerned that someone might see us and inform the Germans. He wants to make sure that there is no one dangerous in the vicinity," explained Michael.

After a short time, we heard the sound of the Pole's footsteps and his heavy breathing. He held a cup of milk and two slices of bread. He served us the meal, asking us to share it between us. My friend gave me one slice and handed me the cup so that I could drink first. He suggested that I take a sip of milk and a bite of the bread. A sip and a bite. And so I did.

The Pole suddenly looked serious and he began to whisper his rescue plan to us. He cleared his throat again and said:

"Listen, children. What I am about to do is extremely dangerous. If I fail, your fate and ours will be death. We must act carefully, wisely and shrewdly. You must cooperate with me. I checked the surrounding area and aside from several workers in a faraway field, there's no one here at the moment. There's a hay wagon outside. You must get down from the attic without anyone noticing you, climb onto the hay wagon and lie down in the middle. I'll cover you with additional bales of hay so that you won't be discovered. Lie there without moving or making a sound. You – watch over little Shalom and make sure that he doesn't cry or open his mouth."

The Pole took a deep breath and continued:

"We have a long way ahead of us. I will take you to a spot from which you can cross the German lines and get to the town where, as far as I know, many Jews have gathered, after being expelled from the battle zone. My wife has prepared provisions for the way – half a loaf of bread and two baked potatoes. I will whistle if we encounter any Germans. If you hear me whistle, that means that Germans are in the area and you must be very careful and even hold your breath."

I was very moved by what the Pole said: he was prepared to risk his life in order to save ours. It's too bad that not all Poles are like him, I thought to myself. I thought of "Father's" Pole, who had handed us over to the Germans, and of all the Poles in Pultusk who coveted our possessions during the deportation.

Our host descended from the attic and we awaited his signal. After a short time, we heard him call:

"You can come down. Take the food with you and wait at the entrance to the barn for my instructions."

We descended carefully and quietly. His wife was below, holding a pair of used shoes and socks. She gave them to me and whispered:

"Put them on – I hope they fit you. This is what I found in the storage room. You will need them on the way. The shoes are a bit too big for you, but I hope that together with the socks, they'll prove comfortable. Stay here until my husband calls you."

I thanked the woman warmly. I donned the socks and Michael helped me put on my "new" shoes.

The Pole approached the barn with a pitchfork in his hand and whispered:

"We're ready to set off. The wagon is ready and the horse is harnessed."

"Take care of yourselves and have a safe journey," his wife added.

We said goodbye to the woman and followed her husband. He had hidden the horse and wagon behind the stable. The wagon was partly filled with hay. The farmer lay us down in the middle of the wagon and began to toss the rest of the hay on top of us. We heard the panting of his breath increase as the pile of hay rose. After a while, he declared:

"I'm finished. I hope the piles of hay aren't too heavy for you. Do you remember what I told you? If I whistle, it means that there are Germans in the area. Is everything okay? Let me know now. We won't talk again until we reach our destination. Is that clear?"

"Yes, okay," answered my friend, and gripped my hand tightly.

"We're leaving," said our host, and we heard the crack of the whip that urged the horse on its way.

It was early morning. The noise of planes mingled with the sounds of the galloping and the repeated calls of the Pole spurring his horse on. The ride was extremely uncomfortable. The wagon bounced and tossed from side to side; it seemed we were traveling on an unpaved road. Every bounce brought with it a calming hand squeeze from my friend.

We continued to travel thus for a long time. The horse breathed more heavily and slowed its pace. Apparently we were in a mountainous region, and pulling the wagon had become harder. The cracks of the Pole's whip and his cries to the horse brought us safely to the end of the uphill stretch. From here, the horse returned to an easy gallop. From afar we heard the familiar rumble of motorcycles. A squeeze from my friend, along with the Pole's whistle, spelled out danger. Germans were near.

We lay motionless under the pile of hay and tried to hold our breath. The Pole's whistling grew louder, as did the roar of the approaching motorcycles. The Pole stopped the horse. The motorcycles – two, from the sound of it – came to a halt near us. The blood froze in my veins. "That's it," I told myself. "We're about to be discovered; this is the end of us." I believed our fate to be sealed, and the image of the human slaughter in the forest clearing burst into my mind. I broke out in a cold sweat. Michael, lying next to me under the pile of hay, read my thoughts and caressed my palm softly as if to say, calm down, child, everything will be all right.

We heard the Germans speaking with the Pole. They stopped and walked toward the hay wagon. We held our breath as they circled the wagon and barked out some sentences in German. The Pole mumbled something unclear. He got down from the wagon and the Germans began to inspect it, thrusting the bayoneted rifles into the hay. We lay in silence, but my heart pounded wildly. My friend's handclasp gave me a sense of security and courage. I lay quietly, buried under the hay piles.

The Nazis sniffed around the wagon for what felt like an eternity. After they completed their task, we heard the sound of the motorcycle engines starting up and, with a deafening roar, they took off in the opposite direction.

"We passed the German inspection successfully. Were either of you hurt by the bayonets?" asked our friend in concern.

"No," we responded in unison.

"Very good!" said our escort with obvious satisfaction, adding: "We still have a long way ahead of us. Hold fast. Remember what we said at the start of our journey – you must not be discovered by the Germans!"

He climbed onto the wagon and the horse galloped onward. Michael and I quietly sighed in relief. The tension eased and this time the heart leaped in joy. But for how long … ?

After traveling for two hours, the Pole stopped the wagon and alighted, explaining:

"We have to let the horse rest and eat so that he'll have strength to continue. The trip is taking longer because I'm trying to detour around villages and main roads to avoid detection."

To our surprise, through the sounds of the horse's breathing and chewing, we detected the trickling of flowing water. The wagon driver had apparently stopped near a stream to quench the horse's thirst. We lay quietly, waiting for him to finish his meal. My eyes closed and I fell into a deep sleep. The horse was not the only one who needed to rest; I did, too, after all I had been through. Again, I do not know how long I had been asleep when a powerful jolt awakened me.

"Sorry," came the voice of the Pole, "I had to cross the gully in order to skirt the village on the route. I hope you weren't hurt." The horse pulled the wagon through the gully with his remaining strength and the wheels bounced from stone to stone, tossing us heavily from left to right.

"We'll be on the other side in just another few meters," the Pole reassured us. It seems he was an experienced wagon driver. He knew how to control the horse and was very familiar with the route. "We are nearing our destination. We'll travel for about an hour along the length of the stream in the hopes of encountering no Germans on the way. We will look for a suitable place from which you can get to the village where the deported Jews seem to have gathered. Are you okay?" he added, with great concern.

"Yes," we responded together.

We endured a bumpy, tension-filled hour of travel. The Pole diverted his route into a nearby forest. In a well-hidden spot in the depths of the woods, our friend told us to come out from under the pile of hay.

"I think this is the safest place to drop you off. I'll explain to you how and where to go. In the meantime, sip a bit of water and help me pick up the hay that fell as you got out of the wagon," said the Pole, giving us a water canteen to quench our thirst.

My friend warmly thanked our escort for his assistance and, together, we began to put the hay back into the wagon. The driver tied the horse to one of the trees, placed a bowl with some handfuls of barley in front of it and asked us to accompany him to the edge of the forest. Before we left, he gave us a bag of food his wife had prepared, with half a loaf of bread and two baked potatoes.

"Take care of the bag and of yourselves. Now follow me and I'll explain where to go," said our friend, starting to walk toward the periphery of the forest, with us at his heels. After a few minutes, we reached the edge of a thicket. Spread out before us was familiar scenery, similar to that I had known in Pultusk. Our escort lifted his eyes toward the horizon on the right, raised his hand and pointed to a building in the distance:

"Look over there, at the town in the right-hand corner – that's your destination, a town under Russian control. At the moment, we are in a German-occupied area. A stream separates the two sides. There is a small break in the fence opposite, and all you have to do is pass through the break, advance in the direction of the town and cross the stream. From the moment you cross it, you will be in a safe area under Russian rule. Go to your house of prayer in the town, and you'll surely find one of your relatives there, perhaps even your parents."

After a short pause, he added:

"I'm leaving you now; I must return home and it's a long trip. It's best that you wait for the cover of darkness to walk toward the town. Be careful of the German patrol along the length of the stream. Walk with your eyes wide open and a great deal of caution. If you notice any suspicious movement in the area, hide in the thick shrubbery, there's plenty of it. When you reach the stream, continue along its length and I'm sure you'll find an easy spot to cross it. I wish you much success and all the best," concluded the Pole, embracing us warmly and then heading for his waiting horse in the forest.

Michael and I stood at the edge of the forest, watching the figure of our friend disappearing among the trees. Michael pulled me into the forest and said:

"The Pole is right, we must hide here until evening and only then set out. Let's look for a corner where we can eat and sleep. We have to gather our strength, because a difficult night awaits us."

I nodded my head in agreement and followed him. I could not understand how he could find his way so easily in the deep forest.

After a short while we found ourselves in a hollowed-out space surrounded by thick bushes, resembling the "living room" of a house – an ideal place to hide and rest. My friend suggested that we stop here. He gathered some of the many nearby soft branches and built a kind of mattress to rest on. We sat down on the bed of leaves he had arranged and opened the bag of food. Michael took a potato out of the bag and divided it in half. Afterwards, he tore off two chunks of bread and gave me one, saying:

"Eat slowly. A little bread and a bite of potato."

I obeyed him. The meal was tasty. We ate slowly.

As I write these words, decades after those turbulent times, I think of these situations, now etched in my memory, and of my behavior then as a young boy. Those were indeed unfathomable and inexplicable experiences. For every hour that elapsed, I felt myself mature by a day; for every day, by a month; and for every month, by a year. We were abandoned as children in the forest at the height of war, in a region controlled by a cruel enemy who stopped at nothing, making no distinction between man or woman, soldier or civilian, elderly or newborn. Everyone faced the same fatal end, and particularly the Jews. It was difficult for me to digest the horrible events of the past month, and I was only partially successful at banishing the visions of death that repeatedly came to mind at random moments. My yearnings for Mother and for my family intensified from one minute to the next. Luckily, my friend sensed my distress and always knew to inject a hopeful comment at such taxing moments.

"According to the Pole, there is a good chance that we will find our families in the town over the border," my friend interrupted my musings.

"I hope so. I miss Mother and Father and my sisters so much," I answered sadly.

"I hope you'll see them soon. The Pole said that many Jews expelled from Pultusk have gathered in the town. I'm convinced that your father wouldn't leave without first establishing what had become of you," he responded. The words uttered by my young, experienced friend calmed me down and instilled new hope in me.

With each passing day, I became increasingly aware that I was surrounded by Jew-haters. It stood out everywhere we went. The sole exception was the kind Pole, who had put his and his family's lives at risk and smuggled us out. We had been lucky.

There were several hours left until nightfall. My companion said that we should do what our friend had suggested and take advantage of the time to rest. After our meal, I stretched out on the bed of leaves and fell into a deep sleep.

Chapter **5**

Stealing Across the Border

"For your own sake, therefore,
be most careful"

Deuteronomy 4:15

A small motion in the region of my arm awakened me. I opened my eyes and saw my friend, his face again radiating like that of an angel. Having woken up before me, he sat by my side, holding my hand. He seemed to have an alarm clock hidden inside him. Perhaps he really was an angel.

"You should get up; it's beginning to get dark and we have to set out," he whispered in my ear.

"Okay. I was dead tired," I said, sitting up next to him. "When did you wake up?"

"A long time ago," he answered, continuing: "You slept very deeply. Apparently you needed it, but it's important that you stay awake now, because we're going to cross the border and reach the town that the Pole mentioned. Perhaps we really will find our families there."

I rose to my feet and stretched. The pains in my body had disappeared. The hope that I would soon be able to meet my father and sisters revived me, and I was ready to start out.

"We'd better wait another half hour so that we can leave when it's completely dark," suggested my friend. We left our hiding place and walked toward the edge of the forest where we had parted from our Polish friend. Total darkness fell upon the entire area. Distant lights flickered in the town that was our destination.

Michael pointed the way. "We'll walk in this direction until we reach the stream."

Our nighttime trek began with our passage through the break in the fence the Pole had mentioned. I had trouble walking. The shoes his wife had given me were a little too big, though certainly more comfortable than going barefoot. We passed by thick bushes, struggled with impenetrable vegetation and evaded obstacles. Mindful of the darkness enveloping us, Michael proceeded cautiously, out of concern for hidden pits and unanticipated traps.

Somehow, the lights of the town seemed farther away the closer we got. My friend was determined, however, and pressed on, unflagging. Despair was alien to him. The main thing was that we were advancing carefully and avoiding German eyes. There were no paths on our route. He was cautious to avoid them, claiming that using them in this area was a recipe for disaster. The moment we hit a paved road or path, the lad was quick to distance us from it as much as possible, like an experienced scout.

We stopped after a few hours and climbed a nearby hill from where we could look down at our destination. This time, the lights of the town were distinctly visible. My friend decided to take a break.

"Are you tired?" he asked.

"No, I can go on," I answered.

"Very well, we'll continue walking straight, until we reach the stream."

While we were talking, we saw the lights of two approaching vehicles and could also hear the sound of their engines.

"I don't know if the vehicles are traveling on this side of the stream or the other," said Michael, "so we can't tell if they're German or Russian. Let's climb down the hill and hide in the thick bushes nearby. We can also rest until the danger passes."

Like seasoned survivors, we proceeded downhill straight into a large thicket of bushes. We cleared a path through them and created a space in which to sit next to each other. The sound of the cars' engines grew louder and their lights bounced up, down and sideways.

"Germans," whispered my friend, adding: "They're approaching from the right, traveling the same route we took an hour ago. I think we're far from them. We'll wait here until they pass and then continue toward the stream."

No further explanation was needed. My survivor's instinct sized up the situation accurately and I was unbelievably calm. This time I relied on both my friend and myself, having apparently begun to think and act like an adult. We waited a short while and the vehicles passed. Michael rose, took my hand and explained with satisfaction that it was evidently a German patrol that had passed and we should not delay in taking advantage of this fact.

"We must hurry and reach the stream before the patrol returns. There may be an additional route along the stream, via which the patrol is liable to come back," my friend said, assessing the situation and hurrying me along.

This time we walked quickly, again avoiding traps and thick bushes. Michael explained that the dense vegetation resulted from winter flooding and the stream that had overflowed. The thicker the plants, the closer we were to the stream. We walked without stopping and, just as my friend had anticipated, reached a point from which the stream was visible. We clearly heard the flowing water.

"We must hurry and get to the other side before the patrol returns," said Michael, searching with his eagle eye for an easy crossing point.

We traversed the road, and with extreme difficulty, cleared a way among the bushes toward the stream. Our goal was to gain distance from that spot and get as close to the stream as possible. The sound of flowing water grew louder until our feet eventually touched the water itself. We stopped and my friend looked for a place to cross. The current was not strong and the water did not seem deep. We continued to walk along the stream in the direction of the town, hoping to find a suitable crossing point.

We reached a bend in the stream. In the stream's center were large pieces of driftwood that had been swept away and gotten stuck on mounds of rocks protruding from the water. Michael stopped walking and noted that this looked like an ideal place to cross safely. He suggested we remove our shoes and roll up our pant cuffs. Sitting on a piece of wood, he took off his shoes, tied the laces together, put his socks inside and hung them around his neck.

"Do just as I did. We'll put our shoes on again once we get to the other side and continue toward the town. We'll be safer there, as our Polish friend told us. We should hurry, I don't know when the German patrol will return," said my friend, helping me with my shoes.

We got ready to cross the stream. Michael, who was taller than I, hung my shoes around his neck too, and we immersed our feet in the water. It was ice cold. With utmost caution, he climbed onto a piece of wood that looked stable and pulled me toward him with his right hand. We proceeded slowly to a rock that jutted out above the water, while he continued to hold my hand and keep me steady.

"Be careful not to fall. The rock is slippery and we must walk very slowly," he warned.

We advanced a few steps. The water froze the soles of our feet. The darkness made it harder to select the strongest piece of wood, but our survivor's instinct helped us overcome the difficulty. My friend checked every single log before we stepped on it. Thus we straggled onward, from rock to driftwood to rock again, our feet in freezing water while the river's spray drenched our bodies. Our clothes were wet, but it was tolerable; and we eventually reached the other side.

We continued into a thicket, looked for a dry place and sat down. I heard my friend release a long, meaningful sigh. I huddled close to him and he hugged me warmly, saying confidently:

"The dangerous part is already behind us. The Russians are not as cruel as the Germans – the Pole did tell us that Jews are not persecuted on this side of the border as they are on the German side. So we can relax. It is important that we distance ourselves from the border, moving eastward, so that we're not detected by German eyes on the other side of the stream."

While Michael spoke, we saw the approaching lights of the German patrol on the other side of the stream, exactly as he had predicted.

"We'd best stay here until the patrol passes. This is an excellent hiding place, we're already on the eastern bank and they won't notice us from the other side. In the meantime, let's dry our feet and put on our shoes so that we're ready to get going," said my friend encouragingly. The patrol vehicles moved slowly and much time passed before we saw them disappear from the path on the western bank from where we had just come.

At an early hour, before the break of dawn, we arose and set out on our way. We felt safe here and took the first path we happened onto, toward the "promised" town. Michael suggested stopping at a creek that flowed parallel to the stream so that we could drink and quench our thirst. I sat near the creek and drank as my life had taught me to, scooping up a handful of water and drinking it. My friend took the remaining bread out of the bag and broke off two chunks, one for each of us. We ate heartily. These are the moments in life when one learns the true value of a piece of bread – how much pleasure a small amount can provide....

"We'll save the potato and the remaining bread since we don't know what awaits us," said my eleven-year old friend, rich in life experience.

Sated with the bread and water, we started walking on the path along the stream. The lights of the town grew nearer. The Divine Creator chose this hour to illuminate the land and all who dwelt upon it. The lighter it became, the more we discovered what we had missed in the dark: not far from the path we were on was a paved road that apparently led into the town. Visible on the approaching horizon were a few houses alongside structures that looked like grain silos, with a number of cows nearby. Several wagons were already traveling in our direction on the paved road.

"We're better off sticking with this path, not the paved road. I don't know who those people traveling it are; they might be hostile Poles or highway robbers. I would prefer we reach the town via our current path. I think we'll be there in about an hour and we'll be able to blend in with the many residents without arousing suspicion. Let's hope we run into some Jews like us who can help us locate our families," commented Michael – here was the life wisdom of a boy not yet thirteen years old.

We walked for a long time, trying to conceal ourselves from the sight of the wagon drivers who rode along the road that twisted alongside our path. Vehicles also traveled on it, including military ones bearing red flags. We immediately sensed the difference, as the uniforms of these soldiers vastly differed from those of the Germans. There was already cause to breathe easy.

We reached the edge of the awakening town. As we proceeded, we were confronted with the most terrible sights. Numerous people thronging on street corners, sleeping on the sidewalks, and in the adjacent courtyards, families, including children and elderly, had settled. Some were wrapped in blankets; others had nothing but the bare sky above them. It was not hard to guess that these were Jews like us who had been expelled from their homes, or had survived the cruel Nazi occupation. Some still dozed; others were awake. Our eyes sought familiar faces. At first glance we saw no one. My friend stopped near a group of Jews and asked about our families. One older man, with a beard and *peyot* (sidelocks) was praying, swaying from side to side. He looked at us with astonishment and asked us where we had come from.

"From Pultusk," we answered.

"You should go to the synagogue and ask there. Perhaps someone will be able to help you," he suggested, pointing in the direction we needed to go.

It seemed as if our Polish friend had been right. Many Jews had gathered here, refugees from the surrounding towns that had been conquered by the Nazis. The deeper we went into the town, the more distressing were the sights we saw. Hundreds of destitute Jews filled the pavements. Some lay with suitcases next to them, while others only had cloth bundles. Women held babies, trying to soothe them, and crying children in tattered clothing begged for a piece of bread.

We were shocked by what we saw. My friend, who had not let go of my hand, pulled me forward. The street we were on appeared to be one of the main streets. No one paid any attention to us; all were preoccupied with their own needs. The place resembled a refugee town in every way. The hundreds crowding the streets became thousands, and though we searched for people we knew, we identified no one. My friend stopped at a group of boys and asked where the synagogue was. One of them pointed to a nearby street and said:

"Turn right at the next street. You can't miss it; there are lots of Jews there."

Noticing my highly emotional state, Michael grasped my hand even more tightly and continued pulling me forward, trying to be encouraging:

"I'm sure the people in the synagogue will be able to help us find our families. Let's hurry over there. It's early morning now; perhaps we'll find some of the community rabbis praying the morning service and they'll advise us what to do."

We turned right at the next street, as the boy had said, and were quickly engulfed in the mass of people around the synagogue.

Chapter **6**

For Brethren to Dwell Together

"Behold, how good and how pleasant it is
for brethren to dwell together in unity."

Psalms 133:1

The town we had reached had been conquered by Soviet forces immediately upon the Russian invasion of eastern Poland. Thousands of Jewish refugees had headed here after the Nazis expelled them from their homes, as did other refugees who fled, or were deported from, German-occupied territories. They arrived in the cities and towns of eastern Poland in waves. The first such wave occurred immediately after the outbreak of war on September 1, 1939, and we witnessed a part of it in Pultusk before the latter's occupation on September 7, 1939. A second wave of refugees accompanied the Red Army's invasion of eastern Poland from September 17, 1939 until December 1939, when the new German-Russian border was closed.

It became obvious that our Polish friend had known exactly where to send us. Wartime rumors spread more quickly than anticipated. The area to where he had directed us was, indeed, a haven for refugees, amongst them many Jews. Luckily, the Soviet-occupied area was near the Pole's town and the border between the Germans and Russians was still officially open – in December 1939, it was closed at Russian initiative, thus preventing the Germans from deporting residents and refugees across the border from the areas under their control.

It was thus that, on a particularly cold morning in October 1939, accompanied by my friend "the angel," I was able to walk on the streets of the town controlled by Red Army forces and filled with masses of Jews. They all assembled at the entrance to the town's central synagogue, as if hoping to go "home."

With deep sadness and unmitigated amazement, I pondered: How did we – two boys who had undergone such terrifying experiences – survive the constant threat of death under conditions of cold and starvation? How were we able to escape the cruel enemy in wartime and join thousands of our people's refugees in search of relatives? Like us, these refugees had withstood the horror, leaving behind, in towns and forests, in fields and on roads, silent testimony to a community that was eradicated, to a culture that was obliterated and to the cries of Jews murdered in cold blood by beasts in human guise, ever since Germany invaded Poland on September 1, 1939.

The crowd grew denser as we got closer to the synagogue. It seems we had encountered a line of worshippers who awaited the local community's food distribution. Our small size allowed us to slip to the head of the line, and reach the synagogue gates with relative ease. The person standing there, apparently the gatekeeper or community clerk, asked what our business was. My friend answered unhesitatingly:

"We arrived here this morning, alone, from the other side of the border. We're looking for our parents. We are not brothers."

The surprised gatekeeper let us into the synagogue, crowded with worshippers, and presented us to the community's rabbi. Michael related to him what had happened to us. The rabbi checked the list of names in his hand, asked us to come closer and embraced us warmly, tears falling onto his beard. He calmed us down and signaled to one of the worshippers to give us a portion of food. At the same time, the rabbi asked that word be spread among the worshippers and refugees of the arrival of two unaccompanied children from Pultusk, in the hopes that someone would identify us.

The news of our arrival spread quickly in the town. In the meantime, we made a place for ourselves in the synagogue under the watchful eye of the rabbi. My friend sat next to me the whole time, still not letting go of me even though we had found shelter. The rabbi requested blankets for us and assigned us a corner in the synagogue to rest until our relatives could be located.

The stream of refugees coming to ask the rabbi for food and lodging did not cease throughout the day. It was an awful sight. People begged for assistance, their faces conveying fear and desperation. Each one recounted his history and gave the names of his missing family members. The rabbi and his assistant listened, wrote down every detail and promised to help as best they could.

We sat down in the corner allotted to us. Someone brought us food and relieved our anxieties. He said it would take time until our relatives were located, as there were thousands of refugees in the town and its surroundings. After we ate our first hot, cooked meal (unbelievable!), we stretched out in our corner. Michael took the trouble to cover me with a blanket and I fell asleep.

I was awakened by the voice of a tall young man, filtering through to me as if from a dream:

"Domb? … Sholom Domb? … From Pultusk? … Your family is here … Your father is on his way to the synagogue!"

This might sound trite, but there are no words to describe the joy that gripped me! It was as if Shulem Domb had been reborn. Without a doubt, these were among the happiest moments of my life, moments that will never be forgotten. Everyone around me was caught up in the elation. My friend hugged me tightly and exclaimed emotionally:

"I told you we'd been saved. Finally, there is someone to look after you. You behaved like a hero. I'm proud of you!"

Approximately an hour later, I noticed my father making his way through the massive crowd in the synagogue. I got up and leaped towards him. For the first time, Michael let go of my hand.

"Father! Father!" I screamed in a broken voice.

"Shulem!" …

My father's strong embrace enveloped me in the familiar warmth I had missed so much … His whole body trembled … The tears streaming uncontrollably from his eyes onto my arm seared it deeply. I can still feel their impression to this day, many years after we were reunited.

I, however, did not cry. I introduced "my angel" to Father, who shook his hand and hugged him. Father was still in complete ignorance of our experiences.

At this point, someone announced that my friend's family had also been found and they were on their way. I stared into Michael's face, which failed to disguise his emotions. I sneaked a smile at him and ran into his arms in full view of the amazed worshippers. The rabbi blessed us and my father thanked him. Father grasped my hand and we walked out together to the synagogue gate. As we exited, I glanced back at my friend. Our gazes held until I was outside the synagogue walls.

That was the last time I saw him. To this day, I do not know his name or that of his family. Not for naught did I call him an "angel." Only an angel could perform such miracles and deliver me safe and sound to my family. I have no idea what happened to him or his family. I hope that they survived and are leading happy lives. To this day, I believe with all my heart that he was sent to save me. It is a story beyond belief, which I have now retrieved from the depths of my memory for the first time. Although I recounted it in the past, this is the first time I am putting it into writing. Unfortunately, I cannot recall exact names and dates from this period, but there is no doubt that these events occurred in the early months of the war, a war worse than any other – World War Two.

Father took me to where our family was staying. When my sisters saw us approaching, they ran towards us and immediately enveloped me in their warm arms. The tears of joy shed that day would not put to shame the many streams I crossed in my wanderings. Everyone gathered around me and asked about my experiences. I shared everything. Every detail.

The tears did not cease falling from the family's astonished eyes. I don't know where so many tears could have come from. The questions were endless.

"Where did you meet your young friend?' asked my sister Ita, who did not stop hugging me.

"In the cellar of Father's Polish friend's shed, the friend who handed us over to the Germans," I answered.

Upon hearing my tale, a forceful Polish expletive escaped Father's lips, and he said that one day that Pole would receive his divine retribution. He sat down next to us and declared that from now on we must worry about our future. He related that the rumors among those in the know portended evil. The war was still ongoing, and the Germans were scheming to take control over additional territories. To this end, Hitler had marshaled all of Germany's resources and placed its industry entirely at the army's disposal, for the unceasing production of planes, tanks and other military equipment.

Father explained further that after the Polish army had surrendered in Warsaw on September 27th, Hitler had annexed western Poland to the Third Reich. Other areas of Poland, including the districts of Warsaw, Lublin, Radom and Krakow, were designated as the General Government for the Occupied Polish Territories (*Generalgouvernement* in German). Such administrations were established in places conquered by the Germans but not annexed to Germany. It later became clear that these areas housed most of the extermination camps – the "machines" for the annihilation of the Jews during the Holocaust.

My father and sisters set themselves up outdoors, on a street corner at the edge of the town. My father, who had been a grain merchant in Pultusk, knew many merchants in villages throughout eastern Poland. With their assistance, he managed to obtain a horse and wagon, upon which he loaded all the "belongings" he had accumulated since the deportation: several blankets, a few articles of clothing, eating utensils and a small amount of food.

Father was radiant with joy at my return to the bosom of the family. He sat down next to the wagon and informed us of his plans. He spoke quietly and we listened attentively:

"Now that Shulem'keh is back with the family, we must plan our steps carefully. At the moment, we are living under Soviet rule. There is no point in returning to Pultusk, which is under the control of the Germans, who took all our property. The little that remained was looted by our Polish neighbors. We are left with nothing. In my pocket is a little money from previous debts I succeeded in collecting from several merchants."

"The Russians have taken over all of eastern Poland and all forms of private enterprise, in accordance with their socialist principles. They have confiscated property and liquidated the commerce run by many Jews. I cannot predict the final outcome of all this, but it is clear that our situation is grim in every respect. As you can see, there are thousands of refugees in this town, and the stores are empty of merchandise. The lines to purchase basic food – bread, milk, flour and rice – are very long, the black market is flourishing, prices are rising and there is no employment."

Father took a deep breath and continued:

"Only one conclusion presents itself. We must move to a large city and try to find a place to live and work so that I can support the family. The place I deem most suitable for us is Bialystok. The city is under Soviet control, but their policies are still not as cruel as the Germans. Besides, we have no other option. So I now ask you to behave responsibly, as adults. We have to preserve the little food we have and use it sparingly."

Requesting us to prepare for a long trip of several days, Father said that in the meantime, he would try to obtain supplies and food for the coming days. He asked Ita to watch over me, and set out on his way. Ita needed no instructions from Father; her eyes did not leave me. From the moment she saw me, she felt the responsibility of a mother, did not let me budge from her sight, looked after my welfare. Her warm embrace was indeed like that of a mother. She instinctively understood what I had undergone and tried to instill stability in our abnormal situation and a warm, loving family feeling, especially towards me.

During my short existence, I had managed to experience life under German occupation. And now I was in another part of my same native country, but under Soviet rule. I sat on the harnessed wagon and gazed around me. Masses of people filled the streets, Jewish and Polish refugees mingling with the local population. Trucks with red flags, carrying Red Army soldiers, moved along the town's roads. It seemed that the color red had become dominant in those days. The flags displayed the hammer and sickle symbol.

Relations between Russia and Poland had always been strained, full of suspicion and hostility. The Russian's Sovietization of the areas under conquest forced many Poles, primarily the middle class and estate owners, to give up their property. A considerable number also fled to large cities in the *Generalgouvernment* under German control and had no means of existence.

The new Russian regime did not overlook the Jews, many of whom lost their property and businesses. With the completion of the nationalization of private property and capital in November 1939, economic activity was effectively paralyzed. The nationalization process and the communist socialist takeover entailed imprisonment and exile of property holders and business owners, including many Jews.

None of this affected our family in any way. The Germans had already stolen our property and business. What was left to take from us? We remained with a few garments and the small amount of food Father obtained with the little money he had.

A few hours later, Father approached the wagon, loaded with packages. Ita and Sarah ran up and helped him carry everything.

"The lines are long and stores are empty," said Father, adding: "We're lucky – a Pole I know from my travels agreed to sell me some goods at double price. There's no point in staying here. We must hurry to Bialystok, where the situation is more reasonable. The Pole also said that we'll be able to manage better in a large city than in towns and villages packed with refugees."

After we piled the goods onto the wagon, Father helped Ita arrange it as comfortably as possible for the extended sitting that awaited us. The wagon was smaller than that of the Pole who had smuggled us to the border. There was barely enough room for us and for our few belongings. Father sat up front on a special wagon driver's stool.

We set out on our way: Father, my three sisters – Ita, Sara, Zipporah – and I. On this one small, old-fashioned wagon that held all our possessions, we all squeezed in for the trip to the unknown. The wagon's wheels squeaked and it was evident from its appearance that it had traversed many miles in its time. We proceeded on a road leading out of town. Father covered me with a blanket to protect me from the cold wind that blew at us mercilessly.

Throughout the journey, I looked around carefully. When we had placed a considerable distance between ourselves and the town, I drew Ita's attention to a thicket of bushes on the left side of the road and explained:

"This is where I hid with my friend on the way to the town. And there, further on, we crossed the stream. There are Germans on the other side of the stream." As I spoke, I pointed out the spots I had passed with my friend Michael. My sisters sat up straight and Father looked leftward to see the places I showed them.

With a warm hug, Ita said:

"Now you no longer have to hide. You're with us and we will watch over you!"

The horse pulling the wagon was tired, not from lack of strength, but due to its advanced age. I thought, however, how good it was to have a vehicle of any sort, and it seemed to me that our horse was doing its job faithfully. All along the road we saw a long convoy of refugees, many of them on foot. Some walked toward the town we had just left, and others in the opposite direction. Everyone was weighed down with bundles and blankets; the sights were truly heart-breaking. Some tried to stop us and ask for a bit of food, even begging to join us on the wagon. They looked utterly exhausted, but the wagon was too narrow to accommodate additional passengers – our family barely managed to cram ourselves into it.

The line of refugees thinned out as we traveled further, until we were alone on the road. At some point, after hours of travel, we reached an area with open spaces, green fields and pastureland. Here and there were isolated huts, with cows and horses grazing nearby. Father stopped the wagon on the side of the road, descended to a side path near a small creek and suggested:

"Get down and stretch your legs and refresh yourselves with water. We must also give the horse a chance to rest. We still have a long way ahead of us."

We got off, and after washing ourselves in the freezing water and quenching our thirst, we sat down next to Father, close to the wagon. We very much trusted our father. He knew the way, since he had often traveled to Bialystok during his many business trips. Looking pensive, he said:

"The road to Bialystok continues to be dangerous; I've been

told that German forces are still operating on it. We must go as far
eastward as possible from the Narew River, and detour around Ostrow-
Mazowiecka. If we get through this area unharmed and reach Zambrow,
the road to Bialystok will be safe."

And Father continued:

"One of the refugees I met had fled from Ostrow, and he told
me of the utter destruction wreaked by the Germans there. The Nazis
slaughtered the Jews and deported everyone. He also said that before
the Russian invasion of Poland, the Nazis murdered many of the Jews of
Pultusk, who fled for their lives and reached Zambrow and Ostrow. So
we should detour around the city and head far away from it, toward the
Russian side, in the hopes of not encountering Nazis on the way. I know
the road well, having traveled the 140 kilometers from Wyszków to
Bialystok many times. From where we are, the distance to Bialystok is
less than 100 kilometers. If we are lucky and don't run into any unusual
trouble, we will arrive there in two days."

As Father finished updating us and prepared to get back on
the wagon, his face suddenly turned serious. Visible from afar were
two approaching military vehicles, which he identified as Russian. He
signaled with his hand to one of the vehicles to stop. Several uniformed
soldiers sat in the car. We saw Father talking with them, and one soldier
gave him a loaf of bread and pointed his finger in a certain direction.
Father returned to us and spoke confidently:

"The soldiers confirmed my plan. We must detour around
Ostrow from the east and stay far from the German forces, then return
to the main road to Zambrow and from there to Bialystok. This route is
a bit longer, but it's safer. We'd better get moving now so we can take
advantage of daylight and get further before it gets dark."

We continued slowly for many hours. Ita cut some of the
bread and gave us each a slice. Father suggested taking small bites and
chewing slowly. The daylight had waned almost completely when he
diverted the horse off the road onto a side path leading to an adjacent

grove. He stopped the wagon near one of the trees, untied the horse and pronounced:

"Here is where we will sleep. Ita, please take some cooked potatoes from the bag, and we'll also eat a little bread. We must satisfy our hunger and rest. A difficult day awaits us tomorrow."

Darkness enveloped everything; but the dark, and the nighttime sounds, did not frighten me. Father said that my sisters and I should sleep in the wagon and he would doze underneath, next to the horse– the wagon was too narrow for all of us to lie down. It was freezing cold. Ita covered all of us with a blanket and asked Father:

"Are you alright down there? Take the coat and cover yourself with it."

"It's okay, Ita," he replied, "I'm managing fine. First I have to feed and water the horse, and then when I'm finished I'll try to take a nap. Pray that it doesn't rain. We have nothing between us and the bare sky. Try to fall asleep. We will leave at dawn and I hope we can make it to Zambrow tomorrow."

At dawn, Father harnessed the horse and we started out. We detoured off the main road and took a side road for a few hours. We passed several huts, apparently farms. Father stopped the wagon at one of the huts and asked us to wait a few minutes. We saw him go inside the house and come out with a jug of milk, which he asked Ita to distribute to everyone, along with a slice of bread. An older Polish woman who had come out of her house sneaked us a look of pity and said a few words to Father, pointing in the direction in which he led the horse.

For several hours, we continued traveling on a dirt path, among forests and groves. We had passed green fields and plowed lands, when suddenly residential structures appeared on the horizon.

"This is Zambrow," said Father with satisfaction, adding: "We'll reach the main road soon and arrive in the city in a short while." After several minutes, we encountered the main road, on which Russian military vehicles and farmers' wagons traveled. We breathed a sigh of relief. Father noted again that our extensive detour had prolonged our trip. Toward evening, we indeed arrived in Zambrow. Many military vehicles were parked at the edge of the city, surrounded by soldiers who cast curious looks in our direction. Father did not stop, but continued to the center of town. He was very familiar with it and said he would take us to the house of a Jewish acquaintance.

The town's Jewish population numbered around 3,000. Who knew what fate had befallen them during this period? Signs of the German bombings were well evident. Some of the buildings we passed looked totally destroyed.

It was early evening. Father stopped the wagon on one of the streets, entered the acquaintance's house and, emerging with a blank expression, said:

"No one is home. We'll go to the synagogue, where perhaps we can get updated and receive information of some sort."

Many Jews had gathered around the synagogue, all refugees like us who had arrived from cities and towns in the area, having been expelled from their homes. They related the Germans' horrific acts: the indiscriminate murder, the deliberate burning of homes and synagogues. Father went inside and returned after a little while.

"There's no point in remaining here," he said in disappointment. While guiding the horse to the center of town, he explained to us:

"The place is packed with refugees and the lack of food is obvious everywhere. We must stick to our plan. We'll spend the night here and leave for Bialystok tomorrow. The place is safe, full of Russian armed forces. In Bialystok we'll arrange for permanent housing until the war ends."

We departed the next morning. This time we were free of fear and could travel on the main road. Father expected us to arrive in

Bialystok by evening. The ride was long and exhausting. We passed villages large and small on both sides of the road, as well as isolated houses located next to streams and small bridges. There was increased wagon traffic hauling goods such as wheat and coal, or transporting people. We also saw carriages harnessed to one horse. We stopped a few times to rest and stretch our legs. It seemed as if there was no end in sight to our trip.

The many military vehicles traveling in both directions instilled in us a sense of security. Here, too, we saw many refugees winding their way on foot. We traveled in tandem with the stream of refugees who were also migrating to the city; until at last we caught sight of it from afar.

We arrived in Bialystok toward evening.

Chapter 7
Bialystok

"Arise and go now to the city of slaughter;
into its courtyard wind thy way;
... and with the eyes of thine head, behold."

"Be'Ir ha-Haregah" ("City of Slaughter") by H.N. Bialik

Bialystok was a huge city. I had never visited such a large city before. Here, too, the heavy hand of the Nazis was clearly in evidence. At the outbreak of the war, the Germans had attacked the city and several buildings had collapsed during the bombings. The Nazis entered the city on September 15th and retreated a week later. Under the terms of the Molotov-Ribbentrop Pact, the city came under control of the Soviet forces.

The city resembled a battlefield. Hundreds of Red Army tanks and military vehicles were scattered everywhere and battalions of soldiers roamed the city. Worst of all were the enormous numbers of refugees who flooded the city. Most, if not all, were Jews who had run for their lives from the claws of the Nazi predator, or had been expelled from their homes in the cities and villages and savagely crushed. The stream of refugees into the city was endless, like the powerful current of an overflowing river.

At first, Father thought we could manage here; but it quickly became apparent that even the Russian conqueror was unable to restore order and cope with such a large population crying out for food and housing. Every synagogue, school and *beit midrash* (study hall) was filled with Jewish families who had arrived empty-handed. All public auditoriums housed refugees; families wallowed in hallways and public areas, under appalling sanitary conditions. Bialystok Jews opened their homes to relatives and acquaintances. Social service institutions and philanthropic organizations did their best to help their Jewish brethren. Although the large community of 50,000 Jews was well-organized, the burden was much too heavy for its institutions to bear.

Our wagon made its way through the masses and Father looked for a convenient place to park. He was very familiar with Bialystok. He thought he would contact his acquaintances in the city, but first wanted to locate a good spot for the wagon and convert it into a home during the coming days. All its problems notwithstanding, the city was safe and protected by Red Army forces and there was no fear of cruelty towards Jews. Although the Russians also ruled with a heavy hand, they tried, in contrast to the Germans, to cope in their own fashion with the suffering that had been created.

Father set up our temporary living quarters on a street corner not far from the synagogue; we stayed there for several days. We met many Pultusk residents who had fled for their lives. They scoured the city as we did, looking for solutions to the grim situation. Most difficult and painful was the sight of prominent community members, depressed, broken and humiliated, standing on an endless line for a bowl of soup and a portion of food.

How moving it was when Father encountered some of his brothers. But the joy quickly disappeared and dissolved into bitterness when we heard of relatives who had not survived. I closed my ears when they recounted the brutal methods used by the Nazis to murder our family members. But it was necessary to continue and survive, come what may.

Father succeeded in obtaining a little food, but searched for work to ensure our continued existence. Between the food distributed by the Jewish community and that trickling in from the Soviet army, we managed to survive our first weeks in Bialystok.

In order to ease the hardship, the Soviet authorities offered all Polish refugees in the city free travel for whoever wished, to the

Ukraine and Belarus. Masses of people stood in line for entire days to register for the program. As stated, the situation in Bialystok was very difficult and many wanted to try their luck elsewhere. The army placed hundreds of trucks at the disposal of those interested, to transport them and their families to the designated destinations.

Many of the refugees from Pultusk went to Lithuania. Lithuania had been occupied by the Russians along with Eastern Poland, and in accordance with the Molotov-Ribbentrop Pact, annexed to the Soviet Union in 1940. The rumor spread that it was possible to travel from Lithuania to Eretz Israel (Palestine). We also heard that Rabbi Lowenthal, the rabbi of Pultusk, had moved to Vilna with his family and other community members. With a population of 200,000, half of whom were Jews, Vilna was considered a large city. Not for naught was it referred to as the "Jerusalem of Lithuania." It was a modern, bustling city, although we heard first-hand from people who wandered from city to city that anti-Semitism existed there, too. Father decided to remain in Bialystok. In retrospect, this proved to be a wise gamble.

Although the evacuation of many refugees led to some measure of relief, the situation remained dire. Many people were still without employment and signs of the approaching winter forced us to find a roof over our heads. Father returned one day and reported that he had found a hiding place with other refugees on an unused truck at the edge of the city. Its canvas cover could protect us from the cold of winter. This truck was an ideal housing solution for us, even if we had to share it with other refugees. We received appropriate compensation for the horse and wagon that Father sold, but from now on we had to pack our "belongings" in bundles and carry them from place to place ourselves, like the other refugees.

"I must find a job if we do not want to end up dependent on the charity of others – perhaps one of the local farmers has something for me. While I work, Ita will watch over you," said Father, adding: "I'll try to reach one of the villages I visited before the war; maybe I'll have a chance there. Don't worry if I'm delayed in returning. I will be back, no matter what, even if it's late at night."

Ita looked at Father and reassured him:

"Don't worry about us, Father, I'll watch over everyone. Go safely and I hope you are successful. We'll stay here and wait for you."

Father left us and set out on his way. The stress and tension he was under was evident in his body language and the way he spoke. His determination to do everything to survive knew no bounds. He had run around for entire days to obtain a bit of food for us and to arrange a place to sleep. Not for one moment had he ceased to search for work within the city. But his efforts were unsuccessful.

"What kind of work is Father looking for?" I asked Ita worriedly.

"These days, one can't be too picky, one takes whatever work is available. Father said he would look in one of the villages. Perhaps he'll get a job cutting wood or on one of the farms. I hope he finds something, because our money is running out," answered Ita, looking concerned.

All of Father's attempts to obtain employment in Bialystok and its environs proved useless. The Russians had liquidated many businesses and nationalized factories. Anyone considered "bourgeois" was arrested and exiled to Siberia. The Polish "zloty" had collapsed, becoming almost worthless; all liquid assets disappeared and a barter system developed. Long lines of people waited outside stores that had merchandise.

One day, Father returned from his regular search for work with good news:

"Children, I'm delighted to report that I found a job! Tomorrow I'll begin to work at a military gas station. One of my tasks will be to use a hand pump to provide gas for army vehicles passing through Bialystok."

We were very happy to hear this. In the course of his work,

Father developed connections with military personnel and many of the drivers who knew him gave him some food from time to time. In those crazy days, this was also something.

We endured a harsh winter. Ultimately, we were at the mercy of the Jewish community and its institutions, which provided us with minimum essentials – a small amount of food and some basic clothing. The Russians made life even harder with their new laws and procedures. They forbade all activity of a national or religious nature. In line with their system of socialism, they nationalized all factories privately owned by Jews and others. Furthermore, Russian soldiers also stole many Jewish possessions, including Father's watch.

The Nazi monster sat on the border, several kilometers from Bialystok, and continued to hunt for more and more prey. Its appetite knew no bounds. We were extremely disturbed by reports from Russian soldiers detailing Hitler's successes as he occupied Holland, Belgium, Luxembourg and France. The rumors circulating about the Jews from those countries described an accelerated process of concentrating them in ghettos, confiscation of their property, merciless slaughter and deportation to labor and death camps.

New refugees who had succeeded against all odds in crossing the roadblocks and borders appeared daily and arrived in Bialystok on their last legs. They were an important source of information for us about the Nazis' actions in occupied Poland. From them we learned of the "labor camp" set up in April 1940, which became the concentration and extermination camp, Auschwitz. Later, we heard of the Warsaw Ghetto, established in November 1940.

This period we spent wandering around Bialystok as refugees was terrible. We all prayed for an end to the war, but there was no indication of this then, in early 1941. Radio reports told of additional German conquests, this time in Greece and Yugoslavia. One by one, countries fell into German hands; and everywhere, the stories repeated themselves – unrestrained murder of Jews, confiscation of their property and concentration of Jewish populations in ghettos.

April 1941 was marked by increased Soviet military activity in Bialystok. Numerous tanks and military vehicles loaded with soldiers filled the streets and stationed themselves around the city. Positions changed every few days.

"I have a bad feeling," I heard Father musing aloud.

"What do you mean?" asked Ita.

"The intensive military movement in the area indicates that something is about to happen. I hope there won't be another flare-up. I tried to see if anyone at the synagogue understands the meaning of all this military deployment, but no one could explain it."

"Maybe the Russians know what is about to transpire, but want to keep it from the civilian population?" asked Ita.

"Perhaps," Father responded. "The news of many European countries falling to the Nazis one after another is surely worrying to the Russians. In any case, my instinct tells me that things do not bode well for the future."

The conditions under which we lived in the city, along with our helplessness, left no alternative but to maintain our desperate attempts to survive and to hope for an end to this hell. But the shocking reports from the other side of the border stole from us all peace of mind and left us unable to sleep a wink.

The morning of June 22nd is forever etched in my memory. We were awakened in the pre-dawn hours by the deafening wail of sirens. Minutes later, the familiar noise of planes filled the air. German Messerschmitt aircraft conquered the city's skies and powerful explosions were heard all over.

In a dramatic radio report, Russian foreign minister Molotov announced that the Germans had opened attack on Russia and were bombing its cities. The agreement he had signed with the German foreign minister over a year ago was not worth the paper it was printed on.

"Germany is invading Russia! Germany declared war on Russia!" was heard from all sides as people scurried, panic-stricken, in search of a hiding place.

Father gathered us together as soon as the bombings began and at his instructions, we immediately packed our belongings and awaited his word. As another wave of planes pounded the city endlessly with heavy bombs, Father declared agitatedly:

"We will stay here until the bombing ends, then flee the city eastward, because the Germans will arrive afterwards. I have no idea if the Russian army will succeed in stopping them. We must leave immediately!"

The explosions destroyed buildings, which collapsed on their residents. Hundreds of bodies were scattered throughout the city. Burning tanks blocked roads and wrecked military vehicles were abandoned with their wounded and dead soldiers inside. Heart-wrenching cries and wails were heard all over. Flames engulfed many buildings, smoke spiraling towards the sky. Father waited for a lull and when it came he rushed to get us out of the city.

We barely managed to make our way through the rubble. The images were horrifying. Dismembered corpses were scattered everywhere. The wounded, bleeding heavily, cried out in pain and called for help. Military vehicles undamaged by the bombing were seen escaping from Bialystok. Pandemonium reigned and the city lay in ruins, its streets in bedlam. Father asked us not to look around and instead to focus on following him quickly. Sounds of explosions and machine gun fire were heard clearly from the western side of the city. Father said we must distance ourselves from the main road and military vehicles as these were targets for enemy planes.

We walked eastward under the cover of darkness towards the retreating Soviet forces. Bursts of shells and rounds of machine gun fire were still blasting in the background. We veered off the main road onto a side path, near a grove. From there we witnessed lines of Red Army tanks and vehicles retreating to the east on the main road. Russian officials and security personnel escaped with their families in cars, wagons or on horseback. Masses abandoned the city and fled like lost sheep. The goal was to get as far away as possible from the approaching enemy. Looking backward, Bialystok was seen going up in fire, enveloped in a cloud of smoke.

Father urged us to keep walking. We walked all night almost without stopping. He apparently knew something that he kept from us. Just before dawn broke, a mighty wave of German planes swooped down on the retreating Russian convoy, and explosions accompanied by fire and columns of smoke were visible along the length of the main road which Father had been determined to avoid. We escaped to the nearby grove, looking at the horror transpiring before our eyes. The planes had no mercy on Bialystok. We looked behind us and saw the "bats of steel" raining heavy fire on the city over and over again. I thought how wise my father had been to urge us to escape so quickly. Wave after wave, the planes descended on the city, as if the death and destruction we had witnessed several hours earlier were not enough. The planes unleashed their wrath and disappeared. Father repeated that we must continue eastward by roundabout paths.

We walked along a winding road that reached a creek. We stopped to quench our thirst, wash ourselves and rest a bit. A long line of refugees trailed behind us. We were among the first to flee Bialystok. Not one of us understood the situation; all we knew was that the Germans had declared war on the Russians, the ramifications of which act we were now witnessing with our own eyes, all around us. We did not know what our own fate would be. If the Germans occupied the area, it would be catastrophic for us to be under their control. We had already witnessed their barbaric behavior in Pultusk and on the roads. As stated, we were terrified by the accounts of their horrific acts, which we had heard repeatedly from refugees arriving in Bialystok.

German planes conquered the skies. Squadron after squadron flew eastward over our heads. Refugees began to slowly gather around us and we again saw appalling sights. Some refugees were wounded, some bandaged. Father was determined to continue on our way without stopping, and constantly urged us on:

"We should leave here as soon as possible, before the Germans arrive. They have vehicles and tanks, while we're on foot. They are liable to catch up with us at any moment. Perhaps, in spite of everything, our best option now is to return to the main road in case we find someone willing to give us a ride eastward," suggested Father, while carrying our bundles on his back.

I stood looking at my father and sisters. At that moment I was not fully aware of the enormity of the tragedy that had befallen me. My childhood and youth were over; the joy of childhood had ended for me before it had even begun.

Several of the refugees walking with us were convinced that everything would work out fine, exactly as the songs of that era implied: Stalin would give the order and the Red Army would clear the area of the cruel German invader. They harbored the hope in their hearts that all would be safely restored in a short time. Their disappointment was as great as their expectations. By contrast, Father was a realist and viewed things more clearly: whenever the Germans initiated an air attack, invasion followed immediately. He therefore felt that we should leave the city quickly and resume our travel on the roads.

"Ita, you hold Shulem'keh and make sure he doesn't trip," instructed father. "Sarah and Zipporah, walk behind me, holding hands. This time, we will go as fast as possible. I hope you drank enough water; we are going to walk without stopping."

"Father, you don't think it's dangerous to be on the main road? After all, the Germans bombed the convoy traveling on it," Ita reminded him.

"Yes, you're right, it's no small gamble. But I assume that if they bombed the convoy on this road, they'll set their sights on other places and won't return. In any case, we'll keep our eyes open and if we see planes approaching, we will immediately run to the side, far from the road. Our only option for a quick escape before the Germans come is in some kind of vehicle. I might be able to stop one of the drivers I met when I worked at the military gas station. We must find someone who will agree to give us a ride!" explained Father determinedly. He was knowingly taking a calculated risk.

After walking a long time, Father stopped us and said:

"Unfortunately, I don't see any Russian resistance."

"Why did the Russians flee and not fight back?" asked Ita.

"I don't know. Apparently, the attack surprised them and they weren't sufficiently prepared. But who can withstand an attack as massive as that of the Germans? I didn't see a single Russian plane in the sky. The Germans are doing as they please in the area. This is total war – they mercilessly bombed and shelled a city along with its residents. I am convinced that thousands were killed in the bombings," sighed Father, looking behind him.

Bialystok was going up in flames.

Chapter **8**

Minsk – Parting from Father

"Take me in under your wing
and be unto me mother and sister"

H.N. Bialik

None of us knew that the attack begun on June 22, 1941 was the result of a plan meticulously prepared by the Germans in utmost secrecy and the start of the Nazis' Operation Barbarossa. The German attack took the Red Army and the Soviet authorities by surprise, almost totally obliterating the Russian air force in a lightning strike. Many planes were destroyed on the ground. Entire corps of the Red Army were surrounded and wiped out, and hundreds of thousands of soldiers fell into German captivity. Many Jews who had managed to escape eastward at the beginning of the war, and had found haven under the protection of the Red Army, were trapped in the line of German tanks rolling toward the east. As a result, they found themselves under German occupation once again.

About three million Wehrmacht (German armed forces from 1935-1945) soldiers and their allies took part in this battle. They were grouped into 190 divisions and opened attack along a 2900-kilometer (1800-mile) border. Among them were SS forces whose fanatical devotion to Nazi ideology was manifested in the mass slaughter of captives and civilians, particularly Jews.

Although we walked a very long way eastward, fortunately we did this as quickly as possible. We left Bialystok just in time. German forces entered and occupied the city on June 27th, which gave us a chance to flee deep into Russian territory. At some point, we succeeded in getting a ride in a Russian military vehicle. As Father had hoped, a driver he knew from his work in the military gas station in Bialystok stopped his vehicle and, that night, drove us the long distance to the city of Minsk.

Despite being heavily hit by the German air force, Minsk was bustling with people. Many refugees gathered on its streets and Russian soldiers could be seen stopping civilians and drafting them into the army. As early as April, government authorities had announced a mandatory draft of men into the Red Army. Father had so far managed to escape it somehow, but now, at the height of war, with the enemy on the doorstep, it did not seem possible to avoid the call-up. And indeed, eventually the Russian soldiers stopped us too.

Father was taken from us together with his brother, my uncle Shalom Domb, and both were immediately drafted into the Russian army. All Father's attempts to explain to the military that his children would be abandoned if he went into the army proved useless. He had no choice but to ask a female acquaintance from Pultusk whom he had met in Minsk to look after us. Father also succeeded in extracting a promise from the Russian officer who had inducted him that a military vehicle would take us to the east, far from the battle zone.

We got into the vehicle and, tears streaming, parted from Father while he waved goodbye until he disappeared from sight. Father was drafted and we children were placed in the trustworthy hands of my fifteen-year-old sister, Ita. The vehicle traveled eastward, but we had no idea of its destination. Fear gripped us. We did not know where Father had been taken, but we noticed that all the new recruits were driven out of the city on military vehicles, also eastward.

Later we realized that Father's determination to leave Bialystok immediately saved our lives the first time, while his insistence upon our traveling east, far from Minsk, in an army vehicle saved our lives a second time, both in the same week.

It transpired that, the day after Bialystok was occupied by the

Germans, 3,000 Jews were herded into the central synagogue. The Nazis set fire to this holy site, and all inside were burned alive. Minsk was conquered on June 28th and German soldiers who had been parachuted east of the city succeeded in intercepting thousands of Jewish refugees, forcing them to retrace their steps westward. To our relief, by then we were very far from Minsk, deep in Russian territory. Four children with no mother and no father, on their own, weak and starving, at the height of a world war.

After hours of travel, we reached a town with a heavy concentration of armed forces. It was early morning. The driver stopped and told us to get off, as we had arrived at our destination. Jewish refugees had gathered in the center of town. Noticing us – four unaccompanied children – getting out of the military vehicle, a Russian officer took pity on us, and handed us half a loaf of bread. We wandered around town, weighed down by our bundles and with only a little food in our possession.

Many military vehicles drove by on the main street. This town had also been bombed from the air, and the further into the city we walked, the more overpowering the unbearable odor became. Even the winds were unable to erase the stench of death, the horrible smell of both explosives and burned human flesh. Ita spotted a line of refugees making its way out of town and, with her excellent instincts, decided to join them. She went to speak with them and returned after a few minutes.

"Where are we going?" Sara asked Ita.

"I wish I knew. Like us, they also came here after escaping the German bombings. They say the Germans are advancing quickly and suggested continuing eastward in the direction of the retreating Russian army. Father would also do the same. He said we should follow the Russian soldiers because they are the only ones who can protect us. Please stay near me so that we can be together the whole time. No one should get lost and we must not waste time," said Ita firmly, taking charge.

So much responsibility was placed on this fifteen-year-old girl's shoulders! At those moments, she showed her true greatness. She was both mother and father to us, and our sister-leader. Like a seasoned soldier, she displayed courage, organizational skills, responsible thinking, adaptability and the survivor's instinct. We obeyed her every instruction. She distributed the bundles among us and we joined the line of refugees leaving town toward the east, in the direction of the Red Army vehicles.

Here begins a journey of wandering and survival that is difficult to describe. This was a journey that stretched for four years over thousands of long kilometers. If not for Ita's leadership, wisdom and sense of responsibility, it is doubtful that we would have survived. Time had no meaning for us. We were fated to wander, but we did not know to where. All we knew was that the direction had to be eastward, as mentioned, because the predators waited in ambush in the west. They were advancing toward us like a hurricane, destroying all that stood in their way, leaving destruction, ruin and mountains of dead in their wake. Whoever escaped early enough and found any sort of hiding place was saved; whoever did not, found their death.

As we were walking, German warplanes flew overhead in our direction. The sounds of explosions reverberated from all sides and wherever we looked, we saw billowing smoke. Along the route were the remains of burnt military vehicles and Russian tanks in flames. Corpses and body parts were scattered around. During one segment of our walk, we passed a genuine battlefield – a field full of dismembered bodies spread over a large area. A cloud of black crows swooped down on the corpses, covering everything.

We walked many kilometers. Those whose strength gave way were abandoned to their fate. We did not know where we were, only that we were in Russian territory, walking eastward. Toward evening we reached a small village near a forest. We were tired, starving and weak.

"I think this place looks safe for resting and sleeping. I see that people are preparing to stop here," said Ita in her soothing voice, turning onto a side road that led to the nearby forest.

Somewhere in the forest, together with a few other Jews, Ita spread out a blanket, thus marking the territory of the Domb refugees for the night. We placed our belongings near us and in her usual manner, Ita gave each of us a portion of bread. She repeated Father's famous sentence:

"Chew slowly and swallow."

After we stretched out on the blanket, Ita covered us and we fell asleep. The exhaustion, starvation, the hardships of the road and the difficult experiences of the last few days took their toll. We slept many hours, and it was already daylight when we opened our eyes. I lay on my back, staring at the treetops above, frightened and agitated from my nightmares. When I calmed down a bit, the terrors of the recent days began to penetrate my consciousness. Reality mingled with dream, and became almost as one.

Ita re-packed our belongings for easier carrying. She sat down next to us, a pitcher of water and cup of milk in hand, and gave us each a portion, saying:

"While you were sleeping, I dropped by one of the farmers in the village, who was kind enough to give me a cup of milk, a potato and a bit of bread. We will leave after we've eaten. The farmer told me that the Red Army forces are fighting very heroically, and in some places are succeeding in stopping the Germans and causing them great losses. I hope this is the case; perhaps it will bring the war closer to its end."

I do not know how long we wandered, but I can certainly say that it was many months. I cannot name all the places we passed through, but I can safely say that we traversed dozens of towns, villages and cities. We also passed through countless forests and crossed rivers and streams. At times we would spend only one night in one location, while at others we would remain for several weeks. The roads were dangerous and we tried to stay close to the Red Army forces deployed everywhere. Frequently we spotted German military vehicles traveling on the roads. At such times, we were careful to hide until they passed, and tried to choose a different walking route.

We had no map and only knew that we had to go as far eastward as possible. This was "the code." In one of the forests in which we hid, other Jews were hiding, as usual, and they warned us of sudden inspections by Nazi units. We also had to watch out for the Gestapo who swarmed throughout the area. It seems that local informers would notify them of Jewish refugees in the forest. In such instances, the Nazis would systematically encircle the forest, cutting off any possible escape route and trapping the Jews who were hiding. Whoever tried to flee was shot and killed on the spot. It was impossible to avoid the chain of beasts in human form who surrounded those hiding in the woods.

Early one morning before dawn, after spending several days in a forest, we heard the din of a large number of cars approaching our hiding place. Still half asleep, we found ourselves blocked on all sides by SS soldiers. They commanded us all make our way out to the main forest path. Great panic ensued. The hundreds hiding out there included many children, women and elderly, as well as handicapped people who were carried on their relatives' shoulders. It was a horrifying scene. Ita hastily gathered us together and encouraged us to blend in among the hundreds of people on the path.

Volleys of machine-gun fire in the forest were accompanied by bloodcurdling human screams. My heart pounded. Ita hugged us all, placing me in the center. The roars of the Gestapo soldiers were terrifying. They ordered us to start walking in the direction of a road that led to a town visible in the distance. German military vehicles rode at the head of the long line of marchers, and two jeeps in the rear forced the stragglers to catch up to the group. We marched thus for several hours until we reached the main road.

Suddenly, like saviors, Russian fighter planes burst from the sky. They had apparently tracked the convoy and now rained heavy fire on the German forces at the head of the line. Great pandemonium ensued. We threw ourselves down on the ground. Some of the Germans were killed on the spot; others began to flee. We remained in the area for a while, shocked at what had transpired. As always, Ita made sure we stayed together. The sight of the dismembered bodies of the SS soldiers scattered on the smoking vehicles was revolting. From afar we saw a line of Russian soldiers approaching. They provided us with a little food and escorted us to a place of safety.

Most of the time, we marched on foot. To the best of my recollection, we stopped once in a town where Russian soldiers sent us to the local train station, to board a train. After traveling for several hours, we were let off to continue our wanderings. They had removed us from the battle zone, but we could still clearly hear the roar of artillery fire from our location.

Part of the time, we rode on horse-drawn wagons we encountered along the way. Once, the Russian soldiers directed us to a dirt path and instructed us to continue on it. The path led to a roaring, impassable river. Russian military vessels transported us to the other bank, from where we continued to nowhere. We always walked in the direction indicated by the soldiers, usually joining the wave of refugees marching in that same direction.

One day, we reached a forest after having walked for almost twenty-four hours. Nearby was a small agricultural village. Ita always preferred sleeping in forests, near small villages. She felt that there was a greater chance of finding someone who would agree to give us shelter or a bit of food. From what I recall, she was usually correct. Accordingly, we prepared to sleep along with other people who were with us. Suddenly, about ten Jewish boys, aged ten to thirteen, burst forth from the forest and asked to join us. We had no idea how they had gotten there or how they had survived. From afar, they had noticed Ita leading us and sensed that she was someone they could trust.

Without a word, Ita cleared a space next to us and told them to sit down. The stories we heard from them were hair-raising. They had been abandoned at one stage or another of the war in various places, and fate brought them together here in the forest. As we sat and listened to them, another few boys emerged out of nowhere. They related that deep in the forest was a kind man who occasionally gave them potatoes and a little bread. They gathered berries, and sometimes received bread and a little food from local farmers. Like us, they all appeared starved and emaciated.

The boys did not leave us, and Ita was now taking care of about twenty boys. During our long journey, we had encountered many refugees, but this was the first time we had joined up with such a large group of youngsters who, like us, were without parents. We stayed in the forest for a few days, and through the kindness of several local Russian families, received a little food for sustenance. The boys became dependent on Ita and refused to part from her. When we left after a few days, they came with us.

A Red Army vehicle picked us up along the way and brought us to the train station in one of the surrounding cities. The station was crowded with thousands of refugees and many soldiers, all waiting for eastward-bound trains. We were swallowed up in the crowd. Ita tirelessly and constantly made sure that we were by her side. We waited along with everyone else for the salvation that might appear from some mysterious quarter; but all in vain. Instead, we heard an ear-piercing siren informing us of an impending air attack. Once again, there was a great commotion, with people scattering in all directions. Ita decided that it was safer to get as far away as possible from the station. We did that. Luckily, though, the planes were heading elsewhere and passed overhead with a thundering noise.

There was no chance of boarding the train. The throngs of people gathered in the station created unbearable, almost life-threatening, congestion. So we continued our endless walking. Our attempts to stop a military vehicle met with no success. Such a ride would have held many advantages for us. There was a certain chance of encountering a Russian Jewish soldier or officer who would undoubtedly treat us well and, in particular, give us a good portion of food. We would also be able to hear updates on the battle situation, as well as warnings of places to avoid. Perhaps most importantly, such a ride would save us days of walking exhaustedly on foot. In our poor physical condition, an opportunity like this would have been extremely beneficial. In the meantime, however, these were merely "dreams" that we entertained.

On one occasion, we arrived in a smoke-filled town; a battle had obviously ended there just a few hours earlier. Vehicles damaged during the fighting were trapped in the ruins. The sounds of gunfire still reverberated on the outskirts of the town. It seems that the Russians had succeeded in repelling the German attack, causing losses to the enemy. Armed Russian soldiers roamed the streets and asked us to hide in one of the houses.

Ita brought us to the train station at the entrance to the city where we found a corner in which to hide. On the way, I noticed the body of a fallen German soldier lying on the ground. My eyes were drawn to his shiny, new shoes and the knapsack he carried on his back. With my vivid imagination, I pictured the bread and other food items in the knapsack....

When things calmed down, we saw Russian tanks and red-flagged military vehicles moving through the city, and understood that the Russians had beaten back the attack and emerged from their hiding places. Encouraged by this, I approached the German's body, pulled off his knapsack, and started to remove his shoes. As I struggled with his right shoe, which stubbornly refused to come off his foot, the German opened his eyes! I ran for dear life, leaving the knapsack and shoes behind, probably to the benefit of another refugee.

Many times, we happened upon battle zones. An incident strongly etched in my memory occurred in one of these areas, which was under German control. This was deep in Russian territory, not far from a large city whose name I cannot recall. As a result of the fighting and the major destruction sown in the surrounding cities, tens of thousands of refugees flocked toward a river in the vicinity. To our surprise, the place was filled with large German forces.

Many tens of thousands of families were present, including children, the elderly, the ailing and handicapped being transported in carts, pregnant women and babies – a mixed multitude of refugees. The Germans concentrated everyone on the river bank and surrounded the mass with tanks and machine guns. Squads of Gestapo soldiers strode among the crowds, snatching every young person who looked like a soldier. These young people were all placed to one side, and then shot to death in front of everyone. The cry that went up from the crowd at the sight of the slaughter raised goosebumps all over my body. The rest of the people were ordered to the other side of the river. We merged with the crowds and were swept up with them to the other side.

"The area is infested with Germans and is apparently controlled by them. We have to hurry and get far away from here. We absolutely must not fall into their hands. Perhaps we should hide in one of the surrounding forests until the situation clears up," Ita mused aloud, turning to consult with an older Jewish woman walking next to us, then reporting to us what she had heard.

"The woman said that many of the Jews who fled are hiding in the forests for fear of the Germans. Rumor has it that the Germans are focusing on a search for Jews. They are concentrating Jews in ghettos and sending them to forced labor and to extermination camps."

We had no radio or newspapers, and received war news

primarily via rumors. When one has no means to verify a situation, rumors are the only alternative. We gleaned the facts regarding the situation primarily via the testimony of refugees who managed to escape the inferno, and recounted what they had seen with their own eyes and the shocking experiences they had undergone. We also had information from Russian soldiers we met along the way, who were updated directly by their commanders or from their military radios. Village farmers were another important source. Whoever owned a radio in those days heard the news and the reports straight from the battlefield.

Our wanderings did not end. For months, we continued marching from place to place together with other refugees, sleeping each night in a different location. We ran out of food and relieved our hunger with grass, berries and stalks of wheat we happened to find on the way. The forest dwellers we met resembled shadows, as did we. The hunger, wanderings and frequent changes of hiding place exhausted our energy. Despair began to eat away at us and to deplete even further our already minimal desire to live. We faced death many times. My sister Ita stubbornly and persistently fought against this somber mood and constantly reminded us of Father's command – not to surrender under any circumstances and to do everything to survive!

Already by the end of 1941, the rumor had arrived: the Germans had activated the machinery of destruction and begun the mass slaughter of Jews in Polish concentration camps. We learned this from survivors' accounts. The rumors spoke of Hitler's outright order to begin implementing the Final Solution to the Jewish Question. This meant one thing only – the annihilation of the Jewish nation.

And as for us … we continued our wanderings. Through endless expanses; with no clear destination; under cloudy skies, under blue skies. On we went.

Chapter 9

In the Forests and Hollows of the Earth

*"And they shall come into the caves of the rocks
and into the hollows of the earth"*

Isaiah 2:19

As we wandered, many thoughts raced through our heads during the endless walking. One thought that never left us was where to sleep at night.

We felt lonely and exposed in the open air, walking for an entire day with short breaks to rest and stretch our limbs. Apparently we were in a hostile area under German control, deep in unfamiliar Russian territory and far from population centers. Ita said we were going towards the forests, where, according to rumor, many Jews were hiding.

Evening descended and darkness began to reign. The forest, our destination for that day, seemed very far away, literally on the horizon. As usual, we walked on side paths rather than on the main road. Whenever a vehicle appeared on the road, we were careful to hide in order to avoid being discovered. Now, under the cover of darkness it was easier to make progress.

"We should rest a bit and then continue walking. We've avoided being detected by the Germans until now, and we must not be caught by them. If we continue we can still get to the forest tonight," said Ita, spreading a blanket on the ground. We all fell on it, exhausted and drained. I fell asleep instantly.

We reached the forest that night. It would become our home-fortress for several months.

We had come across many forests by then, but had never seen one like this. This forest held an entire colony of Jews. There was a family in every corner. Some people gathered in groups. Our common denominator was that we were homeless refugees, hiding from the ceaseless German pursuit of Jews. Ita said it was best to go deep into the forest, where it would be safer. Many of the refugees dug pits to hide in and protect themselves from the cold of the approaching winter.

"It seems we will have to stay here for a long time, until the situation clears up. As long as the Germans control the area, it is very dangerous to be on the roads, especially for Jews. The Nazis are searching high and low for us, and killing every Jew they find," said Ita while walking into the depths of the forest. We passed families and individuals who had already staked out their territory.

"It looks like these people have been here for a long time," commented Sara, asking: "How long will we be here?"

"I don't know. We'll act just as the others do. First, let's organize a comfortable and suitable place for ourselves. Afterwards, I'll inquire among the forest veterans and see if they have information that will help us understand the situation," answered Ita, urging us on.

This was a huge virgin forest, many kilometers in length and breadth. There were tall conifers and leafy trees whose branches extended both horizontally and upwards. It was obvious that no human had trod in the depths of this forest. One could see enormous tree trunks from storm-toppled trees lying on the ground, blocking all passage to the forest center. This was a world unto itself – dark, frightening and uncivilized, a habitat for animals such as foxes, wolves, snakes and wild boars.

Ita drew us deep, very deep, into the forest, where we set up our home amidst trees and thick vegetation. Judging by the arrangements strictly orchestrated by Ita, it looked as if we would remain here for a long time. We removed any obstacle preventing us from spreading out the blanket, then lay down on it and fell asleep for a very long time.

I cannot estimate the size of the forest, but, as stated, it was huge, truly endless and far from civilization. Even from its edges, it was impossible to observe any kind of populated area. Only on the very distant horizon were vehicles visible, traveling on a road. We maintained a fixed daily routine here. Each day, we gathered blueberries, raspberries, blackberries and mushrooms. Ita strictly demanded that we not stray too far from our "home"; and under no circumstances did she me to go by myself. We became experts in all types of mushrooms. Ita would cook soup from some of the harvest, which warmed us up on cold days.

As I write these words today, thoughts come to my mind about the lifestyle, culture, good manners and norms accepted by our society. The encounter with the reality of life – that which exists beneath the veneer of culture – lent a wholly different significance to everything. Time meant something else, behavior was different. In the real life in which we "starred," we were willing to do everything to obtain a piece of bread or a rotten potato. Even if it meant stealing, lying or removing articles of clothing from dead or dying people. Real life meant survival and nothing else, exactly as it did for the beasts of the forest which we now called home.

Since we left Bialystok, I had heard many stories about partisans and their acts of bravery and revenge, and I very much admired their courage. With my active imagination, I pictured the partisan as tall and thick-bearded, with a muscular body that instilled fear in the enemy. I envisioned him holding a weapon, living in the forest and helping the weak. I wondered if there were partisans in our forest as well.

I received my answer when a rumor spread that a group of partisans was coming to our area. When I spied on them from behind a tree, they looked different from what I had imagined. They were young bearded men in their twenties and thirties, carrying bundles on their back and holding weapons. They stopped near us, distributed potatoes and bread, and melted away again into the thick forest bushes.

It seems that every so often, the partisans would raid one of the distant villages and, after their fashion, would obtain food for themselves and the refugees in the forest. They knew that we had no possibility of leaving the forest, in this hostile area under Nazi control. The death sentence imposed on the Jews by the Germans and their collaborators, and the cruel, highly efficient mechanism they had established for its implementation, left us no choice but to hide here. We knew that any Jew caught faced death.

At times, the partisans were accompanied by youngsters aged thirteen to fifteen, also carrying bundles and arms. I very much wanted to join them. Someone in the forest claimed that the weapons these boys carried were real. Someone else argued that the rifles they had were of carved wood and only resembled real ones. Everything to do with the partisans was mysterious. No one knew where they came from and to where they disappeared. Every conversation about them was held in a quiet, almost whispered, voice. When I tried asking Ita something about the partisans, she immediately hushed me, saying there are things that are not discussed, and changed the topic.

I learned that the partisans also provided us with information. They communicated with the outside world via a wireless transmitter and were able to report on events and on the latest news, including the war in Stalingrad. They warned us of German raids on the forests and suggested that we change our hiding places frequently.

Ita borrowed shovels from our neighbor and, together, we dug a pit. We covered it with trees and branches for camouflage, but also, of course, to conserve our body heat during the cold weather.

The more I think of it today, many years after those terrifying times, the more my admiration for my eldest sister Ita grows. From where did she derive the wisdom to accumulate enough suitable clothing during our wanderings to prevent us from freezing in wintertime? As I pen these lines, unfathomable images come to mind, such as Ita rummaging among the corpses of bombings victims, removing clothing and various articles that would be useful to us. To her everything had value – sweaters, coats, socks, blankets, pants, shirts and what not.

I recall one incident when, while on our way to a forest, we found ourselves in a town that was under aerial attack. We hid in one of the destroyed buildings. During a bombing, a woman wrapped in a blanket who was crossing the street near us was hit and killed, and her whole body began hemorrhaging. This time, I mustered up the courage to run up to her and peel the blood-stained blanket off her. To this day, I remember the angry look on Ita's face due to my "irresponsible" actions; yet this blanket served us well later during the cold nights.

One of the items Father "bequeathed" to us when he was drafted into the Russian army was a sack. Made of a strong weave, it was reminiscent of the army "kitbag" familiar to every soldier. Ita made sure to carry this bag throughout our years of wandering. It served as our clothes closet as well as our kitchen cabinet. In it were a vessel for water, cups, plates, a small pot and other items. It was also our pantry, where we hid a few potatoes and, sometimes, when our situation improved, bread that we had received.

We were extremely worried about informers throughout our stay in the forest, fearing that some farmer would hear about us and turn us over to the Germans. There was no shortage of hostile elements who collaborated with the Germans. But luckily, the Germans did not fare well in this region, as the Russians managed to recover and launch a counterattack.

Hunger and cold were our worst enemies. Among those hiding in the forest were older people who died after their strength gave out, while the young managed to survive. We were all very gaunt. Some of the adults required medicines; but since these, of course, were unattainable, their bodies weakened. Thus passed many months. We had become shadows of our former selves. What awaited us? All gates were closed before us – both the gates of mercy and the gates of vengeance. We were like broken vessels. Our strength was totally depleted from the many wanderings decreed upon us, and from the entire situation.

We clearly heard the echoes of battles in the area, and the thunderous explosions of shells grew more frequent. At night, in addition to the sounds of explosions, we also saw flashes of fire. Frequently, we heard the noise of planes pouring out their wrath upon the surroundings via massive bombings. From our hiding place we were unable to discern whose planes these were, but it was obvious that heavy fighting was going on somewhere, outside of the forest.

A rumor spread one morning that the Russians had conquered the area. The forest refugees began to congregate immediately to clarify the source of the rumor, which held great significance for us – it meant that we could finally leave the forest! A sneaking suspicion crept into our hearts that this might be a trick designed to turn us over to the Germans. Not one of us dared leave the place until we heard confirmation of the rumor from the partisans themselves.

The partisans related that the Russians had recovered from the initial blow and had begun to repel the Germans in various spots. They had regained control of the region, and the Germans suffered defeat and heavy losses. No words can describe the joy that gripped us. A spark of hope appeared. "We are leaving the forest! Perhaps the war has even ended …!" we rejoiced. However, the truth was that although the Russians had beaten back the Germans in that area, the war was far from over. Apparently the Germans had attacked Leningrad and Moscow, but had not succeeded in penetrating the strongholds.

We resumed our wanderings, but this time under the protection of the Russian army. An indelible memory comes to mind here. We were being taken somewhere in a Russian military vehicle and along the way saw a long line of posts bearing the hanging bodies of German officers, captured in battle. It was a frightening sight. Ita, sensing that I was upset, covered my eyes with her hands, and said, "These are German officers. They deserve to die after sowing death throughout Europe!"

The tremendous number of refugees roaming the area posed a problem for the Russian forces and interfered with their maneuvers. The military directed the stream of refugees to a huge compound near one of the cities. To maintain order, thousands of soldiers were stationed in the compound, which stretched over a wide territory. We numbered among the tens of thousands of refugees, mostly Jews who had hidden in the area, who were assembled there.

During this period, the Russian soldiers tried to give us food and to demonstrate that matters were under control. We were in the first of many groups transported here by hundreds of trucks. We were told that we were being taken to a safe place, far from the battle zones.

After traveling a considerable distance, the convoy of trucks stopped in an open field near railroad tracks. A large number of soldiers stood around the field's perimeter to maintain order. After we alighted from the trucks, they organized us into groups. Ita made sure that we stayed together and did not get separated. A freight train approached from afar and stopped in the open field. We were ordered to board the cars, in the groups that had been formed.

We all wanted to know where we were being taken. The train started to move and we set out. It was a long trip and it was hot and stuffy in the freight car, which reeked of the sour stench of human sweat. We traveled for hours. A person who recognized the route said we were heading northward towards Siberia. On the one hand, we were happy to be heading so far from the fighting; on the other, the name Siberia brought up unpleasant associations of exile. It was linked in our minds to hard labor and freezing cold, and we knew it as a place for prisoners, criminals and opponents of the regime. We felt unsettled and extremely worried.

Each time the train stopped, we left the car for a short break, to stretch our legs and to relieve ourselves, after which we were called to re-board. The engine would start up slowly, laboring heavily, and then gather speed and accelerate. I looked out through the cracks and saw forests and more forests, countless forests. Here and there a few houses could be seen, their smoking chimneys indicating some sign of life in this godforsaken region. Sometimes, the engine's steam penetrated the cars, resulting in an intolerable odor and feeling of suffocation. As the trip wore on, temperatures dropped further. Someone mentioned that the train routes in Russia were among the longest in the world.

After days of travel interrupted only by short breaks, we reached our destination – a place called Arkhangelsk. This was not a mistake: we were completely surrounded by snow and ice. We inhaled the cold, trembled from the cold.

"Arkhangelsk?" Ita asked one of the travelers.

"Yes, we've arrived in Arkhangelsk. We're not alone, this is a labor camp. I heard one of the soldiers say that conditions are not so terrible," answered the traveler. He took his belongings and approached the soldier organizing the group. We stood outside, in the cold, awaiting instructions.

The many policemen and armed soldiers were charged with guarding and maintaining order in the camp, which was home to a large refugee population. The person responsible for our car took us to a huge wooden barracks housing about two hundred refugees in crowded conditions. Ita located a spot for us, where we placed our possessions. At long last we were settled in proper quarters, with wooden beds, an enclosed space that was heated, and with our own corner. There was, however, no electricity, and light was provided by lamps which burned a special oil made from fish.

We were soon made aware of the camp's rules. The men were taken out to work every day, primarily to chop down trees. Some worked in camp services such as cleaning, maintenance, etc. Young boys also had jobs. They had to gather the short branches and scraps of wood that piled up after the hewing and sawing, and bring them to the heating stoves in the barracks. These were wood-burning stoves with chimneys that connected to other barracks, and thus the heat was retained – fortunate for us, as the cold here was intolerable. Ita made sure that we dressed properly in the harsh winter, and watched over me especially. Whenever she saw me about to leave the barracks, she insisted that I wear appropriate clothing.

We slowly adjusted to conditions. We discovered that a not insignificant percentage of the camp population included exiled political prisoners, many of whom were Ukrainian. Trains arrived very frequently and the stream of refugees and prisoners was unending. The train station was inside the camp. However, these were no ordinary passenger trains. Rather, they were freight trains, discharging refugees and prisoners, unloading equipment for the camp and then returning to the front with military supplies on board.

The camp was an army base that spread over several kilometers and was surrounded by high wooden walls. Permission was required to leave the camp grounds, and it was granted only for work purposes. There were some advantages to being here. The first was the personal security: we were no longer pursued, nor were we concerned for our lives, so far from the Germans and the fighting. The second was having a roof over our heads, and no longer having to worry about finding a place to sleep, as we did previously when we slept in the open air, in fields or forests. Another benefit was the food, distributed weekly – bread, dried mushrooms, corn flour. True, it was insufficient for our needs; but at least we did not have to go hunting for food. We considered our stay, temporary as it was, a tolerable one until the war should end.

To our great surprise and sorrow, we learned after some time that our paternal grandfather, Yaakov Domb, along with our grandmother, had been exiled here, to Arkhangelsk. Suffering from cold and hunger, they met their death inside the camp, both dying on the same day. This story touched us deeply and caused us great pain.

One day, my sister Sara and I went out to the forest with a group of adults and an accompanying guide, to pick cherries and mushrooms. As usual, Ita made sure we were dressed warmly from head to toe. The forest, one of the virgin forests typical to the area, was filled with tall conifers. Focused on our task, we all entered the thick forest.

It was early wintertime, and we were struck by the bitter cold. When we completed our assignment at the designated time, the guide collected us and we began marching back to the camp. After we had walked for hours without reaching our destination, the guide understood that he had lost his way. Several of the youngsters in the group began to display signs of distress and burst into tears. We saw bears in the area trying to approach us, but the older members of the group, together with the guide, cut some long branches in order to chase them away. We all shook with fear. The guide decided that we should light a fire, both for warmth and so that the smoke would signal our location to those looking for us.

We sat in a tight circle around a tree, near the fire. My sister Sara did not leave me throughout this time and we sat huddled with the group to preserve our body heat and – purportedly – to protect ourselves from the bears. A full twenty-four hours passed, with no food, in the freezing cold of the forest. Seeing that we did not return, our families alerted the police and soldiers, who went to search for us. It took them twenty-four hours to find us, hours of unmitigated fear and tension for all. The soldiers who reached us immediately wrapped us in blankets, gave us hot drinks and calmed us down.

Here in the camp we were also introduced for the first time to a unique phenomenon of nature, called "white nights." Arkhangelsk is located in northwestern Russia, near the Arctic Circle (66.5° north latitude). At certain points during the summer, the sun sinks below the horizon for a short time only. Daylight is considerably increased, and darkness is almost non-existent. The reverse occurs in the winter, when, at various periods, the nights are long and there is practically no daylight. The adjustment was difficult for those not used to these conditions, but, ultimately, they became tolerable.

As time went on, we learned of Arkhangelsk's importance as a port city. During the war, it served as a major transfer point on the route used by the Americans and British to provide the Russian forces with military and civilian aid. With naval battles raging in the Mediterranean, and with the western European coast and the skies now under German control, the sole remaining route for transporting supplies to the Russian army was the Arctic one. The railroad to Arkhangelsk, built in the late nineteenth century, was also used for this purpose.

Aware of the Arctic naval aid convoys sailing under harsh conditions, the Germans attacked them mercilessly from the air and from submarines quickly summoned to the area. A large number of supply ships were thus sunk to the bottom of the sea. The Germans also sabotaged the railroad tracks between Arkhangelsk and Moscow. Many camp residents were conscripted for repair work on the bombed-out tracks to allow the military supplies to reach their destination.

The subject of the Arctic convoys stirred the imagination of authors such as Alistair MacLean, in his novel HMS *Ulysses*, and Nicholas Monsarrat, in *The Cruel Sea*. The latter describes the fierce naval battles conducted against the convoys en route to Arkhangelsk.

We came to terms with the fact that we now lived in a land of snow and ice, a frozen, threatening land. There was no place to flee. Around us lay an unbroken monotonous view of endless virgin forests and horizonless plateaus, a land of brown bears and gray wolves. The area was infamous for being a place of exile for millions of people out of favor with various ruling governments, transported here to meet their deaths.

The local winter was cruel and merciless, with blinding, five foot-high snow covering vast spaces. Temperatures dropped to about -58° Fahrenheit and fierce winds gusted; their howling was terrifying. To someone who was not used to living here, it seemed as if the world was on the verge of destruction. It was hard to breathe and the frost burned our faces. No living creature could be outside and anyone without shelter would freeze to death in a very short time. Fortunately, we spent this period in heated barracks, awaiting the end of God's wrath.

For many months, we lived with the hope that the Americans and their allies would prove victorious in the war. We yearned for an end to the ongoing nightmare.

Chapter 10

From Arkhangelsk to Kutaisi

"Who knows the tears that have yet to be shed,
the storms that have yet to strike?"

"Mishut ba-Merhakim" (Back From the Distance), H.N. Bialik

Our stay in Arkhangelsk was, as mentioned, not easy. I varied the daily routine by means of all sorts of activities with my sisters and other boys whom I met. I have already described Ita's role, but I must reiterate and emphasize that in our long stay in this godforsaken location, she truly outdid herself and inspired admiration. She continued to be both mother and sister to us, and none of us questioned her position. She took us under her wing and, in this freezing cold, showered us with her love and warmth.

Throughout the time we lived here, the trains never ceased arriving, bringing with them a stream of refugees, with news and updates. From them we heard about the concentration camps and the mass murders carried out by the Nazis. We had known about the atrocities and had even witnessed some ourselves, but not one of us could have guessed the extent of the slaughter in these camps. Later we learned that in Treblinka itself, the Nazis had cremated 900,000 Jews! The human mind cannot fathom such numbers.

Despite the change on the battlefield in winter 1942, which signaled the end of Germany's victories and rapid advance, the Nazi extermination machinery continued to operate at full steam in the occupied areas, as we later heard.

At a certain stage of the war, the Germans were fighting against three great powers that had consolidated their civilian and military resources – Russia, Great Britain and the United States. Field Marshal Montgomery's forces eventually crushed Rommel and his army in the Battle of El Alamein. The Russians revived and initiated counterattacks that eroded the strength of the German military.

Having heard nothing from Father, we did not know where he was stationed and on which front he was fighting. All we knew was that he had been conscripted in Minsk. We were very worried about him. Whenever I asked about him, Ita would reassure me, saying that we would certainly meet him after the war was over. Here in the intolerable cold, however, no end to the war was in sight, as evidenced by the ceaseless arrival of refugees and the horrifying news they brought.

It is not clear to me exactly how long the duration of our stay in Arkhangelsk was, but I am positive that it spanned many months – more than a year, perhaps even two. It was an unforgettable period. I remember many events and details, but not their exact dates. My account here is based on my best attempt at recollection and on stories I heard, primarily from my sister Ita, of blessed memory.

Once it became impossible for the camp to take in additional refugees, it was decided to release groups and individuals who were only marginally productive, such as families with children, the elderly and others. One day, the officer in charge came into our barracks and informed us that we were leaving. He turned to Ita and said: "You must report with your belongings tomorrow morning. You will be transferred to a safe area in east Russia. There is nothing to fear, as your destination is far from the battle zones and you will be out of danger there."

The officer then turned to a number of others in our barracks with the same information. Ita asked:

"Where exactly are they taking us?"

The officer hesitated. After a short pause, he responded:

"To be honest, I'm not really sure. But it was decided to send you to a safe place, with more suitable conditions. The train leaves tomorrow morning, and you are to report to the platform at 8 a.m."

He left. The other families who were told to leave gathered around us, and one frightened-looking woman grumbled:

"The Russians are sick of us. They're going to abandon us far from the camp, where we'll freeze to death!"

"Nonsense," said a French prisoner to put her at ease. "The Russians are tough, but they aren't cruel like the Germans. I think they just want to make things easier for themselves and for us."

We had long been acquainted with this Frenchman, ever since the initial days of our arrival in Arkhangelsk, when he was already living in our barracks. Noticing that we were alone and unaccompanied by adults, he had offered his help to Ita. Every day, upon returning from work, he asked how we were; and on days when not required to work, he was available for conversation and assistance. Topics of discussion included our life in the camp, the war and our future. Many people enjoyed conversing with him and a circle of listeners formed wherever he stopped to talk. A pleasant, wise and learned man, knowledgeable in many fields, he spoke gently and never argued with others. He always had the upper hand in the occasional disagreements that transpired; but he never insulted or harmed his listeners.

On this occasion, however, his words failed to placate the frightened woman and she burst out crying.

I was unable to sleep that whole night. Thoughts raced through my head and the woman's words echoed in my ears: "They're going to abandon us … we'll freeze to death …. " I recalled the night we had gotten lost in the forest, the freezing cold and the terrifying bear attack. I preferred to dwell on the Frenchman's calming voice: "Nonsense … they just want to make things easier for themselves and for us."

Reading my thoughts, Ita approached my bed and said:

"It's important that you try to sleep. I agree with the Frenchman,

I also think they have good intentions. We're of no use here, and who knows, perhaps they'll take us to a place near Father."

Many families could be seen packing their belongings in the early morning. The Frenchman, also released by the Russians, offered to help us pack. Ita was delighted and, together, they folded the blankets and packed our things. Experienced by now and knowing that the trip could take days, Ita made sure that we dressed appropriately.

The platform was bustling with people by the time we arrived. The Frenchman carried some of the bundles and tried to stay near us at all times. Soldiers maintained order and organized us in groups. The Frenchman insisted upon being in with us.

The train arrived, a freight train with no seats. Ita grabbed a corner near the door where we placed our possessions and sat down with the Frenchman, who had boarded with us. Behind the passengers' blank expressions lay the unanswered question weighing on all of our minds: "Where are they taking us?" Here we heard from one of the Russian soldiers that military headquarters had decided to evacuate the camp to make room for German prisoners-of-war, captured in battle.

The train began to move and left the camp gates. The freight cars proved very uncomfortable, with dozens of people crowded inside each one. The Frenchman calmed us and told Ita not to worry; from now on, he would watch over us and help as much as he could.

After several hours' journey, the train stopped in the center of a town that looked populated, where we received a little food. At the station where we had stopped, we saw the Frenchman talking with one of the officers and with someone in civilian garb. After a short break, the train proceeded.

"Indeed, we are going south. I spoke with the officer, who told me that they plan to bring us to the Caucasus," said the Frenchman, offering Ita some of the food he had received.

Ita thanked him and asked: "Where is the Caucasus? What

country is it in?"

"It's a mountain chain in southeast Russia, in an area famous for its oil wells. Most of the mountain chain is in a state called Georgia, east of the Black Sea," answered the Frenchman, impressing his listeners with his expertise.

"I hope the Germans haven't reached there," said Ita.

"I don't think so. From what I understand, the Russians have succeeded in repelling the German attacks on most of the fronts. Rumor has it that the German situation on the Leningrad front is terrible and supplies are not reaching the soldiers," explained the Frenchman, winking at me encouragingly.

"How far is it to the Caucasus?" someone asked.

"If I'm not mistaken, about 1,900 miles. A great distance, even if we don't have to detour around war obstacles on the way," responded the learned fellow, precisely as if he had a map in front of him.

"What's happening in Moscow? Have the Russians managed to push back the Germans?" inquired one of the travelers.

"The Russians are fighting heroically there and the Germans have failed to penetrate the city. The Russian at the station told me that the Germans are suffering heavy losses, but there have also been many Russian casualties in the attacks," replied the Frenchman.

The train continued on its way. Once again, the same scenery: endless forests, boundless spaces. After hours of traveling in the middle of nowhere, the train slowed and stopped. We were shocked. What was the meaning of this? Nothing could be seen all around except forests and desolation.

"What happened?" asked a traveler.

"Why did the train stop here?" asked another.

"I told you, the Russians decided to get rid of us! They are about to abandon us in the forests to starve and freeze to death. I told you! I told you!" wailed the older woman, who had scared us from the beginning.

Trying to restore calm, the Frenchman declared:

"I'll clarify the situation as soon as they let us open the doors. I suggest that we don't rush to draw conclusions."

I believed the Frenchman. For some reason, his words made sense to me. His approach toward us and his pleasant manner instilled confidence, and we trusted him implicitly. He always spoke logically and demonstrated great knowledge about almost everything.

After long moments of fear, the doors opened and soldiers boarded to explain that the stop would be brief. The officer in charge added:

"We have reached a section where the tracks have been destroyed by German bombing. Luckily, it is a short section. Hundreds of workers who arrived before us are now repairing the track and I hope it will be fixed quickly."

A sigh of relief was heard from everyone in the car. One traveler asked:

"How long do you think it will take?"

"I don't know, but the work has been going on for several days and is progressing rapidly. It could take a few days, perhaps less. We will let you know when we are updated. In the meantime, you can get out and freshen up a bit near the train. You must wait for an announcement from us."

The officer and soldiers moved on to the next car and we breathed a sigh of relief. We alighted from the car. The train looked completely out of place here. The Frenchman helped Ita out, and, as they set off in the direction of the engine, Ita turned to us and said:

"I want you to stay here and guard our possessions. Don't go far from our car. I'm going with the Frenchman to clarify something and I'll be back very soon."

After a short while they returned with news, and people crowded around them to hear the update. Leaning on the car, the Frenchman related:

"The officer spoke the truth – the Germans did, indeed, bomb the track several days ago, and we just saw workers busy repairing it. One of them told us that the work is almost done. Within a day or two at the most, our train can resume traveling. The officer said that they'll distribute food in the evening."

The Frenchman finished speaking and everyone near him continued talking among themselves, each with his own opinion about when the repair job would be finished. The Frenchman explained further:

"We had best be ready for a wait of a day or two. The worker told me that the damage isn't that great and there remain only about 300 feet to fix. They've been working for several days."

Toward evening, Russian soldiers visited all the groups of refugees in the cars and distributed horse meat and bread. The Frenchman joined us and helped Ita prepare the "feast." He reminded us again that he had decided to help us as much as we needed during this period and asked that we not be afraid of him.

For the first time, our friend began to talk about himself. It turned out that he had been a medical student who, shortly before the end of his degree, had been arrested by the Russians on suspicion of spying and exiled with others to the Arkhangelsk labor camp. Ita, in turn, related all our suffering since being expelled from Pultusk: Mother's murder, Father's conscription in Minsk and all our wanderings. Her words moved him and with tears in his eyes, he reiterated his promise:

"I will take care of you from now on, until we reach a safe place."

He put his hand firmly into mine.

After a nerve-wracking two days, they told us to re-board the train, where we sat for a long time before it began its journey. It moved very slowly, crawling along like a snail. The Frenchman looked at me and explained:

"The train's speed has been limited in order to make sure that the newly repaired track can bear the weight."

After several long minutes of traveling at snail's pace, the engine began to belch steam, gathered momentum and proceeded to move faster. We all breathed a sigh of relief. This leg of the trip lasted a long time, taking all night. Toward morning, the train stopped at a station, where we saw soldiers and some civilians. Around the station were a few houses with smoking chimneys, another small enclave of civilization in a godforsaken place. Several travelers got off to fill their vessels with water, as did the Frenchman. We knew that besides water, he would gather updated information about the place, about the direction in which we were going and – most importantly – about the situation on the war front.

The Frenchman returned, this time with hot water in a kettle Ita had given him. Each of us sipped from the improvised tea she prepared. Wherever we went, Ita would gather bunches of weeds from which she made a tea-like drink. In any case, this tea warmed our hearts in the freezing air. Our friend also drank the tea and left to walk around the platform again. We finally heard the boarding call, and the sound of the whistle pierced the air. The Frenchman returned and sat down next to us, mentioning the name of the place we had reached, a strange name that escapes my memory.

The noise of the train wheels became louder. The second cup of tea Ita had poured for the Frenchman grew cold because he preferred to tell us the good news he had heard about the front:

"Everything we heard in Arkhangelsk was true. It seems that there was a turning point in the war and the German forces and their allies have suffered harsh defeats. The Russian forces have succeeded in overpowering the German army in a bloody battle in the Stalingrad area. Using heavy forces, the Germans besieged the city and tried to conquer it, but failed. Both sides incurred hundreds of thousands of casualties and injuries in this battle."

Later, we learned that more than two million soldiers and civilians were killed and wounded in the battle. The Russian counterattack destroyed the German Sixth Army and a large part of the auxiliary forces attached to it by the Wehrmacht. In February 1943, the Germans in this area surrendered.

When the refugees in the car heard the Frenchman's lecture, they gathered around us and began showering him with questions, as if he were the Red Army spokesman. He was an interesting man, this Frenchman, young, learned and intelligent. He knew how to obtain information and construct an overall picture that served to disperse the fog of ignorance in which we lived.

"Who is fighting on the German side?" asked one of our neighbors in the car.

"Hitler won the Axis states over to his side: Fascist Italy under Mussolini, distant Japan and from what I understood, Finland, Bulgaria, Romania, Hungary and others," responded the Frenchman expertly, just as if he had a war map in front of him.

"Who is on the Russian side?" asked another, who had also listened attentively.

"The Russians are with a good, strong group. They are fighting alongside Great Britain, the United States, and my own country, free France, as well as Canada and others," answered the Frenchman, adding: "While we froze in Arkhangelsk, the Germans began to retreat after suffering a crushing blow in Stalingrad. In the central region, the Red Army had pushed the Germans back to the Polish border by the end of 1943."

"In other words, the war has ended?" asked a young woman in our car naively.

"The war is at its height. I do not know the situation at the moment, but from what I understood when speaking with people, the Germans are continuing to fight despite their heavy losses. The Russians succeeded in breaking the three-year German siege around Leningrad.

They had managed to hold out all that time, thanks to the line of fortifications hundreds of miles long that they built to protect the city. There was a severe shortage of food and fuel in the city, and hundreds of thousands died in the bombings and from cold and hunger, but the Russians' determination and their counterattacks led to the breaking of the siege; and the city was able to again breathe a 'sigh of relief.' I believe that the German supply lines for food and military equipment have been heavily damaged."

"And what's happening in Poland?" asked Ita.

"The situation there is terrible. A Russian officer told me that the Germans are destroying everything. They have established camps and facilities for mass murder and are systematically killing Jews, Gypsies and Communists. A German named Himmler has been placed in charge of the annihilation program and operating under him are SS units called *Einsatzgruppen*. The officer recounted hair-raising testimony regarding the terrifying atrocities carried out by these groups."

Silence reigned in the car after the Frenchman spoke, as everyone returned to his or her place and thoughts. My mind was once again flooded with visions of those German acts of murder and cruelty that I myself had experienced. I resisted the drowsiness brought on by the monotonous motions of the train's wheels. I did not want to fall asleep with my thoughts full of the horrible images I had recalled; these usually gave me terrible nightmares. In the end, I did fall asleep.

Time passed as our train continued on its way. In one of the remote villages, we were transferred to another military train, with no change in our routine or in the passing scenery. Apparently, someone forgot to mention the forests in the Book of Genesis's Creation story. Here was a divine creation of its own, whose description defied words: an enormous, mind-boggling number of virgin forests, filled with endless trees. The train devoured mile after mile and the forests just went on and on.

We stopped at a station where we were once again asked to

get off and wait for another, southbound, train. In his usual way, the Frenchman again went to fish for information, after first setting us up in a comfortable spot together with our belongings. He knew no rest. In every station, he could be seen circulating among the officers and local civilians to pump them for news, which he would cross-check with what he already knew.

This time, the soldiers gave us larger portions of food, as well as horse meat. We all looked gaunt, and some of us had stomachs bloated from malnutrition. The wait for the train lasted many hours. An interesting fact came to our attention: we had not heard the thunder of artillery and the sounds of shells the entire time. Apparently the war was far away from us now.

The long-awaited train finally arrived in the station, looking exactly like the one before it: an old freight train, blackened with soot, pulled by an ancient engine. Before it even stopped at the platform, the Frenchman rushed to help us get organized and find a good spot in the car, assisting us, as usual, in bringing our belongings aboard.

My sister Sara complained that her whole body ached. Checking her forehead, the Frenchman realized that she had a very high fever.

"We have to lower her temperature immediately or she won't last the long journey," he whispered to Ita, and hurried off to the soldiers before the train started out again.

Our friend returned to the car with a little alcohol which the medic had agreed to give him. The Russians had no medicines or proper medical equipment. Throughout the trip, the Frenchman never left Sara's side and, applying a technique he had learned involving water and alcohol, he succeeded in bringing down her temperature. We worried the whole time. Ita's face said it all – she had always tried to protect us from various illnesses and now this ailment had gone and befallen us.

Among the masses of refugees we were with during our wanderings, including in Arkhangelsk, disease outbreaks occurred as a result of poisoning or contamination, often fatally. Ita was very careful, and tried to maintain the highest standard of hygiene possible, even under the poor conditions in which we lived. She took particular care that we not catch the "third plague" of Egypt (lice), from which many of the refugees suffered.

After tending to Sara for hours, our friend reassured Ita:

"I used cold compresses to lower the fever and I'm happy to say that it worked wonders. She's a strong girl and is now totally out of danger. She must rest, eat and regain her strength."

Ita thanked our doctor and quickly gave Sara water and a slice of bread.

Our trip to the Caucasus lasted many days, even weeks, although exactly how long I cannot say. Often, our trains were forced to stop because of tracks damaged by German bombings. In such cases, we walked for a few days until we reached tracks that were safe, where we boarded another military train traveling toward our destination.

The scenery began to change somewhat. We saw more and more populated areas, although there were still very large expanses of unsettled territory. The long journey weakened many people who had trouble withstanding the conditions. Russian soldiers accompanied us the whole time. During the last few days, we heard the noise of German military planes overhead and we feared that they would attack the train. Fortunately, this did not occur.

After extensive traveling, one of the officers informed us at last that we were approaching our destination and would probably arrive in a day or two. Great joy followed this announcement. We hoped to reach a safe place, far from the areas of fighting. However, about an hour after the train set out, it suddenly stopped. No one inquired as to the cause, as we were used to such stops; but this time, we were left in the cars for a long time, with no explanation. According to the learned Frenchman's calculations, our destination was still far away. Officers and soldiers could be seen through the cracks, conversing as if in consultation.

"Strange. Something must have happened," our friend mused aloud.

The doors opened abruptly and we were asked to exit the cars. The Russian officer stood in front of us, pointing in the direction of the trip, and said:

"I'm sorry to report that we have reached the end of the road. The tracks ahead have been bombed out in various places, as you will see, and the repairs will last a long time. As far as we have been able to learn, even the preparatory work has not yet begun, which means that repairs could take weeks, if not months. It has been decided, therefore, to continue the rest of the way by foot, together with the food and equipment. Luckily, we are near our destination – Kutaisi, Georgia. I request your cooperation so that we can arrive together as soon as possible. We are stopping here to rest and get organized, and I will inform you of our plans later."

We were all in shock. The refugees included children and older people. Despair overtook many of them. Would they survive the difficulties along the way? Had they not endured enough till now? Our small group had gained much experience from our years of wanderings, but what would become of them? The officer calmed everyone down and told us that this time we were truly at the end of the trip. He promised that we would find relief at our destination, since it was very far from the fighting.

Here I must give credit to the Soviet rail system. Throughout the war, as we also learned afterwards, the trains continued to operate ceaselessly and unobstructedly. The Russians had enough coal to fuel thousands of engines, which pulled tens of thousands of cars loaded with soldiers and refugees fleeing for their lives from the war zone, in addition to transporting war materials, arms and food to the fronts. Damaged tracks were repaired and trains that had been attacked and were no longer serviceable were replaced with others. It must be said that these trains stood the test of the horrors of war.

More than anything else, however, I was thinking that our years of suffering and wandering would never end. Every time it seemed as if my sisters and I had reached a place where we could settle and begin to rebuild our lives anew, something transpired that forced us to continue our journey, our course of endless suffering. And now, who knew how long it would take to reach Kutaisi, and what else awaited us along the way? Nevertheless, it was somewhat comforting that we were under the protection of the Russian army, and that the soldiers accompanying us took care of us. We assumed that they would continue to do so along the way.

"Kutaisi? Where is this city? I've never heard of it, nor of the country in which it is located!" cried one of the women desperately.

Our wise French friend quickly jumped in:

"If my memory serves and from what I learned in geography classes in school, Georgia lies east of the Black Sea, at an interesting juncture of the peaks of the Caucasian Mountains and the warm waters of the Black Sea, amidst green slopes and fertile valleys. The scenery we see around us is a sign that we are very close to our destination. Kutaisi is a large city, considered the second largest in Georgia, whose capital is Tbilisi."

The Frenchman's knowledge and expertise knew no bounds; he was like a walking encyclopedia. As he spoke of his school days, it suddenly occurred to me that I, in the first decade of my life, had still not seen the inside of a school building. I consoled myself with the fact that I was learning in the "school of life," an open school with no walls....

We walked for days. The soldiers led us along the tracks, where we discovered that the officer had, indeed, been correct, for we saw the results of the German bombings along the full length of the tracks, which had been damaged in various places. We often came across duds and unexploded shells. The soldiers would alert us to these early enough and we would be forced to take a detour. The weather cooperated and was consistently pleasant.

Our friend did not leave our side the entire time. He constantly looked after us, helped Ita carry our traveling sack and knew how to provide encouragement during moments of crisis. Every day, he calculated the number of miles we had walked and told us how many remained. Not only did he instill a spirit of optimism among the wandering refugees, he was also well-liked by the military personnel.

The sub-zero blinding white scenery to which we had become accustomed in Arkhangelsk had been replaced by green surroundings; and this, at least, was reassuring. The soldiers distributed tiny portions of food whenever we would stop for the night, but we walked around starved and weak.

After many days of walking, we came upon a magnificent expanse of green fields. In the course of our journey we crossed a considerable number of bridges. One morning we came to a bridge spanning a river. With some of the refugees already on the other side, my sisters and I suddenly heard the deafening sound of German planes circling above us. We all panicked, including the Russian soldiers. We had learned from previous experience with planes that it was best to run as far as possible from the area under attack. As a result of the pandemonium and the ear-splitting noise, I fled back while Ita and my sisters ran ahead, to the other side of the bridge – we had no time to look around, for the planes had already started to drop their bombs on the bridge. Powerful explosions were heard from all sides and a huge hole opened in the middle of the bridge. The planes disappeared immediately and Red Army aircraft were seen flying in the skies.

Fear gripped me. I had emerged from the attack in one piece, but where were my sisters? My heart pounded and was almost torn from my chest. After recovering for several minutes, I spotted my sisters on the other side of the river, searching for me. Noticing me first, the

Frenchman pacified them and pointed toward me, standing on the other side of the river. Without thinking too much, in my fierce desire to join my sisters I leapt into the hole in the bridge and, to their amazement, swam across the river. To this day, I do not know how I gathered the courage to do this and how I managed to cross the river waters. Over the years, I learned that at certain moments in life, when one's life is at stake, one discovers unimaginable strengths and abilities. This was one such moment.

The Frenchman pulled me out of the water, and Ita and my sisters pounced on me as if I was a hero returning from battle. Luckily, none of us had been injured in the attack. Ita changed my wet clothes and restored calm. The Frenchman went to offer aid to the soldiers and some of the wounded. Fortunately, there were only a few lightly wounded people, who were treated by the accompanying soldiers.

The soldiers gathered all of us at a place far from the bridge. Many people had lost possessions. The soldiers reassured us that we were very close to the city and would already arrive that night. The officer who had led the march came over and, pointing to the bridge, said:

"This German air attack indicates that the war is not over. We must all remain together. We have reached the end of the trip and just a few miles away is the main road to Kutaisi, from where Red Army vehicles will take us to the city. We will leave in about an hour."

We were still agitated from the attack, and I believe we were unable to digest the officer's words. I heard the Frenchman whisper to Ita:

"That's it. We've reached the end. At long last, we'll see urban landscape, people, public squares, buildings and marketplaces."

"What does it mean that the war has not ended? How long will it last? Why did it reach here? They said they were bringing us to a safe place and yet the Germans attacked the area!?" asked Ita.

"If I understand the situation correctly, we are not in the battle zones. It's true that the Germans launched an air attack, but they're not physically here. This place is important from a strategic point of view, as it boasts oil wells and serves as a source for food supplies to the fighters on the front. The Germans have been bombing the railroad tracks and bridges in their attempt to disrupt the supply routes. This is one of the reasons for Hitler's occupation of the Ukraine and all the surroundings. He viewed them as a strategic goal, important for sustaining the war effort, because they are a source of food and military supplies for Germany, and is an important base from which to continue toward the Caucasus and its oil wells. His plans were upset with his defeats at Stalingrad," analyzed the Frenchman.

We waited for many hours at the bridge. Red Army trucks arrived at the bombed area carrying iron tracks and tin planks, which they placed on the bridge so that the remaining refugees could cross safely to the other side. The refugees arranged themselves in a long line and walked over the bridge one at a time. The next evening we arrived in Kutaisi.

Chapter 11

Georgia – Kutaisi

"All Jews are responsible for one another"

Babylonian Talmud, Shavuot 39a

I felt the difference as soon as I entered the city. Laid out before our eyes was a city in its full glory, a beautiful and well-organized city. Aside from the military air field, which had been damaged in the German bombings, we saw no destroyed buildings; nor did we encounter the masses of refugees we had become accustomed to seeing. The city was vibrant and full of life.

The military trucks that had picked us up brought us to an army base outside the city, which apparently served as a Red Army military school and had spacious barracks and storerooms. Here we met other refugees who, like us, had arrived from various locations near the areas of fighting. The base seemed orderly and well set up.

We were welcomed by the city's Jews, who provided us with food and clothing. One of the women, who knew the officer in charge, decided to help us. She took pity on us, four orphans dressed in rags, battered and exhausted, and asked the officer to house us in the base storeroom. The officer approved her request, but noted that he had no beds or mattresses for us.

"Don't worry, I'll take care of their needs. I thank you for your cooperation," she said. Taking the initiative, our hostess went from one Jewish home to another collecting food, clothing, mattresses and blankets. She returned to the storeroom after a short while with the donated supplies.

Weakened from the fatigue, hunger and difficulties we had experienced on the way, I went to sleep. I awoke to a completely different world: my sisters sat on their beds all washed and clean, wearing fresh, "new" clothes. On my bed were clean clothes for me. My sister Sara urged me: "Get up, wash yourself and put on the new clothes we've received. Soon they will also bring us food."

The clothes were clean, but not new. Ita interrupted Sara:

"Get up, Sholem'keh. This place is great, different from what we've become used to. There is a wonderful Jewish community that looks after us. I chose clothing that would fit you. Go outside to the faucet, freshen up and put on the 'new' clothes. We're also going to receive food from the community shortly."

I did as Ita directed. Finally, a faucet with running water! What a refreshing feeling! I took off my old, dirty clothes and put on the new ones. Evident in my old garments were all the signs of the suffering and hardships we had endured. I was so pleased that the clothes fit me and that Ita had even included clean socks in the items she chose for me.

My sisters greeted me joyfully when I returned wearing my new clothes, admiring my new appearance at length. This was the first time in years that I had such attire and no one was happier than I in those moments.

Representatives of a refugee organization, apparently UNRRA (United Nations Relief and Rehabilitation Administration), arrived at the base and recorded all our personal details. Ita made sure that all our names were registered and provided precise information.

"It's very important to keep the details exact, to make it easier in case Father or any other relative looks for us," she explained after the officials had left.

We were called to get our food a short while later. I don't recall ever having eaten such a meal in my life. The aromas and taste were wonderful. The meal included soup and vegetables, freshly baked bread and fruit. This was the first time in all our years of wandering that we ate fresh, hot food, which was provided by the Jewish community of Kutaisi, who spared no effort in fulfilling our needs. Since we were not the first group of refugees to arrive, they were fully aware of the events of the war and all the suffering we had endured. Many had come previously and been taken in by this warm Jewish community, which opened its heart and assisted as much as it could.

The local Jews had settled among one of the most cultured peoples in the Union of Soviet Socialist Republics. The Georgian nation boasted a history spanning more than two thousand years, and was particularly proud of its glorious heritage, which had produced great literature and poetry. They were honored to note that Stalin (Iosif Vissarionovich Dzhugashvili) was born in their state, in the town of Gori, though they bore little love for him due to his Great Purge in which many of the Georgian intelligentsia, as well as numerous others suspected of hostility to his regime, were murdered.

Georgian Jews occupied a respectable place in the state's economy and were involved with the wine industry and various types of commerce. It was difficult to distinguish between a Georgian Jew and a Georgian national. Both were tall, with a shock of black hair and a typical Georgian mustache, like Stalin. The women had tall, aristocratic bodies and long, flowing hair that lent them a unique charm.

Having been used to typical Jewish names such as Lederman, Pinchuk, Feibush, Applebaum, Goldberg and the like, we were now exposed to others that ended with Shvili and Adze, exactly like the names of Georgian nationals. The language they spoke was also identical to that spoken by their compatriots, in contrast to the Yiddish we used to speak. This shows that this ancient Jewish community preserved its Judaism, but at the same time blended into the local life.

In addition, it became clear to us that anti-Semitism had seeped into Kutaisi, albeit not to the degree with which we were familiar. It reared its head primarily during the Stalin era. We did not sense it; the

Jewish community was free to live as all other locals.

Kutaisi, the second largest city in Georgia after the capital Tbilisi, sat on both banks of the Rioni River. During the war period, the city's population numbered about 150,000, of which 15,000 were Jews. Most of the Jews lived in their own ancient quarter, near the riverbank. It was an organized community, complete with institutions for conducting Jewish life. There were three synagogues in the Jewish quarter, the largest and grandest of which was at its edge, near the city's other quarters.

We were very impressed by the warm hospitality of community members, who opened their hearts and pockets to support their Jewish brethren, survivors of the terrible, still ongoing war. It turned out that many of its members had been drafted into the war, together with the 700,000 Georgians who were fighting in the ranks of the Red Army, half of whom fell in various battles. Here we felt freer, had a roof over our heads, were able to roam the city and see its life, and were protected by soldiers. Our daily food ration consisted of potatoes, bread and soup, and an occasional slice of salami as a "bonus."

We went into the city one day, exploring one of its lively markets, where the aromas and the sight of all the fruits and vegetables piled on the stands drove me crazy. My eyes were, in particular, drawn to a stand filled with bars of soap. I sniffed around it and, exploiting the owner's momentary absence, went over and, in a split-second decision, snatched two soap bars and left. Heart pounding and terrified of being caught by the merchant, I hurriedly disappeared in another area of the market, where I sold the soap and used the money to buy fresh bread, whose aroma wafted all around me. The wonderful taste of the Georgian bread, purchased in exchange for the stolen soap, remains with me to this day. Of course, I shared the bread with my sisters.

Here in Kutaisi, we received continuous news from the war fronts and were no longer depended on rumors and reports from incoming refugees. The daily war reports from the radio or newspapers reached us immediately and the news spread among the refugees like wildfire. All wanted to be updated on what was transpiring and to learn about those dear to them who were fighting on the front. Many had close family and relatives caught in the areas of battle, with no opportunity to escape.

In my estimation, we arrived in Kutaisi at the end of 1944. The news we received was most encouraging. It was here that we first heard about Operation Overlord, launched in June 1944 when Allied forces landed in Normandy, France under the command of the American General Eisenhower. Before and during the campaign, Allied aircraft had bombed major German cities, greatly damaging their infrastructure as well as German morale.

We eagerly absorbed every scrap of information and rejoiced at every Allied advance and German defeat. A British force led by Montgomery, together with an American force, conquered Brittany; and another, Canadian, force, took over Falaise. Paris fell in late August 1944.

The joy of our French friend knew no bounds. He added his own interpretation of events. No one was happier than he to hear that his country had been liberated from German occupation. On a piece of paper, he drew for us a map of France and its neighbors and, with the aid of arrows that he had added, explained the progress of the war. Even more impressively, he came to the barracks one day holding a newspaper cutting with a map of Europe and the USSR. He indicated our location in Kutaisi and, with a pencil, outlined the torturous route we had taken from Arkhangelsk to Kutaisi.

"According to my calculations," he noted emotionally, "we traveled about 3,000 kilometers during our difficult journey. That's a very long distance!"

"Even longer if we take into account how far we had to go on foot.... "Ita mused.

"Very true," agreed the Frenchman, as he continued to trace the course of the war on the map he held. From his responses to our questions, he appeared to have kept quite up to date about the war ever since we arrived in Kutaisi. Having finished, he folded the map carefully and placed it in his pocket. This map of Europe, the first I ever saw in my life, is etched in my memory.

A few days later, we heard that the Russians had conquered Yugoslavia and were preparing to take over Poland. The news that our home was going to be liberated thrilled us. We followed the Russians' progress in Poland daily, excited to learn of familiar cities falling into their hands one by one. We celebrated every German defeat and our mood soared, as was also evident everywhere in Kutaisi, though the joy was mixed with sadness and worry over the rumors about the number of war casualties per day.

The radio reported the fall of Poland and the surrender of tens of thousands of German soldiers to the western military powers. All were taken captive and put under heavy guard. Russian forces opened another attack and conquered first Hungary and then Czechoslovakia and Germany. The German military was in retreat and under total collapse, with the Russians attacking from the east and the Americans and British from the west. In April 1945, after the conquest of Austria, Russian forces met with the Americans and British on German soil.

We all understood that this was the end of Nazi Germany, but had not yet heard an official announcement. The officers' club on the base where we lived had a radio from which the command received news updates.On May 8, 1945, the radio announcer informed the world of Germany's unconditional surrender. We understood from the officers' shouts of jubilation, echoing throughout the base, that something significant had occurred. The officers eventually emerged and apprised us of **Germany's surrender and the end of the war.**

The event was celebrated in the base with the opening of vodka bottles and endless drinking. The outburst of joy that we witnessed in Kutaisi knew no bounds and was shared by all, without exception. People hugged each other and blessed this marvelous hour. The masses spread throughout the city streets in celebration and it seemed as if no one remained at home. Soldiers were lifted in the air and flags flew all over. Improvised bands played national songs and dance circles were seen everywhere.

With the waves of euphoria having subsided somewhat, reports began to arrive about the true magnitude of the Nazi extermination machine. Having failed to destroy all the evidence, the Nazis had their methods of deception and destruction exposed to the whole world. The death camps were opened to the liberating forces, who were shocked to discover one of the cruelest horrors in human history: the systematic annihilation of millions of Jews in gas chambers and crematoria. Not knowing who among our relatives had survived and who had found death in the camps, we were terrified.

All our thoughts were now focused on Father, where he was and whether or not he had survived the war. Ita never ceased asking the soldiers. They tried to reassure us, and said that millions of people were as anxious as we were to learn the whereabouts of those dear to them. They explained that the registration set up when we arrived in the city would assist Father in locating us, and we must wait patiently. In several days, everything would be clearer.

Indeed, one morning we were called to report to the base offices. The receiving officer looked straight at us and said:

"I am pleased to report to you that we were notified this morning by the refugee organization that your father has tried to find you using their services, and they gave him your exact location. He asked to convey to you that as soon as he is discharged, he will come immediately to Kutaisi. He sent you his love and longs to see you."

We all burst out crying, not disguising our emotions. The soldiers present became as emotional as we were – some even shed tears.

"Thank you, Officer sir," exclaimed Ita emphatically. "How long do you estimate it would take Father to arrive?"

"I have no idea, but I do know that entire units are in the process of being discharged. Most of the roads throughout Europe are open and many damaged railroad tracks in the USSR have been repaired; the trains are moving freely. In any case, trains are entering Kutaisi without disruption. You just have to wait patiently. I promise to pass on any piece of information that reaches my desk. The news your father received that you are alive and well surely made him happy, and just as he knew to find you, so too he will undoubtedly make his way here as soon as possible," concluded the officer.

While shaking our hands in parting, he asked:

"By the way, how long has it been since you saw your father?"

Ita was embarrassed and tried to make a quick calculation:

"We were separated from Father when he was drafted in Minsk … about four years, in my estimation."

"And you were alone this entire time?" asked the officer.

"Yes, all alone. Four years of suffering, of survival and of wandering," said Ita, overcome with emotion and wiping away tears.

The officer looked at us admiringly, shook our hands and we left.

Several days after our conversation with the officer, and without any prior announcement, Father arrived at the Kutaisi camp. It is hard for me to describe the emotional reunion. He hugged us over and over with all his might and with his familiar warmth. I do not recall if he cried, but his feelings did not abate for many hours. Not only did he live to see his children alive, but he found them healthy and sound.

We had grown up in those four years since leaving Father in Minsk. Four years of war had toughened both him and us. He told us about the war zones in which he had served, about his desperate attempts to obtain any scrap of information about our fate, all of which were for naught. The truth is there had been no one to ask. The relief organizations had only recently begun to function, and it took them time to set things up. They were not always able to operate due to the bombings and heavy battles in the areas of fighting. They were also not accessible, especially to soldiers stationed at the front.

Father related that he had heard of UNRRA only in the last few months and as soon as he could, had submitted a request to them to locate us.

"They responded almost immediately. The representatives apparently knew of your exact location from the precise details you gave when registering in Kutaisi," Father complimented us. He said that in order to arrive here, he exploited his good ties with Russian

The Jewish synagogue in Kutaisi (photo: Jonah Moritz, 2010)

officers, who allowed him to board a military train bound for Kutaisi.

Father wanted to know everything that had happened to us. He did not stop hugging me or looking at me. We all looked gaunt and our bodies showed signs of the distress of the war years. Father said, thinking aloud:

"Now that the war is over, we must plan for the future. I've examined several possibilities. There is no point in returning to Pultusk or any other city in Poland. I don't know what you saw during your years of wandering, but the infrastructure of a sizeable number of Polish cities is destroyed, and many years will be required for Poland to rehabilitate herself after this terrible war. Europe is full of millions of refugees like us – penniless and homeless. I heard that various relief organizations, under American and UN sponsorship, are trying to solve the problems of the masses of refugees."

"We must first register with one of the organizations, preferably one sponsored by America, and request their protection. In the meantime, I noticed that UNRRA is operating smoothly. I see no reason to remain in Russia and at the moment, Palestine (Eretz Israel) is not an option. The British have closed its gates and the only way to get there is through illegal means. Therefore, we must organize ourselves as soon as possible and with the small amount of money I managed to save, go to Lodz and register as refugees. There is a large registration and counseling center there, assisted by various relief groups."

Father met with Jewish community activists over the next few days, who helped him with supplies and arrangements for our trip. The officer in charge of the base also promised assistance. After Father completed all his preparations, he assembled us for an update:

"And so, children, the moment has arrived. We depart tomorrow on a military train to Warsaw and from there to Lodz. As I said, we will register there and they will advise us further. We have to get our belongings ready for travel and report to the train station tomorrow morning. The officer in charge promised to be at the station especially, to guarantee our place on the train."

As if we had not wandered enough until now, we were fated to resume our journey into the unknown. This time however, Father was with us.

We awoke to a new day, filled with hope. Packing our possessions, we said goodbye to everyone we had met in Kutaisi. The parting was very emotional. The Frenchman was also there, shedding tears and telling Father:

"You should thank God for blessing you with such special children. They survived the inferno until now, thanks to their courage and determination, and thanks to Ita's devotion, wisdom and leadership. May you be successful in everything. And may Divine Providence continue to watch over you and your children and protect you from all evil, as He has until now. Take care of yourselves and have a safe journey."

Father thanked our friend profusely for all his assistance and blessings, embraced him warmly and we said goodbye.

I will always remember Kutaisi well. And I will particularly remember the Jews of that dear community, who spared no effort to help us. They fulfilled the Talmudic verse, whose essence has accompanied our nation throughout history: "All Jews are responsible for one another." They proved that this, far from an empty saying, is indeed a supreme, fundamental value which has guided our people wherever we were throughout the generations. Its practical application is mutual responsibility in every situation and under any circumstance.

The Jewish community of Kutaisi truly taught us an important lesson on this topic.

Chapter 12

Lodz – Under the Aegis
of the Relief Organizations

*"Victory was to be bought so dear as to be
almost indistinguishable from defeat"*

Winston Churchill, The World Crisis

Everything went well. The Russian officer stood by his word and
saw to it that we got on the military train. This time we traveled with
Father. Although she no longer bore the same heavy responsibility,
Ita continued to maintain firm control over the situation; and Father,
who had always known she was reliable, admired her performance. He
was also very impressed with the level of our cooperation. Ita issued
few instructions; a facial expression or simple hint was sufficient for
everyone to understand their task. After four years of wandering, we
had learned to obey her.

Each sibling knew what to carry and which place to occupy
as we walked. Sara carried one bundle, Zipporah the other and I, of
course, also had something small to carry. Our walking pattern was also
clear. Ita was always in the rear, with me in front of her and Sara and
Zipporah ahead of me, holding hands. Ita carried the heavy traveling
sack and occasionally held my hand. I walked next to, or in front of her.
This system gave Ita full control of the group, allowing her to maintain
constant eye contact with us. This is how we now walked to the train
station in Kutaisi, although this time, Father carried the heavy bundle.

The train departed and we breathed a sigh of relief. The trip to
Lodz was not short and it took many days to travel the almost 1,250-
mile distance from Kutaisi. We had to get to Warsaw first and then

board another train to Lodz. It stopped at many stations along the way and we had to change trains occasionally, sometimes being forced to wait several days until the next one arrived.

This time we were calmer and did not fear explosions or bombings. Father and Ita supplied us with food we had received from the Jewish community and from the army. No one rushed us or tyrannized us now, but the unknown future and the effect of our sad situation – utter poverty and dependence on relief organizations – was visible on Father's face. Ita attempted to ease some of the tension:

"This war involved many countries, and many people lost their dear ones and all their property, becoming refugees like us. The numbers are not small – even if we only consider what we ourselves witnessed firsthand, we're talking about hundreds of thousands of refugees. It makes no sense that a solution cannot be found for these people, innocent citizens caught up in a situation not of their own making. The countries involved will, surely assume responsibility and try to find answers. It will take some time, but a solution will eventually be found."

Nodding, Father responded:

"I definitely agree with you that a solution must be found. This cursed war brought misery to tens of millions of people, destroying entire countries, and that is no simple matter. The question is how long it will take to find a solution and how will the refugees be treated and their lives rehabilitated. We must remember that this was not an ordinary war, but a world war in which a large number of countries took part, something that has never happened before. Civilian populations suffered in previous wars, but not as in this one. Never before were special concentration camps established for human slaughter using poisonous gas. In this war, people were separated from their families, exiled, deported and cruelly murdered for no reason. Millions were killed, first and foremost amongst them Jews, out of pure racist ideology, with meticulous planning, torture and starvation; and all of it by means of a wide variety of deceptions, in order to disguise the atrocities."

Ita opened one of the food packages and distributed our portions of food. In giving Father his, she said:

"I hope that the rehabilitation will be conducted with the same diligence as the unwavering decision to defeat Germany. Indeed, the Germans should pay for the horrible injustice they inflicted and all the murderers and their collaborators should be put on trial. It's inconceivable that they will emerge innocent from this war that they forced upon the whole world."

Father was moved by Ita's words:

"You are correct, my daughter. Let us hope that justice will prevail. I cannot even think what a suitable price would be for the Nazis' barbarism. I recall the biblical commandment regarding *Amalek*: "Remember what *Amalek* did to you..... You shall blot out the memory of *Amalek* from under heaven. Do not forget!" (Deuteronomy 25: 17-19). I never understood this biblical commandment – to eradicate the memory of a nation. Today, after witnessing the horrors inflicted by the Nazi beast during the war they imposed on us, I am beginning to understand this divine commandment. Some people estimate the number of war victims to be fifty million – an unfathomable sum! The brutal slaughter of Jews and the vicious murder of other peoples who had gone to war in defense of the world."

The train slowed down and stopped in the center of some city whose station was packed with what looked like refugees wanting to return home. There were ruined houses and huge collapsed buildings on both sides of the track. Amidst the ruins, I detected many people rummaging through the piles.

From experience with long, difficult train journeys, we knew how to pass the time. I listened to the conversations Father held with Ita and did not stop thinking about them for even a moment. Father, too, was deep in his thoughts and occasionally shared them with us. With a deeply pained look, he said:

"One of the things distressing me so much is that I was deprived of the opportunity to educate my children properly – both at home and also in formal school education. For this, too, I will never forgive the Germans." He cleared his throat and his voice caught before he continued, speaking as if testifying in some court:

"In their critical years, my children did not have the chance to attend school, nor did they experience a tiny bit of the love and warmth of a father's home. Here, my young son, Shulem'keh, in his first decade of life has not yet been to school to learn how to read and write, like every normal child the world over. Ita, Sara and Zipporah had their education interrupted at its beginning. Their childhood years, meant to be filled with the joy of youth and abundant family love and warmth, were stolen from them and replaced with evil, cruelty, suffering and wandering. How can we recuperate what was lost while we are still wandering empty-handed?"

Seeing how Father's words affected all of us, Ita, in her great wisdom, interrupted his ponderings and tried to generate more optimism:

"Father, it's pointless to dwell on what was. We're young and capable of doing anything. This was not the first war ever, nor do I assume it will be the last. People have rehabilitated their lives after wars, and countries have recovered. I recall your telling us how terrible World War One was; yet, despite its difficult outcome, people were able to resume their lives after that war as well. I know it will not be easy, but look around you: Sara, Zipporah, Shulem'keh and I accomplished the impossible during the last five terrifying years, surviving without parents."

Taking a deep breath and sighing deeply, Ita continued:

"Do you doubt our ability to withstand the challenges awaiting us after the war? True, it's unfortunate that we were denied a formal education and the parental warmth and love to which every child is entitled, but we're older now and will know how to overcome this. Don't torture yourself with unnecessary thoughts. Although it's important to remember what was, it is no less important to rebuild our family. Every day is valuable; and since we are penniless, we must first find an organization that will help us. Your decision to bring us to Lodz was, therefore, very wise. I see Shulem'keh and my sisters: after all we endured together, there is no obstacle to success that we cannot surmount. I know that difficult days await us, but nothing can compare to what we have already been through. A person who knows how to cross rushing rivers and survive, will be able to easily skip over small streams."

Having concluded speaking, Ita looked at me and gave me a secret wink as a reminder of when I crossed the river. She handed Father a cup of water to calm him down. I was very moved by my oldest sister's wise words. Once again, the image of the bombed bridge on the way to Kutaisi, when I crossed the river, came to my mind. It seems that Ita's optimism pacified us all. I noticed that she did not mention Mother, probably to avoid adding to my father's and our sorrow.

The trip to Warsaw lasted several weeks. We often stopped on the way to change trains and by the time we arrived at our final station in the capital, the major destruction sowed there by the German bombs was clearly visible. We had seen many bombed cities during the trip, but had never encountered the extensive ruins we saw in Warsaw.

Father related that upon its occupation by the Germans, the city became part of the *Generalgouvernement* – territory that was under German control. On that same day, the order was given to close all schools and to round up the Jewish population – 300,000 residents – in a ghetto (The Warsaw Ghetto). When the Germans decided to liquidate it as part of the Final Solution, an uprising of the Jews broke out in the ghetto (The Warsaw Ghetto Uprising), and a bloody battle ensued. The resistance fighters held out for a month but, in the end, the Germans cruelly suppressed the revolt and almost all the rebels were murdered.

Father also recounted what he had heard in the Russian army base where he had served, that in July 1944, the Red Army in Poland liberated extensive territories from the Germans. The Russians advanced and reached a point eighteen miles from Warsaw. The Polish government-in-exile, sitting in London, instructed the Polish underground to try and take control of the capital before the Red Army entered. The underground began a rebellion against the Germans (known as The Warsaw Rebellion), which lasted sixty-three days, but ultimately failed. Although located near Warsaw, the Soviets did nothing to assist the rebels. In reaction to the rebellion, Hitler ordered the total destruction of Warsaw, for which a special unit was established, tasked with bombing all government structures in the city as well as many residential buildings. 800,000 people met their death in the battle for the city! "All this explains the degree of terrible destruction we are seeing," Father pointed out. We were shocked at what he said. How could any human being contemplate carrying out such acts?

We remained in Warsaw for several days and Father reported to the UNRRA offices to receive assistance. He appeared troubled throughout our stay in the city. The mystery was resolved when he finally explained:

"We will depart for Lodz in two days. I have pondered this a great deal, and have decided to go to Pultusk to see if any of our property remains. Perhaps I'll locate Mother's grave, in the event that someone made the effort to bury her. We are really very close to Pultusk, which is about forty-three miles north of Warsaw. I will leave in the morning and return in the evening. You will stay here and Ita will watch over you until I come back."

"I don't understand the purpose of this trip! It's dangerous, who knows who controls the area and how order is maintained in Pultusk?! Who is in charge there – the Poles, the Russians? I think it's much too early to go there – please reconsider your decision!" Ita requested vehemently.

There were many Russian troops on the streets of Warsaw. Military vehicles traveled back and forth, and tanks and armored vehicles were positioned at key intersections. Tractors were seen repairing traffic routes damaged during the bombings. Father was very familiar with the region from his frequent trips to Warsaw. He pointed northward.

"This is the way to Pultusk. I see no risk in traveling there, but in any event, I will check the situation with the soldiers stationed at the crossroad," he said, approaching the nearby military position. After speaking with the soldiers for a short while, he returned.

"All the roads to Pultusk are blocked and the Russian army is not allowing anyone to go there. Perhaps it is for the best," he sighed.

Masses of people crowded into the Warsaw depot waiting for the train to Lodz. As in every station, we searched for a spot where we could put our things down and get organized. Next to us sat a lone woman, looking at us intently. It was obvious that she, too, had undergone difficult experiences during the war. After she introduced herself as Leah, Father began talking with her, and we learned about the tragedy that had befallen her. The woman had survived the Majdanek concentration camp and arrived in Warsaw alone. The Germans had murdered her husband, her two children and her entire family, while she herself had managed to survive somehow, against all odds.

Leah said that she was also going to Lodz, where she might find some relative who had survived and, perhaps, gain a roof over her head. Father suggested that she join us and promised to help her make her way through the tens of thousands of refugees in the station to board the train. Leah expressed an interest in this plan and in a desire to likewise help us.

After a long wait, we succeeded in boarding the train to Lodz with Leah, who from then on became a permanent part of our group.

The sight of the ruins and destruction en route to Lodz and in every town we passed through was shocking. Columns of refugees were visible on every road the train crossed, and blackened tanks and burnt cars were an inseparable part of the "scenery" that we saw during the trip.

Father had visited Lodz often before the war and began to tell us about the city and its history. We learned that Lodz was Poland's third largest city, located southwest of Warsaw. A large industrial city, it was known for its textile industry and had become famous throughout Europe. There were sixty-one factories in operation in 1910, more than half owned by Jews, and all an important source of livelihood for tens of thousands of workers. Until World War Two, there was a large Jewish community there, comprising 230,000 people, one third of the city's entire population. The community boasted a vast network of Jewish schools, Jewish newspapers, and even a Yiddish theater to which visitors flocked; and it was also the home of famous *hassidic* courts, such as Gur and Chabad.

Lodz was conquered by the Germans on September 8, 1939, one day after our town Pultusk was occupied. On February 8, 1940 a formal order was issued to establish the ghetto. The area allotted for this was in the poverty-stricken section, Baluty, into which 164,000 of the city's Jews were packed under disgraceful conditions. The rest escaped or were deported eastward, and many were murdered. The Germans forced the *Judenrat* (specially appointed Jewish community leaders), led by Chaim Mordechai Rumkowski, to take responsibility for the day-to-day management of ghetto life. The *Judenrat* tended to matters of food, health, education and labor. They organized the labor groups for the Germans, as well as the "death groups" – the Jews sent by the Nazis to their death. About a quarter of the ghetto's residents died of starvation and of diseases that broke out there.

We arrived in Lodz and were barely able to make our way out of the train station. Thousands of refugees swarmed the place and the congestion was stifling. It seems that people had been waiting entire days for their turn to board the train.

Father had chosen Lodz because he had heard that its "Jewish Committee" was recognized by the Polish authorities as officially representing the Jews. One of its first actions was an organized registration of refugees in order to help in the search for family members. Lodz had an enormous concentration of survivors – 20,000 Jews on the day we arrived, according to the committee's list.

The Jewish Committee was the first post-war institution established in Lodz. Its role was to help the survivors find shelter, and to provide medical assistance, food, clothing and even aid in the search for employment. When we arrived at the committee's office on Srodmiescie Street, we found many refugees sitting on the steps of the building awaiting their turn to receive housing. It seems that the committee had acquired a thousand apartments abandoned by the Germans, in which they intended to resettle the survivors. The stream of refugees from the USSR was unending, and every day more problems awaiting solutions piled up on the committee's desk.

This was during the first few weeks after Germany surrendered. The relief organizations had only just begun to get set up, and this required much coordination and staff. Like the others, we took a place in line at the entrance to the committee's offices. It was a strange sensation. Thousands of emaciated Jews had gathered all around, their torn clothing and facial expressions speaking volumes; hopeless people, remnants of communities attempting to rebuild their interrupted lives and awaken from the unimaginable loss.

After several days of waiting, we finally obtained a roof over our heads – a room in a building with a large courtyard. In the corner of the courtyard was a bicycle repair shop owned by one of the building's residents, a Pole. I recall that whenever I passed by the store, he would call me "dirty Jew." I now realized that hatred of Jews had not disappeared, despite the fact that the war had ended.

One event etched in my memory, and from which I learned a valuable lesson, pertained to the son of that Polish bicycle repairman. That day, when I went down to the courtyard, as usual, I saw the son, who was a few years my elder, walking around holding a rifle. As soon as I neared the bicycle shop, he called out to me: "Dirty Jew! Get out of here, dirty Jew!" While shouting thus, he aimed the weapon and shot a live bullet in my direction. Luckily, the bullet hit the floor between my legs, and I was uninjured.

Extremely unnerved, I ran toward the building of the Jewish Committee, where many Jews in search of their relatives and of assistance gathered daily. I met a young boy, and, still highly agitated from the shooting experience, told him what had transpired. He seized my hand and brought me to an older friend of his, a member of the Beitar movement. Outraged at my story, the latter immediately organized a group of twenty fellow Beitar members. They went to the Pole's house, destroyed it and the shop, and gave the father and son a beating they would never forget!

I was so happy that someone was able to react so quickly to this act of anti-Semitism, warning the Jew haters not to repeat their actions. The efficacy of this was proven by the radical change in the behavior of the Pole and his son, after the lesson they learned....

Additional relief organizations began to operate in refugee-filled Lodz, distributing food, articles of clothing and money via the central committee. Father also registered at the UNRRA offices, which offered various solutions for rehabilitation, among them in the displaced persons camps in Germany which they sponsored. Father hoped to reach one of the camps under American sponsorship. He believed that this type of organization would help find temporary solutions to our distress, and perhaps even get us to America.

The relationship between Father and Leah grew closer. They had a lot in common and they shared a mutual respect for one another. We were delighted to witness Father's happiness at having found a sympathetic ear and an understanding friend in this difficult period. Of course, Leah, too, had Father's support and attention. Fate had brought them together on the train platform, crowded with refugees amidst the ruins of Warsaw.

Leah told us about her experiences during the war. She spoke of the cruelty of the Nazis, the frequent *aktions* (harsh anti-Jewish operations) in her area, the murders at the burial pits and the forced labor in which she was involved. Particularly painful was her account of the Majdanek extermination camp, where her husband and two children were killed in the crematoria.

We were shocked at the traumas Leah had endured. We had heard many stories from survivors whom we had encountered on our way, but this was the first testimony we heard from a survivor who had arrived directly from the death furnaces. From her we learned that Majdanek had been built about two miles from the center of the Polish city Lublin and, in contrast to other camps, was visible to all. It was established in November 1941 under the command of the arch-enemy, Heinrich Himmler.

Majdanek was first used to house prisoners-of-war, and only later transformed into an extermination camp where people were killed in gas chambers and crematoria. Leah's husband, children and other family members were among the 60,000 Jews who met their end there through burning and suffocation. The camp also held Soviet and Polish prisoners-of-war, who provided slave labor for the munitions plants and for the Steyr-Daimler-Puch weapons factory. Majdanek was the first concentration camp captured by the Soviet army, its secrets thereby exposed to the whole world. The Soviet government released widespread reports about the shocking discoveries there, thus notifying the world for the first time about the concrete details of the horrors perpetrated in the Nazi extermination camps.

We lived in Lodz for several months, waiting for approval to transfer to the refugee camps in Berlin. Along with other refugees, we received food and clothing during this time from the Jewish Committee, UNRRA and the Joint Distribution Committee, who also provided medical care and medicines to those who needed them.

One day, Father came to our room looking very happy. He was holding the transit certificates to Berlin. We all rejoiced, knowing that the refugee camps in Germany were well-run. Rumor had it that families were helped there with their rehabilitation: returning them to their native countries or transferring them to others, where they could build new lives.

"We have to get organized. I have all the necessary papers and we leave tomorrow," Father informed us, and rushed out to the UNRRA offices to obtain information about travel arrangements.

We indeed left the next day. Leah did not join us, but Father took her address, promising to maintain contact with her and update her about everything after we should reach Germany. We returned to the familiar train platform in Lodz. On the previous occasion, it had been difficult to make our way through the crowds; but, now, thanks to the soldiers and policemen, everything was more orderly, the thousands of waiting passengers notwithstanding.

After a long, impatient wait, the arrival of the Berlin train was finally announced. Masses of people swarmed to the doors even before the train came to a halt, and the police and soldiers were unable to control the pandemonium. Noticing what was happening, Father pulled us toward the back of the train, where he managed to board a car with the bags he was carrying and to save us places. After several long minutes, and with the aid of the police, everyone managed to get on the train and we departed. This time, the destination was Berlin.

Chapter 13

Zeilsheim

"Our hope is not yet lost, the ancient hope –
to return to the land of our fathers,
the city where David encamped"

Naftali Herz Imber

It was difficult not to be impressed by Berlin's dimensions. In my short life I had managed to visit such large cities as Warsaw, Bialystok and Kutaisi, but this was the first time I was exposed to one of this size. Traveling through the suburbs, the train had already begun to slow down. Berlin, Germany's largest city, had until a few months earlier been the capital of the Third Reich. It was also considered one of the largest cities in Europe.

The effects of the war that had ravaged Berlin until Germany's surrender were evident everywhere. As a result of the heavy bombings, large areas had been completely destroyed and huge buildings had collapsed, burying everything within. Walls of buildings that still stood were pockmarked by bullets and shells. It was unmistakable that a deadly battle had occurred here.

"From this place came the proclamation of war that caused misery for millions of families. From here came the commands to murder and annihilate that shocked the world," pondered Father aloud.

Pointing to a huge building, half of which had collapsed into its other half, Ita added: "I'm so happy to see this city devastated, subdued and defeated. Yet all this is no consolation for our personal tragedies, and, of course for the horrific catastrophe that befell our people."

On the way to Berlin, Father had told us about Kristallnacht, perhaps to prepare us for what we would see in the city. Kristallnacht had taken place seven years earlier, on the night of November 8, 1938. On this night, he related, almost all the synagogues, as well as the cemeteries and Jewish institutions in Germany had been destroyed. Thousands of stores had been broken into, looted and set on fire. Hundreds of Jews were killed in these pogroms and tens of thousands were arrested and brought to concentration camps. Before the Nazis took over the government, Berlin had had an organized Jewish community, numbering 160,000 people.

"In Warsaw, I heard that all of Berlin's Jews were sent to the death camps during the war, and that no Jewish community remains in the city," Ita remarked, drawing our attention to a long line of refugees winding its way along the main road.

Father pointed out that these were refugees who had fled the areas under Soviet control. They carried their possessions on their backs. Some were on foot, some in loaded wagons and a few were in vehicles. Although some of the streets damaged in the bombings had been repaired, the overall appearance of the city was one of destruction and devastation. After being conquered, Berlin was divided into four occupation zones. Those that were under American, British and French control were unified and formed West Berlin. The eastern sector was under Russian control.

The train came to a halt and crowds of passengers spilled out of it. We, too, took our belongings and walked over to the offices of UNRRA, joining the procession of refugees making its way there. Such refugee processions were the most common sight in Europe in those days. They were seen everywhere, moving like columns of ants trying to reach their nest. The route to the offices was not short and passed through destroyed buildings and structures with shattered windows. It looked as if the authorities had managed to remove some of the ruins that had blocked the roads, and had repaired other buildings damaged in the bombings. There was indeed an attempt to return to a life of normalcy.

We stood on line at the entrance to the UNRRA offices. The agency clerks who received us explained the intake process; we underwent interviews and various registration procedures. Files were opened, and all our personal details recorded. We were taken for medical exams immediately afterwards, had rudimentary haircuts, were treated with anti-lice powder and given disease-prevention care. We also had an opportunity to bathe here, and received clean clothing and a hot meal from the relief services.

We remained in Berlin for several months, in housing allotted to us in the Displaced Persons (DP) camp in the Zehlendorf neighborhood. Here we met many Jewish refugees who had arrived from all over Poland and from the areas under Soviet occupation. The tales they related shocked us all. Those who had hurried to visit their native cities had ended up at the Displaced Persons camps in Germany bearing tragic news: "There is nowhere to return to." This, in effect, is how the westward flight of refugees and their infiltration into the DP camps began.

Various statistics on the extent of the murder and ruin exacted by the war began to be made public, numbers no human mind could digest: here in Berlin, 50,000 buildings were destroyed and another 25,000 damaged; 100,000 civilians fell in the battles for the city; during the Allied bombings of the city, 50,000 of its residents were killed. Moreover, six million Jews, one-third of our people, were systematically annihilated in the death camps. The human toll exacted by this war, from all the nations involved, was fifty million people. Millions of refugees remained homeless, families were shattered and masses of orphans and widows were left as survivors of the inferno. This was the calamity inflicted by the Nazis on their fellow countrymen and on the rest of the world in this cruel war, the product of warped minds.

The relief organizations were prohibited from entering the refugee camps during the first months after Germany surrendered. The initial relief efforts were provided by the Red Cross; later, relief and rehabilitation services were transferred to UNRRA. Only thereafter were the Joint and other organizations permitted to enter the camps, in coordination with UNRRA and the military.

A rumor spread among the refugees in Berlin that an organized camp, with all required services, had been set up in Zeilsheim, a village near Frankfurt. After Father made all the arrangements with the appropriate authorities, he informed us with great satisfaction that he had received approval to transfer to Zeilsheim. It turned out that Leah was due to arrive there a week after us, which pleased Father very much.

A military vehicle that UNRRA put at our disposal brought us to Zeilsheim. We traveled in the American sector, on a highway repaired by the United States Army after the war. During the war, the village had served as living quarters for slave laborers, and afterwards became a refugee camp for Jews. Surrounding the village were agricultural fields

With my family in Zeilsheim. Standing: Father in a black suit with Leah to his right and Ita to his left. Center: My sister Sara, seated, wearing a flowery dress

With Holocaust survivor children in the Displaced Persons camp. Zeilsheim, Germany

tended by local German farmers. American flags, and flags bearing the
Star of David, flew at the entrance to the village. Bulletin boards were
decorated with photographs of important sites in Eretz Israel. We were
welcomed by UNRRA representatives, who provided us with housing
and basic needs. The place resembled a Jewish village in every sense.
There was a synagogue and a school, and even youth movements. The
first days in Zeilsheim were devoted to acclimatization. Father quickly
arranged for my education and I entered a school for the first time in my
life. I recall the emotions that seized me when I was given a notebook
and pencil.

Now, after being freed from the daily struggle for survival since
our expulsion from Pultusk, we gradually began to digest everything
that had transpired – the totality of the Holocaust and the destruction

With my sister, Zipporah (in the flowery dress), in Zeilsheim

of our world. Father's desire, and our own, to rebuild our lives, was met with quite a few difficulties. We were completely dependent on the relief organizations. There was no opportunity to create an independent life with such normative basics as citizenship, permanent housing, source of livelihood, etc. All this often led to bitter disappointment for Father; in contrast to his nature, he often found himself in a condition of helplessness, through no choice of his own.

We were Polish citizens, but Father refused to return to Poland. First of all, there was nowhere to return to; our homes had been destroyed and property stolen. Secondly, how can one go back to a country where one is not wanted? How can one settle in a state in which an atmosphere of hatred prevails and which had become a huge cemetery for our families and millions of our brethren? Anti-Semitism in Poland had not ended. According to rumors that reached the camp in Zeilsheim, there were pogroms against Jews who returned to their

With Holocaust survivors in Zeilsheim. Standing on the right is Jerry Wartski's brother, Arnold

homes and places of birth. We saw this with our own eyes during our short stay in Lodz.

The pogrom against Jews who went back to Kielce in Poland was discussed a great deal in the camp. Most of the 25,000 Jews who had lived in the town before the war had been murdered. Several who had survived the inferno arrived there a few weeks after Germany surrendered. The local Poles, afraid of demands to return the Jewish homes and property they had stolen, began a campaign of anti-Semitism. Among other things, a rumor was spread about a Christian boy kidnapped by Jews for ritual purposes. In July 1946, a frenzied mob gathered in front of the Jewish community center and slaughtered the Jews. Forty-two survivors of the atrocities of the Holocaust were butchered by the Polish residents of Kielce. Such stories were heard frequently at various gatherings and in the synagogues. Hence, many of the Zeilsheim refugees rejected the idea of returning to Poland.

Eleanor Roosevelt's visit to Zeilsheim

In our discussions in Kutaisi, Father had already expressed his determination against going back to Poland. The moment this was ruled out, we effectively became stateless refugees, our rehabilitation at the mercy of the relief organizations. Not many options remained. The gates of Eretz Israel were closed to Jews by the British White Paper, whose policy applied throughout the mandate period. This policy set an annual quota of 10,000 people who were permitted to enter the land, and anyone else attempting to arrive took a risk and came as an illegal immigrant. The only way to reach Eretz Israel was through one of the various illegal immigration schemes. Although Father wanted to go to Eretz Israel, he was afraid of getting involved in such an undertaking with a family that had suffered so much during years of wandering.

The situation very much frustrated Father and he was forced to wait for solutions from the relief organizations sponsored by America. At least here in Zeilsheim there were support services that provided

our minimum needs, giving some hope and "breathing space" until a
solution could be found.

In the meantime, life in Zeilsheim slipped into routine. We gradually
became part of Jewish community life, which was being rehabilitated
in every sense. I attended school daily, where we learned Hebrew,
arithmetic and other subjects. There were also *yeshivot* in the town and
even Zionist youth groups, as well as an amateur theater group, a jazz
ensemble and a library. An active Jewish leadership, democratically
chosen, was in place. I also met new friends here: Gedaliah Scheinbrum,
Jerry Wartski, Robert Dessau, Michael Edelstein, Abraham Pomerantz
and others. I am still in contact with most of them.

All the activity in the Jewish community here was supported by the
Joint Distribution Committee, whose assistance was evident in various
areas. The organization provided medical services, supplying doctors,
nurses and a variety of medicines. It also helped set up an educational
system in the camp and rebuild religious life (synagogues, kosher meat,
matzah on Passover, etc). In general, the work of the Joint was a real
blessing and encompassed all the DP camps throughout Europe.

The Joint also collaborated with the ORT organization, working
together in job training for the refugees. There was a branch of ORT in
Zeilsheim, too, which proved very encouraging for the youth in the
camps. Also active in our camp were soldiers of the Jewish Brigade
(a brigade of Jewish soldiers in the British army, mostly from Eretz
Israel, who had fought against the Nazis). They assisted in various
areas, focusing primarily on education, together with Jewish Agency
emissaries and with the productive cooperation of many survivors.

The camp in Zeilsheim was full of young people in their thirties,
assigned by the military to work on renovating the buildings and prepare
them for winter. Many of these people were all alone after the war and

sought new ties; they naturally wanted some kind of compensation for the pain of their loss and bereavement, and searched for a partner with whom to share the burden of life. The wedding ceremonies held in our camp and in many others were tangible expressions of that process. The first signs of new life had begun to sprout from within the abyss of death.

Father and Leah also wed in Zeilsheim. The crises they had endured during the war created a dependency between them. They developed trust, understanding and mutual responsibility, and their

At an anti-British demonstration in Berlin in favor of opening the gates of Eretz Israel to Jewish immigration

bond strengthened. The wedding signified their readiness to give new meaning to their lives and hope for the future. "New Lives and Hope" was not a meaningless expression, but testified to the displaced people's yearning for a new tomorrow. This was also manifested in the titles of the Yiddish newspapers distributed in the DP camps, such as: *Undzer*

Hofenung (Our Hope), *Wiedergeburt* (Rebirth) and *Der Morgen* (The Morning). Two Yiddish newspapers published in Zeilsheim were *Untervegs* (On the Road) and *Undzer Mut* (Our Courage).

UNRRA officials supplied basic food including bread, flour, milk, eggs, oil and sugar. I recall that meat and fish arrived in cans. The Joint also provided various products and I particularly remember chocolate, coffee and cigarettes.

Our village was selected for visits by missions, important people and statesmen from the United Nations and the United States, as well by journalists, high-ranking military officers from the United Nations and the Allied armies. They came to see the results of the war and to witness rehabilitation efforts. The complaints heard after the war, with Europe being flooded by millions of refugees, and the shocking reports of overcrowding and inferior conditions in the DP camps led to the establishment of the Harrison Commission (headed by Earl

Carrying a photo of gallows victim Dov Gruner, at an anti-British demonstration.
Berlin, Germany

Before my immigration to Israel   *With Father in Berlin after the war*

Harrison, dean of the University of Pennsylvania Law School and the United States representative on the Intergovernmental Commission on Refugees).

After pressure was exerted by Jewish organizations in the United States, the Harrison Commission was sent, in July 1945, by President Truman, to tour the camps and present its conclusions. Following the commission's reports, conditions improved in Zeilsheim and the village became a Jewish camp. It was impossible to estimate the number of residents in the village because this changed continuously. Many wandered to other camps searching for relatives, and new refugees arrived in their place. In October 1946, village residents numbered about 3,500 people.

I do not remember the exact date we arrived at Zeilsheim, but I do recall the visit to the camp by David Ben-Gurion, the great excitement in the village and the preparations for his arrival. This was in February 1946 and it seems that we had reached the camp several months prior to that.

David Ben-Gurion, the chairman of the executive committee of the Jewish Agency in Eretz Israel and eventually, the prime minister of Israel, visited the DP camps twice: in October 1945 and in February 1946. On his second trip he stopped at Zeilsheim, and for us it represented a stirring, tangible greeting from the Holy Land, which was still closed to us. For us, Ben-Gurion symbolized the hope for a new life, for Jewish independence in our historical homeland and for the resurrection of our people out of the ashes. Masses of people received him and crowded into the hall to hear his speech.

Ben-Gurion spoke about Eretz Israel as the historic homeland of the Jewish people. He emphasized that the solution for the Jewish refugee problem was to bring them to their natural homeland. For this, he noted, heavy pressure must be imposed on Great Britain to open the gates of the land to the surviving remnant of our people and to lift the blockade preventing the return of tens of thousands of survivors to their land.

Ben-Gurion's visits to the German DP camps formed the basis of the Zionist movement's eventual policy stating that the Jewish refugees should be concentrated in Germany so that their presence would exert pressure on Great Britain to open the gates of Eretz Israel to massive Jewish immigration. However, instead of this happening, the British government decided, on August 7, 1946, to deport to Cyprus all illegal immigrants who had arrived in Eretz Israel or were on their way there, and to place them in detention camps.

Many protests against the British Mandate and its Palestine immigration policy were organized in Zeilsheim and other refugee centers. I remember actively participating in these demonstrations and in one of them, even marched at the head of the protesters carrying a flag bearing a drawing of the Star of David. It later turned out that our contribution to this battle was most important.

One of the factors that helped unite the Jewish community in our refugee camp was the bond with Zionism. The activities of the Zionist movements and their initiative in encouraging future immigration to Eretz Israel contributed greatly to restoring morale and instilling hope among the refugees. The fact is that over two-thirds of the displaced

Carrying a flag at the head of an anti-British demonstration in favor of opening the gates of Eretz Israel to Jewish immigration

With Holocaust survivor children in Berlin

persons eventually reached Eretz Israel.

The Harrison report and other published statistics indicated that about ten million refugees and displaced persons were roaming Europe after the war. They comprised a mix of people that included war captives, partisans, death camp survivors, Jews who lived under false identities and refugees like us who returned from Soviet Russia and other places.

As part of the general rehabilitation program to restore normal life, the Allies made major efforts to convince displaced people to return to their homes. They formulated the Repatriation Program, for which purpose they placed at these people's disposal an enormous system – including equipment, many personnel and vehicles – and opened the borders to free movement, without the need for transit documents. Trains ran non-stop on Europe's tracks and vehicles transported anyone who wished to take advantage of them. Everyone was able to return to their homes, except the Jews. They had nowhere to go; their homes and property had been stolen, mostly by the local population.

In early 1946, about 80,000 Jewish refugees were concentrated in German DP camps. In the summer of 1947, the number of Jewish displaced people in Germany, Austria and Italy alone came to a quarter of a million people – an enormous number of refugees crying out desperately for a solution. The Harrison Report recommended granting 100,000 displaced Jews immigration certificates to Eretz Israel, but the British stood fast, sealing the land to immigrants and exiling to Cyprus those who had arrived or were still en route.

We remained in Zeilsheim for almost three years. During this period, Father tried to locate surviving relatives via UNRRA, the Joint and every other possible organization. Except for his brother and several acquaintances, the entire family perished in the terrible Holocaust. During these years, my sisters also matured and developed relationships with their future spouses, eventually establishing families with them. Of course, I also grew up in those three years. I learned Hebrew, made friends and dreamed of a better future.

One of the events etched in my memory occurred on November 29, 1947. All the refugees without exception gathered in the central square of Zeilsheim to hear the results of the vote in the General Assembly of the United Nations on the Partition Plan and the establishment of a Jewish state. At the end of the vote and the fateful decision, the audience erupted with immense shouts of joy. A generations-old dream had been fulfilled. We finally had a state! Someone recited the blessing "Who has granted us life, sustained us and enabled us to reach this occasion," and everyone responded in a loud voice, "Amen! Amen!"

"It is high time we had a home of our own, so that no one can ever banish us from it again!" cried Father emotionally. This was a an unparalleled moment of excitement and spiritual elevation. Many people wept openly, hugging each other. Many of the young began to dance. Everything was spontaneous, a truly heartfelt rejoicing.

Suddenly, the possibility of making *aliyah* (immigrating) to Israel became very real. The establishment of the State of Israel in May 1948 was a true turning point in the rehabilitation and immigration of those displaced. Father was happy that there were signs of a solution for us, together with hope for a more promising future. But with his experience, he knew that there was still a long way ahead, one with many pitfalls.

"The declaration of an independent state is important, but creating it is very hard. Difficult days await us, but the first step has nevertheless been taken. No force in the world can stop this nation's will to live. From the moment it made the decision, a Jewish state will arise!" proclaimed Father with feeling, and we all nodded in agreement.

Reports of the imminent closure of the Zeilsheim camp disturbed many. The military authorities announced that the camp would be closed and transferred to German control on July 15, 1948, creating much agitation among the refugees. Camp leaders claimed that it was unacceptable to again place concentration camp survivors at the mercy of the Germans. After a pressure campaign, the evacuation was postponed to a later date.

Meanwhile, plans for *aliyah* were set in motion. Father informed me that the *aliyah* of many youth to *kibbutzim* was being organized; there they would study and work. He commented that this would be an excellent program for me. At the same time, he explained, he and my sisters would arrange their immigration to Israel, where we would reunite as one family.

I was delighted with the opportunity being presented to me. I had heard from my friends about these youth groups preparing for *aliyah*, and had long awaited this day. All conversation at that time focused on our trip to Israel. The youth leaders prepared us in group discussions as well as in private meetings. They explained that we would fly to Israel in special American military planes.

Finally, the long-awaited day arrived. Father supplied me with a small knapsack, which Ita filled with everything I might need. Many parents came to say goodbye to their children. The looks in my father's and sisters' eyes reminded me of earlier partings which I had tried to forget. Father hugged me tightly and my sisters could not help but burst into tears. This time, these were tears of excitement and of hope.

I parted from Father and my sisters and, with my friends, climbed onto the military vehicles waiting at the camp gate. The accompanying youth leaders recorded the names of those present and the trip began. We traveled a few hours toward the Belgian border, not far from which was a military base with an airfield. Many planes were parked all over the base, since other youth had arrived here from elsewhere in Germany, it seems.

Everything was organized perfectly. The youth leaders gathered us in a large hall where doctors and reception clerks were waiting. We underwent various medical examinations and registration procedures, and personal files were prepared for each of us. We were divided into groups and approached the planes. It seems that several planes were readied for this trip, I think four. Many hundreds of youth were there, mostly orphans who had lost their families in the Holocaust, as well as youth leaders and staff personnel.

We were all extremely excited. This was to be the first time in my life on a plane, and I had always dreamed of this moment. We were allowed onto the plane one at a time, almost all of us boys my age. The leader calmed us and gave out pre-flight instructions.

The plane's engines roared and it began to taxi before take-off. After minutes of trepidation and silence, we heard the leader wishing us a safe and pleasant flight to our new homeland – Israel.

After several hours of flight, the pilot announced that we would land in Greece to refuel. The excitement reached a new high: landing in a country which I had never visited. We remained in our seats and waited a long time for the refueling to be completed. Once again, the plane taxied on the runway, took off and was swallowed up in the blue skies on its way to the Promised Land.

With Holocaust survivor children in Zeilsheim under UNRRA auspices – group number 503

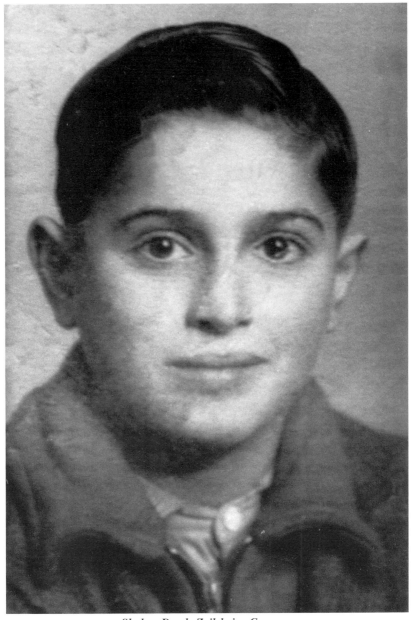

Shalom Domb. Zeilsheim, Germany

Section II

Rebirth

1950-1960

"...and I have broken the bars of your yoke,
and made you go upright."

Leviticus 26:13

Chapter 14

Hanitah

"All is lost, and now
Shall we here too be denied rescue?"

"Hanitah" by Sh. Shalom

Heavily loaded as it was with all the boys, the American plane made sluggish progress. Every time we hit an air pocket, I felt as if my insides were hurtling into my throat. I peered out of the small window on the right, hoping to see the Promised Land on the horizon, but only clouds and sea were visible. I was quite afraid on my very first flight, for up until then my conception of planes had been as frightening steel birds raining bombs, fire and brimstone, sowing destruction and killing people.

Visions of the devastation and death I had experienced resurfaced in me. I again pictured in my mind the bridge that was bombed and split in two, with me on one side and my sisters on the other. Quickly, I banished these disturbing thoughts from my mind. I reflected on the fact that I had left my father and sisters on the western side of the Mediterranean Sea, while I was "galloping" eastward on a plane towards the Jewish state, the State of Israel, our true hope.

The indescribable excitement my fellow passengers and I felt came to a peak when the pilot's voice was heard announcing our imminent landing. Sighs of relief and enthusiastic applause mixed with shouts of joy, and the sound of singing filled the plane as its wheels touched ground on Israeli soil.

"Welcome to Israel!" came the voice of the leader, choked with emotion.

The plane taxied on the runway and stopped not far from a two-story building. This was a military air field in the north of the country, which served the British at that time. Scattered on the field were solitary planes parked some distance from each other.

On that slightly cool morning, January 1, 1950, my feet trod on the holy soil of Eretz Israel for the first time: a young boy with a small knapsack holding all his possessions entering a new world. I kept telling myself: Here I am, little Sholom, embarking upon a new life filled with hope, in my new, nascent country.

Few civilians were to be seen at the air field. Jewish Agency officials and clerks were present, as well as parents and relatives who had come to welcome their dear ones. No one awaited me. All my acquaintances and family members had been left behind, some under piles of earth in the forests of Europe, others in the Nazi crematoria. Only my father and sisters remained somewhere in Germany, awaiting their turn for salvation. Policemen and armed soldiers were on the air field, but this time they were ours, Israeli soldiers – standing in total contrast to the evil Nazi soldiers. The look in our soldiers' eyes said: "Welcome to Israel."

Our leader lined us up and, after completing registration and other administrative matters, we were taken to a waiting bus. There we were received by a wonderful man whose tone and fatherly approach captured my heart immediately. His name was Moshe Yedaya and, he would accompany me as my teacher and educator through a significant part of my life – my stay on the kibbutz.

I was pleased to note that the Hebrew I had learned in Zeilsheim sufficed for me to understand the leader as he explained that we would be traveling northward to Kibbutz Hanitah. Each boy received a bag with a sandwich and candy, and then the bus set out on its long trip. The leader said we'd reach Hanitah in the afternoon.

After stowing my knapsack on the shelf above the seats, I sat down next to the driver, near the front window, so that I could watch the scenery of the new homeland. The bus was very old and had clearly traveled many long miles in its time.

Right from the journey's start I noticed our skilled Israeli driver's "odd" hand movements: Before making a right turn, he pulled a handle to release a red arrow made of iron that was located on the right side of the bus, signaling his intention to turn right. Before turning left, he pulled another handle, near the first, that did the same on the left side of the bus. A further handle, screwed into a diagonal iron post attached to the door, was used to open and close it: pulling it back opened the door, while pushing it forward closed it.

Another item I found interesting was a wire threaded along the entire upper length of the bus, through rings attached to the inner wall of the vehicle above the windows. Pulling the wire released a metal tab tied to a bell in the front of the bus, requesting that the driver stop. These "wonders of Israeli technology" intrigued me.

The trip to Hanitah lasted several hours. No new construction was evident on the narrow road we traveled on. Throughout the journey, my eyes devoured the green expanses, while I listened to the leader's explanations and his account of the War of Independence and the establishment of the state. From him I learned that a great deal of Jewish blood had been spilled in this war. The human toll was 6,000 dead and thousands of wounded, at a time when the entire Jewish population numbered only 600,000.

We passed through towns and villages, and crossed groves, green fields and various fruit orchards. The road wound through the coastal plain and the leader's soothing voice informed us that we were not far from the Mediterranean Sea. All the boys crammed into the bus stared out of both sides of the vehicle in search of the sea, but it was not even visible on the horizon.

"We'll soon reach a stretch of road where you'll be able to view the sea. You'll soon have enough of it," the leader reassured us.

I was very impressed with the leader Moshe's manner of speaking. His Hebrew was fluent and sounded as if it was his native tongue. I tried to compare his speech with that of the teacher in Zeilsheim: it was completely different, but my lessons there had nevertheless provided a basic familiarity with the language, which now allowed me to understand and communicate. Luckily, the expressions in Yiddish, a language I had used with my father and sisters, were similar in pronunciation and meaning to those in Hebrew. But the leader's pronunciation had a special ring to it – a "Sabra" ring to it, as it is called here in Israel.

The quiet moments during the long trip to Hanitah triggered many personal thoughts. Had my wanderings come to an end? I had not had a real roof over my head since the age of five. I had been a homeless, motherless wanderer, mostly fatherless too, and, for lack of choice, only an older sister as a substitute-mother. I considered the fact that I had spent the majority of my life in hiding, in forests, in courtyards, on the streets and roads, constantly fleeing the inhumane Nazi conqueror. I wondered: has my time come, here in Israel, to gain a permanent roof over my head and a safe haven from persecution, pogroms and destruction? Now I find myself in a peculiar situation, not knowing what awaits me, with no family or friends here. Those I once had, ended their lives in mass graves, forests and extermination camps. Those who remain are far from me.

Moshe's soothing voice cut into my thoughts:

"We're approaching Haifa and you'll soon be able to view the sea."

I looked at his face. I trusted this man and, perhaps because his manner of speaking reminded me of my father, felt a strong bond of love toward him from the very first moment. Indeed, "Father" is the name we children in the group gave him – "Father Moshe." He took care of all our needs and listened to our every word. It was evident that he knew exactly where we had come from and what we had endured.

He had been blessed with a fatherly nature, and showered us with much warmth and love.

On the way, Moshe told us about Haifa's history, explaining that it was an important port city, Israel's largest. Many cargo ships were anchored there, loading and unloading merchandise; alongside them were ships that had transported tens of thousands of Jews from all over the world to Israel.

"This is our largest port of entry for immigrants," he explained. "Haifa is a mixed city of Jews and Arabs and is very important to Israel's economy. It sits south of Haifa Bay and its houses are built on the northwestern edges of the Carmel range."

After some time, the sea and the city were finally visible in their full glory, exactly as the teacher had described. Pointing to the mountain on the right, I called out:

"The Carmel!"

Moshe heard me and nodded in my direction, saying:

"Correct, that is Mount Carmel. You should know that you have arrived in Israel during a momentous month which will become famous for a unique historical event. Several days ago, on December 5, 1949, the government of Israel, headed by David Ben-Gurion, decided to move the Knesset to Jerusalem, which will now serve as the nation's capital."

The leader took a newspaper article from his pocket and read excerpts from Prime Minister Ben-Gurion's announcement in the Knesset:

...A nation that, for two thousand and five hundred years, has faithfully adhered to the vow made by the first exiles by the waters of Babylon not to forget Jerusalem, will never agree to be separated from Jerusalem. Jewish Jerusalem will never accept alien rule after thousands of its youngsters liberated their historic homeland for the third time, redeeming Jerusalem from destruction and vandalism...

Moshe explained that this announcement was made in response to a debate held in the United Nations General Assembly on the topic of internationalizing Jerusalem.

To be honest, hearing this concept of "Jerusalem" for the first time awakened in me an inexplicable feeling. I was familiar with the Hatikvah anthem by Naftali Hertz Imber and even knew it by heart from our Hebrew lessons in Zeilsheim. It was one of the first deeply moving songs I had learned, and the name "Jerusalem" appears in it. Each time we sang the song, I trembled, beset by a mysterious emotion. The same familiar feeling returned during this journey through the expanses of "the land of Zion and Jerusalem," as the last line has it. I choked up momentarily, but continued to listen to what our leader had to say:

"Jerusalem is our capital. It is important and holy to us, and to other nations. There are other important cities in our country. Have you heard of Tel Aviv? It is the first Hebrew city, built from the ground up by Jews exactly forty years ago, in 1909. It's a large, modern city with a port, new houses and boulevards, schools, workshops and many commercial structures. There is a boardwalk along the coast, cafés and restaurants and it boasts many Jewish residents. We built all of this with our own hands."

The leader interrupted his lecture to note: "Here on the left is Haifa port, where new immigrants from throughout the world disembark." Everyone looked towards the port.

He added:

"And here is the train station. Until the late 1920s, trains departed from here for Egypt, Syria and Istanbul. This was the 'Mandatory' train run by the British while they governed the country. Now Israel Railways operates here. Last year, new tracks were laid and old lines re-opened, connecting Acre and Nahariya with Haifa and Tel Aviv, and from there to Jerusalem."

Throughout the trip, Moshe did not cease talking about the places and sites we passed. I was very impressed with his expertise regarding the country's geography and history. Like a walking encyclopedia, he remembered dates, names and statistics. We sat open-mouthed, eagerly absorbing everything he said. We heard and saw facts and sites to which we had never been previously exposed. I thought to myself: Who are we? Dozens of boys crammed into a bus, our common denominator the bereavement caused by our Jewishness. We were all survivors of broken, destroyed and wounded families. Moshe's words infused us with confidence and calmed us, as if to say: You have arrived on safe shores in another world, to a new, challenging life, one filled with hope.

From both sides of the bus, a large tent encampment and many long barracks with rounded "tin" roofs was visible. Many people walked among these, and some stood in groups, with young boys of various ages running around them. Some of the boys played ball and some stood at the side of the road waving to us. We waved back in greeting.

The leader explained what we were seeing:

"This was once a British army base. As you know, the British left a year and a half ago, in May 1948. The military barracks you see were converted to an absorption center where new immigrants from Europe now live. The tents serve as temporary housing for the thousands of recently arrived immigrants. Such places are called transit camps, as this is where people will live until a permanent housing solution is found. Our government is making great efforts to move the immigrants as quickly as possible to new housing being constructed in various locations throughout the country. Currently populating this transit camp are Holocaust survivors from Poland, Romania and Hungary, and others who arrived in recent months."

This was the first time I heard of a "transit camp" and saw with my own eyes one of the elements that would eventually, many years after the state was founded, become a subject of much debate, involving accusations of neglect and inaction on the part of the establishment. The transit camps and poor neighborhoods that emerged from them are an issue that has preoccupied the State of Israel for most of its existence, since life there left many of the residents with such deep resentments.

Turning left at one of the curves in the road, the bus entered a city full of old buildings. The street had numerous stores on both sides offering their wares to all. The many people walking around included Arab men with *kaffiyehs* on their heads, sporting long white robes over very wide, white cloth trousers *(sharwal)*; and Jewish women, mingling with Arab women in long black dresses with faces covered by black veils and, on their heads, large clay pots, various packages and tree branches carefully tied with thin rope. This seemed to be the main street of the city. The sidewalks were swarming with people, and on the street were several vehicles, merchandise-filled wagons harnessed to horses and donkeys, and flocks of sheep walking about freely.

"This is the city of Acre," we heard Moshe announce. "Acre is one of the most ancient port cities in the world. A mixed city, it is populated by Arabs, Jews and Christians. According to the Partition Plan, it was included in the territory intended to become the Arab state, but after some tough battles in the War of Independence, it surrendered on May 18, 1948, whereupon most of its Arab residents fled to Lebanon. The walls you see are the fortress that served the British as a prison. Many of the Jewish underground were jailed here, including Ze'ev Jabotinsky, and here, too, the British hanged many of those sentenced to death, the first among them Shlomo Ben-Yosef."

To be honest, I was a little intimidated by the sights of the city. I had not expected to see such a large number of Arabs in the Jewish state. As we traveled on, the scenery and views changed; hearing Moshe's explanations, I began to slowly learn about the land and its customs.

It was late afternoon. Moshe told us about Hanitah, its early days, its economic sectors and the kibbutz's plans for development. Before he could complete his account we had arrived at the kibbutz gates. The houses were built on top of a hill, from which there was an amazing view. Welcomed by kibbutz members, we were given drinks and refreshments. Moshe took us to the slope near the houses where we were assigned our tents, several boys in each. The beds had been made up already – they were "Jewish Agency beds" of heavy iron, with metal slats attached with springs to the bed frame.

"Go rest and organize yourselves in the tents. Please be at the dining hall at six o'clock for supper. Afterwards, we'll have an introductory discussion and decide on tomorrow's schedule."

I put my knapsack under my bed and took a much-needed rest after the flight and the day's experiences. When supper and our meeting were over and Moshe left us, I went to bed, put my head on the pillow and fell asleep. This is how my first day in Israel and my first night in Hanitah passed.

The next day, after we had recovered from our initial shock, we understood that Moshe was, in fact, to be our teacher and educator; we would stick close to him and he to us. He learned our names instantly and related to us like a father to his sons.

It seems that other groups of boys had reached the kibbutz before us. One group was from Italy and another from Germany, where I recognized my friend from Zeilsheim, Avraham Pomerantz.

As fate would have it, while the killing machine had been operating against the Jews of Europe, the seeds of redemption had begun to sprout in Eretz Israel. During this period, the land was under the control of the British Mandate; but the Jews living here were determined to fight for the establishment of a sovereign Jewish state in Eretz Israel, despite Britain's White Paper policy which attempted to halt the process.

Waves of illegal immigration flooded the country's coast. Back in Zeilsheim, too, emissaries and Jewish Brigade soldiers in the camp had tried to organize groups of immigrants to Eretz Israel. The underground organizations in Eretz Israel – the Haganah, Eztel and Lehi – intensified their struggle and their defense activities against the Arab rioters. They also fought relentlessly – politically and militarily – against the British administration which had closed the gates of the land to immigrants and Holocaust survivors. But as throughout Jewish history, the population of the Yishuv was divided in opinion as to the acceptable approach to such operations. Ultimately, however, everyone shared a common goal – the establishment of an independent Jewish state in Eretz Israel.

I learned an interesting and thought-provoking fact from my teacher's tales: While the Nazi boot was trampling heavily on the Jews in my native Polish town Pultusk (as elsewhere) and expelling them from their homes, the settlement of Eretz Israel was growing and taking root everywhere, including in our kibbutz, Hanitah. It was already established back in March 1938 on Israel's northern border with Lebanon, as part of the Tower and Stockade settlement campaign.

The kibbutz of the 1950s differed from that of today. It had all the familiar characteristics of social equality and ideological and economic cooperation. Kibbutz property was jointly owned by all members, who were forbidden to have private property, and everyone was equal in both production and consumption. The atmosphere in the kibbutz was one of pioneering, sacrifice and joint creation and development. There was a feeling that kibbutz membership, in and of itself, made you a partner in guarding the northern border, as well as in building up the land. With this backdrop, a new Hebrew culture developed, one that had not existed previously.

Kibbutz Hanitah sits in a mountainous region about eleven miles from the city of Nahariya and about one mile east of the Mediterranean. Here I received my first exposure, running counter to my earlier experiences, to a different type of Jew: idealistic, imbued with faith and prepared to sacrifice for the good of the nation and the land. Most of the members had participated in founding the kibbutz; it appeared that the hardships they had endured before and after the War of Independence had only strengthened their spirit.

Whenever I speak about the time I spent in Hanitah, I always recall the song by Ya'akov Orland, which expresses the spirit of that period: (composed by Mordecai Ze'ira, 1938). Here is one of its stanzas:

"Night descends, from the mountains a fire
From somewhere erupts a heroes' choir
A fire ignites my heart, with flames my heart abounds
I am for you , Hanitah, for you all around."

Riding to work in the fields of Hanitah

I hold special feelings of affection and admiration for Israel Prize Laureate (1994) Ya'akov Orland, for his songs and his translations. Perhaps this is because he, like me, experienced a traumatic childhood. In his native country he survived a pogrom in which seven family members were murdered before his eyes. Perhaps my fondness for him also stems from the fact that many of his songs were performed by Shoshana Damari, a particularly favorite singer of mine. I loved Orland's lyrical poems and grew up with them. These were songs we sang on various occasions and around the campfire.

At our first meeting with Moshe, we were asked to write letters to our family in Israel and abroad, and to include our new address. In my pants pocket was the note Father gave me before I boarded the plane in Germany with the address for mailing letters from Israel. The address was: UNRRA Offices, Frankfurt, Germany, and included my father's ID number. I wrote the letter that day and gave it to the teacher.

Several weeks later, our group of boys was reduced when parents and relatives came to collect their children. No one came for me. Father was delayed in Germany because my sisters had found partners and their plans were unclear. I remained therefore on the kibbutz, eagerly awaiting them.

Our group of boys was divided into sub-groups. Some reported for kibbutz work in the morning, while others studied in the kibbutz school; this allocation was reversed in the afternoon. The older boys were assigned to construction work. We moved into cabins that had been built near the tents – four boys per room.

We did all kinds of work on the kibbutz. I was placed in the bakery and afterwards did gardening; there were occasional rotations in the kitchen, dining hall, orchard and chicken coop. Gardening brought me much pleasure; anyone searching for the roots of my obsession with flowers and a well-tended garden can find them here in Hanitah. The kibbutz fields were located in the plains at the foot of the mountain. We were taken to work there on an old transport truck belonging to the members. We got into the truck with work tools and since there were no seats, we traveled to the fields standing up and holding onto each other.

The dining room was the main hall; general meetings and key events were also held there. There were times when it was too small to hold all the members, forcing us to eat in shifts. This was a difficult economic period and portions were rationed: half an egg, a tablespoon of oil and a tomato for each person. We sat on benches around long tables. Free time was spent in the cultural lounge which also served as a library and housed a radio and a piano.

I filled my spare time with a variety of activities. I particularly liked sport. The kibbutz gave us a ball to play soccer; I was very drawn to this game and my talent at it soon became evident. I eventually rose to play professional soccer in the national league, becoming the youngest player in the *HaPo'el Kfar Saba* team.

I also did a lot of writing, and I loved to express myself through poetry. I had already attempted to write poems during our Hebrew lessons in Zeilsheim. I wrote copiously; but unfortunately nothing was saved from that period.

One day, we were informed that a large gathering of boys who had survived the Holocaust, organized by the authorities, would be taking place in Kibbutz Manarah in the North. A poetry contest was announced and all participants were asked to write something. Sitting in the shade of one of the trees that looked out over the magnificent scenery of Sulam Tzur, Nahariya and the sea, I wrote a poem conveying thoughts of the past and hopes for the future. This poem won first prize, was put to music in tribute, and was performed at the conference by the famous singer Shimshon Bar-Noy. My excitement knew no bounds. The organizers called me to the stage and I received loud applause from the participants and a certificate of honor. Unfortunately, that poem was

The splendid view from Hanitah (Photo: G. Stav, 2009)

also lost. Everything disappeared in the course of my many journeys and wanderings from place to place, as I will relate further on.

Whenever I felt strong yearnings for my family, or disturbing memories came to mind, I found solace in the shade of the tree overlooking that spectacular view. I was happy that I had managed to continue expressing my feelings in rhyme and in verse.

Of the yearly cycle, I particularly remember liking the Jewish holidays. The first Seder night on kibbutz is well-etched in my memory. With the dining room too small to hold all the members, we emptied all the hay and equipment from the granary and converted it to a dining room for the whole of Passover. It was 1950. The artists among us undertook to paint the Exodus story on white fabric that was hung in the granary, and we added brightly colored paper chains. Festive white cloths were spread on tables decorated with flowers. The choir rehearsed songs from the *Haggadah* and songs about Spring. Members were requested to wear white shirts and the atmosphere was joyous and moving.

Seder night itself was highly enjoyable. We read from the *Haggadah* and sang songs. The food was excellent and included fish, meat, salads and other dishes not served on regular days. Bottles of wine were opened and we all drank the requisite four cups, ending with the *Had Gadya* song.

I also recall other kibbutz holiday celebrations. Purim was a lot of fun – everyone was in costume, and whoever did not dress up was treated to a "helping" of make-up. Independence Day included a special ceremony, after which we went to the main square in Nahariya for folk dancing, followed by all-night song-fests around campfires on the beach.

Another holiday that left an impression on me was *Shavu'ot*. We celebrated the harvest of the first fruits in the field, where bales of hay were strewn all over as decoration. Prepared by the kibbutz's Culture Committee, the ceremony was accompanied by readings of text and dancing. Everyone wore white and each "branch" of the kibbutz brought its first fruits on wagons, tractors, donkeys and horses. Most poignant of all were the mothers wheeling their babies in carriages, presenting all the babies who had been born in the previous year.

Many guests from outside attended the ceremony of the first fruits. Particularly touching was the parade of kindergarten children. Dressed in white festive clothes, heads adorned with bouquets, they held reed baskets with seasonal fruits. It was here that I first heard the song by Levin Kipnis, *Saleinu* (Our Baskets), composed by Yedidyah Admon:

"With baskets on our shoulders
Our heads adorned with flowers
From throughout the land
We've come, first fruits in our hand"

My Hebrew grew stronger during my stay on kibbutz, to the point where I read and wrote fluently and spoke almost like a "Sabra" (native). School lessons and Moshe enriched my knowledge of national history, as well as of basic mathematics and other subjects I missed during the war period.

A year and a half passed very quickly on Hanitah. Returning from work in the orchards with my friends one day, I alighted from the truck and was met by my teacher, who handed me an item of mail. The envelope, studded with unfamiliar stamps, was addressed to me. I immediately recognized my father's handwriting! Sensing my excitement, the teacher placed his hand on my shoulder and whispered:

"Go to your room and read the letter at your leisure; I'm here if you need assistance."

"Thank you," I answered, hurrying back to my room before my friends returned, so I could concentrate on the contents of the letter. Opening it carefully, I read Father's words informing me that he would soon immigrate to Israel. My sisters would, for personal reasons, remain in Germany for now. At this stage he was taking care of the necessary arrangements, and would contact me upon his arrival. He conveyed regards from my sisters, ending with his good wishes and his desire to see me soon. It was a short letter, but one filled with hope. At last the remnants of my family would be reunited! I folded the note and placed it in the pocket of my knapsack for safekeeping.

I ran to the dining room and told Moshe about the contents of the letter. He embraced me warmly, saying how pleased he was to hear the news and offering to help me whenever I asked.

Several months after I received the letter, a phone call arrived at the kibbutz office from the Raanana post office. The reader must remember that the means of communication in those days were very poor. The kibbutz had one telephone, which had a place of honor in the secretariat office. The post office was "Mobile Post" but it was barely mobile, moving rather slowly. Transfer of information and coordination required great efforts, and sometimes even then to no avail.

In this unusual phone conversation, I was informed that my father had arrived in Israel and was living in a Raanana transit camp. I was in ecstasy. The kibbutz decided to send me to meet my father. The next morning, after a restless night, I put on clean clothes and was ready to go. They took me to Haifa where they gave me money for the bus; I waited for a local Egged bus to Tel Aviv, which also stopped in Raanana.

It was a long trip. It seemed as if the bus stopped at every city and town, with passengers getting on and off each time. The further we traveled, the more the bus filled up, forcing some people to remain standing. The mixture of languages I heard made my head spin. I had become accustomed to hearing only one language in Israel – Hebrew – and it felt as if I was in the Tower of Babel.

I heard a couple speaking Polish and understood every word. Others spoke Russian and I understood every word. There were, unmistakably, many Yiddish speakers; again, I understood every word. I could not, however, understand Arabic or the other languages I heard. One thing I learned from this long trip: I spoke four languages: Hebrew, Polish, Yiddish and Russian. I had unintentionally learned Polish and Russian during the war period.

When the bus arrived in Raanana in late afternoon, I got off and inquired about the transit camp. One passerby pointed in the direction of the camp, mumbled something in some unclear tongue and continued on his way. It seemed that the word for "transit camp" was understood in all languages. I thought to myself: Here I am, standing on the main street of Raanana, independent and making my own decisions about what to do, in which direction to go, whom to ask. To be on the safe side, I asked someone else, who responded in Hebrew and pointed in the same direction as others had.

I walked along the street. Residential buildings and stores had been built on both its sides and ornamental trees planted along its length. Orchards and green fields peeked out from behind the houses. Tent tops were already visible at the end of the street on the right, indicating that I had chosen the right direction. My heart pounding from emotion, I quickened my pace. In a short while I would meet my father, from whom I had been forcibly separated several times in my short life.

From afar, the camp resembled an army base. Dozens of tents were lined up and spaced out in orderly fashion. As I neared it, I became aware of the difficult conditions prevailing there. There was one family to each tent, with the number of beds corresponding to the size of the family. Laundry and other items were hung to dry or air out on the lines strung between tents. What I saw was depressing, reminiscent of the unpleasant sights in European refugee centers we had passed through after the war. I recalled Moshe's comment that this was a "transit camp," which meant that it was "temporary housing."

Living in the transit camp were new immigrants from various countries: Poland, Romania, Hungary, Iraq, Morocco and Yemen. At that moment, the mix of people and the sounds of all the surrounding languages seemed to me a unique and impressive phenomenon.

My eyes were drawn to a group of Yemenite Jews gathered in front of one of the tents, singing and drumming on cans. I didn't understand a single word of their song, but it sounded like a prayer. I walked through the rows of tents, asking about my father: Did someone know him, or know which tent was his? No one knew. I went through another row and started to inspect each tent, encountering an older man in one of them.

"Domb?" he asked.

"Yes, I am looking for my father, Avraham Domb," I responded.

"Yes, I know him. He lives there, in the first tent," said the man, pointing to a tent at the end of the row.

I hurried to the tent. No one was there. There were several beds and a cabinet upon which rested a kerosene lamp for use at night; on the beds were folded blankets and some clothes. The neighbor said that Father had left a few hours earlier and suggested that I inquire at the office on the other side of the transit camp.

The person in charge there received me warmly, gave me water and some bread and jam, commenting that he knew Father very well. After a moment, he looked at me and said:

"It seems that your father went to the city to look for work or to visit relatives. In any case, if he does not return this evening you are welcome to stay with me. Your father will come back at some point."

An interesting discussion ensued. I asked how long he thought my father would stay here. He said he didn't know, explaining that in the past year the country had absorbed 900,000 immigrants from many places, and the stream of arrivals was currently still ongoing. He pointed out that the country was still in its infancy and lacked the resources to expedite the building of permanent housing for everyone. For lack of options, these transit camps were established as temporary residences until the housing shortage could be resolved.

While he was still speaking, my father burst into the office, having heard from his neighbor that I was here. This was a great surprise. To this day I still treasure the memory of that long, warm embrace and his tears pouring down on my face with such longing and yearning. His wife Leah entered the room and also gave me a loving hug.

I cannot close this chapter on my life in Hanitah without dedicating a few lines to my much-admired teacher and educator, Moshe Yedaya (Duchovny), a figure who left a powerful impression on me during this period. He undoubtedly deserves even more than the following:

Moshe Yedaya was born in Serbia in 1921. Raised and educated in a traditional Zionist family, he learned Hebrew at school, immigrated to Eretz Israel in 1939 and was among the founders of Kibbutz Hanitah. He married Rachel Gutman, who passed away after illness at age 46.

Moshe studied literature, grammar, Land of Israel studies and archeology. He was a teacher, principal and educator of generations of students. He founded and was principal of the area's Sulam Tzur school, and numbered amongst the founders of Hanitah's Tower and Stockade Museum. In the 1950s he established in Hanitah a regional club for Land of Israel studies, and was a student and admirer of Ze'ev Vilnai. He went on many hikes with his pupils and wrote a series of pamphlets on the subject.

Moshe had three children – Oded, Itai and Yemimah. His son, Itai, fell during the Yom Kippur War in October 1973 in the battle at Kantara, Egypt. His daughter Yemimah died of an illness at age 62. His son, Oded Yedaya, followed his father as an educator and today heads the Minshar for Art college in Tel Aviv. Moshe Yedaya passed away from illness in 1987 at the age of 67, and was buried in Hanitah.

May this chapter in my life story serve as a tribute to all his work.

Chapter **15**

The House on Ahuzah Street

"A rose of Sharon, a lily of the valleys"

Song of Songs, 2:1

Raanana is one of the nicest cities in Israel. Not for naught is she dubbed "The Pearl of the Sharon," for she is truly a lustrous pearl, bathed in green expanses. This is the place where my personal lily of the valley, the love of my life and mother of my children – Sara – grew and blossomed. However, I will not jump ahead of my story.

My first visit to the Raanana transit camp left a very negative impression on me: How is it possible to lead a normal life without a real home, with no shower or attached bathroom? We, of all people, appreciated the importance of living in our own independent country; nevertheless, in order to lead a reasonable family life, basic living conditions are a necessity. Father and Leah also had trouble accepting the circumstances in which they were forced to live – in a tent lacking the bare essentials, let alone privacy.

The bathrooms in the transit camp were open to all and the authorities tried to maintain some level of decent hygiene. One barely trickling faucet served the entire community, and there was always a long line and many people crowding around it. It was amusing to witness the arguments about the line among people speaking different languages. One person made his claims in Yiddish, while his opponent countered in Yemenite-tinged Arabic. Occasionally, we would witness violent outbursts among the residents.

As usual, Father made a determined decision: to make every effort to leave the camp and, above all, to find employment. As soon as there was some income, he claimed, it would be possible to improve living conditions and even move to a new apartment. Father decided that Raanana was the most suitable place for us to build our future. From the moment he had arrived in Israel, he did not cease searching for work. In general, I remember that wherever we went during our wanderings, Father's priority was to find a job.

This was in the early days of the state, the early 1950s, when the Austerity program declared by the government in May 1949 was at its peak. Many unemployed shuffled aimlessly along the streets and the government struggled to come up with solutions. The number of immigrants streaming into the country increased steadily, arriving from all over the world, primarily from Eastern Europe and Arab countries. The wretchedness manifested itself in both lack of housing and unemployment.

The young state was not prepared to absorb the tens of thousands who arrived empty-handed; by the early 1950s, the population had doubled, to 1,300,000. Many were refugees from the death camps. The government had hit a point where foreign currency reserves were dwindling rapidly. There was no choice but to announce rationing of basic food products, intended to stabilize the cost of goods that had risen and to conserve foreign currency.

Dr. Dov Joseph, the Minister of Rationing and Supply, decided that standard bread would not be rationed, but other products would be limited as follows: Corn – 60 grams per day; sugar – 58 grams; flour – 60 grams; rice – 17 grams; margarine and beans – 20 grams; noodles – 8 grams; eggs – 12 per month; meat – 750 grams per month. The public was indeed expected to manage with very little.

In addition to the foreign currency problems, the greatest challenge facing the newly independent country was establishing the Israel Defense Forces and dealing with the never-ending security issues. The majority of the public patiently bore the labor pains of the Jewish state and the personal sacrifice required of each person. For example, Father, Leah and I, who had personally experienced the Holocaust and the humiliating starvation from which we constantly suffered, accepted the order of the day. There were, however, those who strongly cried out against the policy of rationing.

I returned to the kibbutz after my first visit to Raanana, maintaining contact with Father and Leah via letters. Every so often I traveled to visit them. I was happy that they did not remain in the transit camp for too long; within a few months of arrival and after an intensive search, Father found a job in the laundry of a cooperative in Raanana. He was thrilled that he finally had a steady income!

Father had already started to look for housing as soon as he received his first salary. He found something suitable for a family in a building on Ahuzah Street, the main street of Raanana. It was an ideal location: the heart of the city, on the corner of Motzkin Street. Not far were a bus stop, a grocery store, various businesses and the municipality building. Father promptly rented the house.

The joy felt by Father and Leah was indescribable. The last time my family had our own roof overhead was in Pultusk on September 26, 1939. Since being expelled, we had wandered around homeless for over twelve years! This was, therefore, a turning point in our lives – arriving at a permanent residence.

At first, Father and Leah did not speak Hebrew; they spoke Yiddish between themselves, as did I with them. Slowly, they began to learn the language and use it to communicate with others.

During one of my visits to the house on Ahuzah Street, my father sat down with me to discuss my future:

"I understand that you're doing well on the kibbutz, you've made friends and are managing very nicely there. I very much appreciate what this setting has done for you, but it seems to me that you also have to look into your own future. I've been thinking about this a lot lately and I suggest that you leave the kibbutz and come live with us in Raanana. I am about to become a partner in the laundry and I'll need your assistance."

"Yes," I responded, "I've done well on the kibbutz. Quite a few of my friends have left to be with their families who've arrived in Israel. Truthfully, I had no plans for a future on the kibbutz. I had thought to remain there until being drafted into the IDF while you continue in the city, where I would join you later. But having heard your suggestion, I'll consider the matter seriously."

"You're still young. It's worth utilizing these years to acquire a profession, earn some money and thus be able to help me by investing in the business while also saving for the future. Leah has already prepared a room for you in the apartment and we'll take care of all your needs."

During the entire return journey to the kibbutz, I pondered Father's proposal. How could I leave Hanitah and the many friends I had made there? Moving to the city and leading an independent life was very tempting. I thought about Father and all the hardships he had endured. I concluded that since he asked, it must be important that I be with him during this time. The money I would earn from work I find in the city could help Father pay the rent and build up the business.

The next day, I discussed Father's suggestion and my doubts with Moshe. In his unqualified decency, he told me to follow my heart, advising:

"It's important that any decision be made only if your emotions and your conscience leave you at peace with yourself."

After several weeks of deliberation, I left the kibbutz and went to live with Father in the house on Ahuzah Street in Raanana.

Throughout this period, Father and Leah spared no effort in locating surviving relatives. The searches were conducted through the Searching Relatives Bureau, set up by the authorities and through which Father finally found some of his brothers, who had also come to Israel.

In the meantime, my sisters had grown up, gotten married and begun to establish families. My sister Zipporah met her husband, Freddy, also a Pultusk native, in the Zeilsheim DP camp; they moved to the United States. My sister Sara met her husband in Germany and though they moved to Israel and got married, they returned to Germany and lived in Munich for many years. My oldest sister Ita also met her husband in Zeilsheim; once married, they immigrated to Israel.

The transition from kibbutz to Raanana was quite drastic. Life in the city was very different from the cooperative existence on kibbutz. The regular routine was not the same, and neither was the atmosphere or anything else. The daily encounter in Raanana with Jews from various Diasporas gave one the feeling that in this bubbling melting pot something unique would be created which humanity had never before experienced. Jews of about 100 nationalities, speaking different languages, from varying levels of society and with different customs and mentalities, all gathered to rebuild their homes in the land of their forefathers.

The years I lived with Father in Raanana were successful and productive in every way. I worked, made many friends and enjoyed life, just as any teenager of those times did. It seems I had to make up for what I had missed previously.

After searching for days, I found work as a gardener with a Jewish employer who took care of private gardens in Raanana. Aside from me, he also had two Arab workers from local villages. The experience I had gained in this realm on the kibbutz served me well. It was a wonderful feeling to earn a living, save money and help Father.

Everyone who knew me at that time noted that I was much more mature than my peers. I was alert to everything, approaching those I encountered with suspicion and appropriate caution. This instinct was rooted in my boyhood, when I had wandered with no father or mother in the virgin forests and roads of Poland and Russia. Kibbutz life had toughened me further, adding a "Sabra" quality to my developing personality.

I spent my free time after work with friends I met in Raanana. I joined the local *Hamahanot Ha'olim* (immigrant camps) youth movement, whose activities included many ceremonies and evenings of entertainment. A key part of its activities was devoted to singing and dancing, and another central component was to hang out at the *"Hameyu'ash"* falafel stand in Herzliya.

Everyone dressed simply. Popular among my friends was the embroidered shirt. For the most part, this was a black, Russian-style shirt with a modest, hand-embroidered flower decorating the front. In the summer, many wore shorts with pockets hanging down past their cuffs. The girls wore full skirts puffy shorts secured at the thigh with elastic threaded through the hem

In warm summer months, we would frequent the open-air cinema in Herzliya and watch movies under the twinkling stars. In those days, the subtitles did not appear in the film itself, but on a film strip to the left of the screen. They were not always synchronized with the on-screen action – it depended on the level of projectionist's Hebrew. Sometimes the audience would let out an ear-splitting whistle to draw his attention to the problem and urge him to speed up the translation reel.

This is how I spent my first months in Raanana.

One hot Shabbat morning, I went to cool off with my friends at the Herzliya beach. As they did every week, a group of young people had organized a soccer game on a make-shift field, which attracted many spectators. When I inquired why so many people came to watch the game, my friend explained that most of the players were from the *HaPo'el Kfar Saba* team and these were some of its fans. Summoning up courage, I asked to join the game. I played with one of the teams, scoring a goal within the first few minutes. When I scored another goal a few minutes later, the players recognized my talent and began to gather around me, expressing amazement upon hearing that I did not belong to any club.

Someone suggested that I join my hometown's *HaPo'el Raanana*, which I did – that very same week, I reported to the coach,

With the soccer players of the HaPo'el Kfar Saba club

who had already heard about me, and immediately went onto the field in uniform. My successes made me famous in the city and within two months I was traded to *HaPo'el Kfar Saba*, starting a brilliant soccer career. The team's coach was a young man named Edmond Shmilovich who had previously coached *HaPo'el Tel Aviv*. I was not familiar with my new club's history, but later learned that I had joined a respected club, established in 1928, which had made the effort to cultivate a magnificent team that had attracted many fans.

I became one of the key players for *HaPo'el Kfar Saba*. Over time my salary rose from the initial ten liras per game up to twenty. Recognized wherever I went, I was constantly surrounded by fans patting me on the back. My teammates in those days included Emanuel Shefer and Haim Glazer, Shaya Glazer's brother. I believe that Shlomo Scharf and Yitzhak Shum played then on the junior team.

To keep me happy and deter me from a possible transfer to a competitor, the team management offered me a perk – they rented a room for me with a family in the center of Kfar Saba. The hosting family restricted my movements too much and I did not feel comfortable there, so I quickly gave up this "bonus" and returned to our home on Ahuzah Street.

Aware of my playing skill and great popularity, I made major efforts to attend all practice sessions and games, despite the tremendous strain this placed on my daily routine. At some point, however, I gave up, as it was impossible to devote time to both the gardening work and soccer. I began to arrive late to practice, which made things difficult for the coach. Worried that I was being wooed by a competitor, the management tried to offer me various benefits so that I would remain with the team, though, as stated, I had no plans to leave .

Wherever I went, I reaped the rewards of my fame, even at the *"Hameyu'ash"* falafel stand, where Orah, the owner's daughter, would treat me to an extra large portion on the house. I became a celebrity, publicized in the media, was invited to a variety of events and had beautiful girls chasing after me. As I write this, I long for that period, which was special for both the country and for me personally.

From 1952, the *HaPo'el Kfar Saba* team began to play in

Israel's premier league, continuing for thirty-three seasons. The team produced some of Israel's first-rate coaches and players, including my friends Yitzhak Shum and Shlomo Scharf.

In early 2006, Shlomo Scharf, the Israel national team coach, hosted a reception in my honor in his backyard in Kfar Saba. He invited past players of *HaPo'el Kfar Saba*, among them Shefer and Shum. We reminisced about the old days during this very moving reunion.

My friend Gershon Stav had told our mutual friend, then Prime Minister Ehud Olmert, about the reunion beforehand. An avid sports fan, the prime minister surprised me by calling me on the evening of the event to congratulate me and the team's veteran players.

As a former player, I remained devoted to the team and was absolutely thrilled when it won the national cup in 1975. Although a fan of Beitar Jerusalem, I was happy when my team, *HaPo'el Kfar Saba*, defeated Beitar 3:1 in the finals, winning its first national cup. The goal scorers in this game were Yoram Mor and Yitzhak Shum, and the coach was Shlomo Scharf.

Throughout my life, I have followed the victories and defeats of my team, and continue to do so now with the aid of my friend Shlomo Scharf, who updates me periodically on team events.

Shalom Domb, 1956

Chapter 16

In the Israel Defense Forces

"Every fine man to arms
All our youth on guard"

Palmach Anthem, Zerubavel Gilad

In the short time that I lived with my father in Raanana I made many friends. My position as a leading player of the *HaPo'el Kfar Saba* soccer team brought me numerous fans and much recognition. Among my close friends were Aharon Eshel, Yitzhak Golan, Yossi Zim and Ehud Kongret. We were a special group of friends, whom today's Sabras would call the "salt of the earth." I was the only Holocaust survivor of the group.

We were all highly motivated youth, prepared to do everything for the sake of the newly established country. More than once we had discussed joining the Israel Defense Forces, and in the end we all decided to report for regular duty. Aharon Eshel was drafted before me; at seventeen, I was too young to qualify for the army, but I decided to report to the induction office and volunteer to serve before draft age.

This was 1953, five years after independence. The country's security situation was difficult, with endless border incidents claiming quite a few lives. I viewed enlistment in the IDF as a natural step. Many of my friends were older than me and had received draft notices. I recalled the stories heard from soldiers on leave at Kibbutz Hanita, stories which fascinated me. I had always dreamed of the moment when I could experience the army myself. An image from the past comes to mind, of sitting on the grass with my friends, listening open-mouthed to the soldiers' tales. Without too much deliberation, I decided that this was the time to join up and proudly don the IDF uniform.

I arrived at the induction office in Jaffa in early morning. After undergoing various registrations and medical exams, I received a high physical profile classification and was informed in the personal interview that I was fit to serve in a combat unit. I was happy with these results and was told to wait at home for the draft notice, which would be sent soon. I was young, with an athletic body, and in top physical form. The practice sessions and games on the soccer field had helped me to maintain a particularly high level of fitness and to thus be accepted for an early draft. This would also make things relatively easy for me during the basic training period.

Meanwhile, I resumed my routine in Raanana, dividing my time between work and the soccer field while awaiting the longed-for draft notice. Gardening work was a form of "occupational therapy" for me. Although I didn't earn much, I was able to help my father with some of the household expenses, while allowing myself a small sum for pocket money. The additional money I received from *HaPo'el Kfar Saba* helped alleviate some of my father's daily expenditures. As stated, this was during the *Tzena* (Austerity) period in Israel, when so many people still lived in transit camps and food was rationed.

Father kept working hard and the laundry partnership brought in sufficient funds to maintain the apartment on Ahuzah Street and cover daily costs. After all the hardships my father had endured, I felt obliged to help him as much as possible, so that he might stabilize his financial situation. I was troubled by the thought of how I would manage to keep this up during my two-year army service; but Father reassured me that I need not worry, they would manage now that Leah had also found a job.

When I notified the management of *HaPo'el Kfar Saba* of my impending induction date, they immediately started contacting their "connections" so that I could participate in some weekend games during my army stint. They were concerned that, as a star player, my absence would seriously impact the team. Nothing helped, however, and all attempts to release me for the weekends were for naught.

I saw Aharon Eshel during his leaves from the army, and the stories I heard from him stirred my imagination. Aharon (Arol) was a Sabra, born in Raanana in 1934 and drafted into the IDF in 1952.

He was among the founders of the first paratrooper reconnaissance unit. This was a military spearhead, commanded by the most elite and talented IDF officers and comprised of fighters known for their daring and courage, as was my friend Aharon.

Aharon told me a lot about the unit and its exploits. He had begun as a rank-and-file soldier, together with such courageous IDF soldiers as Meir Har-Zion, Aharon Davidi (whom I knew as our neighbor on Ahuzah Street), Shimon Kahaner (Katcha) and many others. In 1960, Aharon was appointed deputy commander of the General Staff Reconnaissance Unit, taking part in its daring operations. Arik Sharon commented to me on more than one occasion that my friend was one of the IDF's most outstanding warriors. He was discharged after a brilliant army career with the rank of colonel and was put in charge of the Fire and Rescue Service in Tel Aviv with the rank of Senior Commander. I have maintained regular contact with Aharon Eshel to this day.

I had very much wanted to join such an elite unit. As stated, the security situation in 1950s Israel was very difficult. Infiltrators were able to enter the country through the porous borders with Jordan, Syria, Lebanon and Egypt; they damaged rail lines, placed mines on roads, set fields aflame and murdered Jews. These attacks caused serious harm to the state's security and to the morale of the populace, most of whom were recently arrived immigrants.

As a soldier in the Israel Defense Forces

In a military coup in Egypt in late February 1954, Gamal Abdel Nasser ousted General Muhammad Naguib and took control. Two weeks later, a terrible massacre occurred at Maaleh Akrabim when a bus en route from Eilat to Tel Aviv was attacked by terrorists who, having apparently entered Israel from Jordan, slaughtered the passengers. Eleven passengers, including women and children, were shot to death at close range, and many others were wounded. Prime Minister Moshe Sharett did not launch a counterattack. This is the atmosphere that prevailed during the period of my military service.

On the day I was drafted, I parted from Father and Leah, as well as from Ita and her husband, who had immigrated to Israel several months earlier. I boarded the bus and went to the induction base at Sarafand, today's Tzrifin. The first day in the army was very busy with registration, medical exams, receipt of military equipment, various instructions and run-arounds, all of which introduced me to the new world I was destined to occupy in the coming years.

At the end of the process, I was assigned to the 10th Infantry Brigade.

The army of the mid-1950s was vastly different from that of today. Although the budget was large, it was tiny relative to the security

With soldiers in my unit, at fitness training

needs. This was evident in the quality of IDF equipment and in the bases themselves, even though the government did its best to provide the maximum, particularly in weaponry. I remember some of the songs that expressed the spirit of those days: "Artillery instead of socks, tanks instead of shoes…. " No one complained, however, for we understood the situation.

After basic training we went through back-breaking additional training in the Jordan Valley in northern Israel. Leaves were infrequent and the sole means of communication with the family was through letters, which first passed through the hands of the military censor. The many friends I made here served as compensation for the distance from home.

Discovering my physical abilities and athletic prowess, my commanders decided to send me to a course for fitness instructors – my fame as a soccer player undoubtedly contributed to this decision. However, all my friends from basic training were placed in combat units: paratroopers, Givati and others.

After some time, I was nevertheless sent to a five-month combat sergeant course in which soldiers from various combat units participated. It was particularly difficult and was conducted in unusually challenging conditions. Even I, who had survived the inferno of World War Two, can testify that the regimen was extremely hard.

During the course, we were taken for routine security patrols. We conducted military operations to prevent the entry of *fedayeen* (terrorist infiltrators), including setting up ambushes to uncover these cells before they became active. On more than one occasion we actually had a run-in with them and fought until they were eliminated.

Despite the limited means of communication available, I tried to maintain contact with Father in Raanana throughout my service. Next to our house was a café called Café Noga that had a telephone. The café was very popular in those days, with many residents attending the dances they held every Saturday night to the music of a record player. I knew the owner, who was kind enough to occasionally convey my regards to my father. Luckily, the company clerk whom I knew from the base sometimes allowed me to use the military switchboard to contact the cafeteria and inquire after my family.

One day, after being instructed to don our Class A uniforms, we were taken to a military base in the center of the country, where Prime Minister David Ben-Gurion was due to visit with a group of American Jewish industrialists. Slated to serve as honor guard for him, we were very excited about the event. I was placed in the front row, giving me an up-close view of the prime minister. I recalled his visit to Zeilsheim after the Holocaust – and now I was privileged to see him in the State of Israel. Then I had been a stateless and homeless refugee lad; now I saw him as a soldier of the Israel Defense Forces!

I contemplated the reversal of my fortunes in less than ten years. On this special occasion, I listened to every word of Ben-Gurion's speech. He emphasized to the visitors from the United States how the Jewish people could not exist without a Jewish state; the stronger our situation in Israel, the more secure that of Diaspora Jewry too. However, if, God forbid, our situation in Israel was to worsen, so too would Diaspora Jewry suffer, for this is the common fate of the Jewish nation.

During the sergeants' course I widened my circle of acquaintances. One of the outstanding fighters was a Yemenite named Zechariah Hetzroni, with whom I formed a special bond. We shared our experiences with each other and I learned that he also lived in Raanana, in the "Yemenite neighborhood." I had heard of the neighborhood but had never visited there. On one of our leaves we hitchhiked together to Raanana, and before each of us went our separate ways, he invited me to visit his home.

I went the next day. The neighborhood was at the other end of Raanana and I had to cross orchards and plowed fields to get there. I met two young girls at the edge of the neighborhood and asked them where Hetzroni's house was. The older one, very pretty with greenish eyes, said that she was going in that direction and would take me there. Who could have guessed that this encounter would bring me the love of my life? This was Sara, who eventually became my beloved wife and mother of my children. She was the only Yemenite with green eyes I had ever met.

After this, I visited the *"Bet Ha'Am"* community center in this Yemenite neighborhood during every army leave, participating

With the IDF national soccer team, mid-nineteen fifties

in evenings of song and dance. The place and atmosphere were wonderful and I could think of no better place to meet Sara. I loved this ethnic group's way of life, one filled with joy and an especially warm hospitality.

The entire period of my military service was packed with security events, courses and training. I was forced to manage on my army wages, which at that time were very low, barely enough to buy a falafel and a glass of soda water. I refrained from asking Father for money; I entered the canteen with my friends on more than one occasion, and did not buy a thing, just eyed the wares from the side. During my army stint, I made a new friend named Aharon Kaplan, who eventually became a famous basketball player with *Maccabi Tel Aviv*. He apparently came from a well-to-do family, and when he saw that I had no money to purchase anything in the canteen, he gave me his military ration booklet so that I could buy some wafers or a soda bottle. I saw this as a friendly, noble act which I very much appreciated.

On July 26, 1956, Egyptian ruler Gamal Abdel Nasser nationalized the Suez Canal. Traffic on the canal had been managed by the Suez Canal Company, owned by France and England, who viewed the Egyptian action as hostile and wished to regain control of the canal. In this context, France and England pressured Israel to declare war on Egypt – they were searching for an excuse to enter the fray and reconquer the canal.

Israel had solid grounds for war against Egypt at that time. It was necessary to eradicate the terror nests in Gaza, which were causing much harm to our innocent citizens. In addition, the threat presented by the massive build-up of Egyptian forces in Sinai needed to be eliminated; these forces were equipped with the best arms purchased in a huge, Russian-inspired deal with Czechoslovakia. Above all, it was important to breach the naval blockade placed by Egypt on Israeli maritime activity in the Straits of Tiran. Ben-Gurion initially rejected the French-Anglo request, but, given Israel's dependency on French arms, ultimately agreed to it.

Thus, I found myself deployed, along with fellow soldiers in my unit, on the Egyptian border before the start of the war, which finally broke out on October 29, 1956. Chief of Staff Moshe Dayan oversaw the battles and the war was conducted in coordination with the French and the British.

The unit in which I served boasted excellent fighters. Particularly memorable was Yonatan from Kfar Saba. Classified as an outstanding soldier, he joined us during the deployment before the Sinai Campaign and served as the unit's bazooka man. Yonatan did not hide the fact that he was an active member of the Israeli communist party. Political arguments were also common amongst us soldiers, and there was always someone raising one topic or other. The members of our unit often teased him, asking what he would do in war if the enemy appeared in tanks or half-tracks made by Mother Russia … He answered definitively: "I am a Jew first and foremost, and then a Communist." Yonatan was killed in an artillery barrage the first night of the Sinai

Campaign while crossing the Sinai border.

On October 29, a paratrooper force was parachuted into the Mitla Pass, about forty-three miles east of the Suez Canal. That same night, IDF forces conquered Kuntillah and Ras al Naqb, and then surrounded Um Katef and Abu Ageila. At this point, the Israeli air force was fighting the Egyptian air force single-handedly. Then, on November 1, England and France joined in with a decisive attack on the Egyptian air force. Panic-stricken, the Egyptian army scattered all over, leaving behind valuable military equipment – tanks, trucks, heavy mechanical equipment, a multitude of weapons and more. This booty was all taken later to IDF storage depots.

During the fighting, while advancing deeper into Sinai, I was sent with three others to bring back water for the unit. We traveled on a dirt road in a command car that served us during war. We were careful to drive along a route previously used by other vehicles, literally following the tread marks in the sand. On the way, we encountered a Bedouin and asked him for the location of a water source. We traveled in the direction he pointed, but this turned out to be a trap, for the path we were on was littered with mines and the command car hit one. The sound of a strong explosion assailed our ears and we were thrown from the vehicle. All four of us were injured. I was wounded in my hands: my right thumb was left hanging, almost torn off, while my left hand was covered in blood. The force of the blast had also injured my lower back, and I lay on the ground practically paralyzed.

After a few minutes we managed to call for help with the radio that had luckily remained undamaged. An evacuation force from our unit arrived and we were treated initially in a makeshift field hospital. Members of our unit searched in vain for the Bedouin. The pains in my back and hands were unrelenting. I was evacuated to a large field hospital set up at the edge of Gaza City, where I received basic care. I underwent an operation on my right hand, from which shrapnel was removed. Signs of the surgery remain on my hand to this day. After the surgery and medical treatments, I was offered a leave to rest and recover. I refused it and returned to my comrades; it did not occur to me to abandon them while the war was going on.

As a result of massive pressure from the superpowers, the United States and the Soviet Union, Ben-Gurion ordered the evacuation of Sinai in March 1957. Before retreating, he declared that any further closing of the Straits of Tiran in the future would constitute a *casus belli.*

The mood of the nation soared as a result of the brilliant victory in Sinai. The radio played a slew of songs that had been composed during and after the war. Pictures were printed in all the newspapers and later, books were sold at the stands. The war, however, took a heavy toll: 171 of our best sons were killed, and hundreds wounded.

The velvet voice of Shoshana Damari singing Mohar and Vilenski's *Mul Har Sinai* (By Mount Sinai) still resonates in my ears:

> ***"It is no dream, my friend, and no passing legend***
> ***For at Mount Sinai the bush is burning….."***

Life in Israel slowly returned to normal. My discharge date from the IDF drew nearer. One of the last events I recall from my service was the Outstanding Marksman competition, held at the shooting range near

With Sara in Raanana, before our marriage

Rishon Lezion. Due to the excellent marksmanship I had displayed in the sergeants course, I was chosen to represent my unit. At the end of the competition, I was awarded the Outstanding Marksman certificate, which I have until this day.

Several weeks before the end of my service, I was called for an interview by representatives of a government authority. They were interested in my history, focusing on my experiences during the Holocaust. They recorded and documented everything I said and thanked me for my cooperation.

My discharge day arrived and I found myself at a crossroads – with no career and no employment. I lived in my father's house in Raanana and spent my free time with Sara. The friendship and the trust between us grew stronger.

I reported to the management offices of *HaPo'el Kfar Saba* where everyone was happy to see me. To my joy, using their good connections in the city, they arranged work for me as a taxi driver in Raanana and its surroundings after I took out a driver's license.

Barely a few months after my discharge, I received my first notice for reserve duty. I hadn't imagined being called up so quickly. Apparently, I had been placed in a Central Command unit. After a brief training period at the Schneller base near the entrance to Jerusalem, we learned that we were slated to go to Mount Scopus – at the time an enclave in Jordanian territory under Israeli control.

According to the cease-fire agreement with Jordan, military forces were not allowed on Mount Scopus, only civilians and police guarding university property. Thus, I spent my first reserve duty there as a "policeman" looking westward at the expanding new city.

I returned to my routine in Raanana immediately afterward. A short while later, I received a registered letter inviting me to another meeting. I reported as instructed for the meeting in Tel Aviv, where my hosts greeted me warmly and explained that I was asked to come as a result of my interview prior to my discharge from the army. My hosts offered me a year of studies and training, and presented me with plans for future work abroad. I was promised a respectable salary, even during my studies.

I considered this offer very seriously and decided to accept the challenge and join the course. It was very interesting but extremely taxing, and I was forced to cope with unusual situations. Luckily, I was in excellent physical shape after the army. I met new friends here and was exposed to a particularly high caliber of people. During the course and on every vacation, I made sure to see Sara. Our meetings became more frequent and our bond grew stronger. I visited her parents' home and she came to ours on Ahuzah Street. I drew a great deal of encouragement from her throughout the arduous course.

After it ended, I was called for an operational briefing of several days and was sent abroad for national service. My first home leave, of course, was spent with Sara. Our mutual longing and the burning love between us made us decide to marry.

Sara's parents were jubilant at our decision and gave us their blessing, and the faces of my father and Leah also shone with happiness at the news. Father offered to hold the event in a wedding hall; however, desiring a modest ceremony including only our families, we refused.

The marriage ceremony was properly conducted in a restaurant on King George Street in Tel Aviv by a rabbi who came from Raanana. Present were Sara's family, Father and Leah and a small number of relatives. Sara displayed her full beauty and radiance and our joy knew no bounds. After the wedding, I resumed my service abroad and Sara remained in Israel.

With my wife Sara on our wedding day

Section III

He Raises
From the Dust

1960-

"He raises up the poor from the dust,
and lifts the needy from the ash heap."

Psalms 113: 7

Chapter 17

America

"America means opportunity,
freedom, power."

Ralph Waldo Emerson

America is known as the land of unlimited opportunities. Ralph Waldo Emerson, the nineteenth century American poet and philosopher, expressed it well. He fought relentlessly against the slavery that was accepted in his time, and demanded that man's freedom be restored. This philosophy was based on his belief in the "infinitude of the private man." Emerson was highly influential and impacted much of the American population. His declaration that "America means Opportunity, Freedom, Power" shaped the character of the United States and the nature of its government.

This doctrine of opportunity and freedom enabled me to establish a thriving and robust economic enterprise, which brought prosperity to me and to my family. Do not think this a trivial matter, dear reader. I toiled and sweated greatly and encountered many periods of difficulty until I acclimated and began to enjoy the fruits of my labors. Indeed, in America money does not grow on trees. It exists, but much energy must be invested, along with persistence, professionalism, and reliability, before it may be earned.

With the completion of my national service in the spring of 1960, I boarded a Pan American flight and flew to the United States to visit my sister Zipporah in New York, intending to return thereafter to Israel. I had not seen Zipporah since Zeilsheim. My wife, the love of my life, was slated to arrive in New York as well.

For the entire duration of the trip I pondered my future. My mission was completed, I was an adult and married, but I lacked an education or a profession. Personal history and circumstances had led me to a crossroads filled with uncertainty but rife with possibilities for building a family and a financial future. Until now, all my thoughts had been focused on assisting the nation abroad, but after years of serving the country with all my heart and soul, I decided it was time to work on behalf of my family. And there was no partner more worthy or suited for me than the beauty waiting for me in Israel, my wife Sara. My longing for her was unbearable. From the day we had wed in Israel, and during the entire period of my mission abroad, she was at the heart of my thoughts and yearnings.

My excitement peaked as the plane's wheels touched down at what is known today as Kennedy Airport. Everything in the United States was big, giant-sized; the runway was unending. The aircraft circled at length until it received clearance to land. Planes landed and took off frequently with a deafening roar.

At last, the plane came to a halt. I disembarked and joined the throngs that had arrived from every corner of the globe. The lines at Immigration were long, and the examination of each passenger proceeded slowly. After about an hour's wait, I reached the Immigration officer, presented my passport and, about a minute later, received my entry visa to the United States. The speed with which I was processed surprised me; apparently an Israeli passport had its advantages.

Though I had no suitcase, only a package, I had to wait a long time for it to arrive. It finally appeared from amongst the huge quantity of luggage. I wasn't worried about my clothes disappearing, but was concerned about all the gifts I had bought abroad for Sara with my hard-earned money. The minute I saw the parcel, I relaxed. As I left the terminal, I breathed easily for the first time – I was a free man. My life was now in my own hands.

At the airport in New York, January 1960

Outside, my brother-in-law Fred Sokol, my sister Zipporah's husband, was waiting for me, and we were both very moved to see each other. Fred had first met my sister in Zeilsheim. They fell in love and decided to marry. Of the two, Fred was the first to obtain his immigration visa to the United States. My sister awaited her turn, and received hers after a few months. Their eldest boy had been born a few months prior to my arrival in the United States

"We have a gorgeous baby named Alan," Fred told me, and added: "Zipporah apologizes for not coming to the airport to welcome you; she stayed home with the baby. How was the flight?"

"I'm happy you've managed here and established a family. I of all people know what it means to look after a baby, and I certainly understand her, I'll see her soon. The flight was fine – the plane was full, it looks like everyone is trying to come to America," I responded, while admiring Fred's car, a 1950 Pontiac.

He opened the car door and said: "True, everyone wants to come to the United States, but life here isn't easy. You have to work hard to survive. People here can't be choosy about the kind of work they do; whoever doesn't work doesn't survive. Unfortunately, there are a lot of unemployed in New York these days, and it's hard to find work."

I placed my belongings on the rear seat and sat next to Fred. I was impressed with the number and size of the vehicles that I saw. Fred started the car and we set out. Everything looked enormous, gargantuan; the roads were wide, the bridges numerous, the buildings were tall and the traffic jams were long. We made our way through an endless bottleneck of cars. Traffic crawled bumper to bumper.

"Welcome to New York, traffic jam city. Start getting used to this. This is rush hour; it's five o'clock, when everyone goes home, so the congestion is impossible," Fred apologized.

"I've seen traffic jams in my short life, but nothing like this," I replied, unable to take my eyes off the thousands of cars surrounding me.

"Have you heard anything from Israel?" I asked. "From Father, Ita, or Sara?"

"Yes, we received a letter from Ita. Things are tough over there but they're managing. Everyone is healthy. They asked if we'd heard from you, and we wrote that you're expected here shortly. As you know, communication with Israel isn't easy and it takes a long time for the response to a letter to come," answered Fred, continuing to drive slowly.

After an hour, we arrived in Brooklyn. My sister was living in a rented house in a mixed neighborhood called Highland Park. The area was reasonable and rents were not high. Fred parked, and we got out to meet Zipporah. We fell upon each other, and her warm hug reminded me of embraces as we wandered during the war years. It was very emotional, and tears poured out of my eyes. The last hug I had been privileged to receive from Zipporah was in Zeilsheim prior to my immigration to Israel, ten years earlier. As we hugged, I recalled her expression and her tearful eyes at that parting.

I was delighted to witness Zipporah and Fred establishing a family and settling down. Zipporah allotted me a corner in their house, where I was able to rest and make plans. I stayed with her a few days. I tried to come to grips with the local lifestyle, and the language, which was foreign to me. I started to leaf through newspapers, in the hopes of understanding the words, and tried to follow conversations by their context.

Within a few days I began to find my way around the neighborhood and on the subways. Accordingly, I left for Manhattan early one morning in the hopes of finding some sort of work. I got off the subway at the bustling Times Square station. It was rush hour and thousands of people spilled out of the trains, hurrying to their destinations. With no specific place to go, I decided to roam the streets.

Purchasing a newspaper, I tried to read the want ads. I read all of them and tried to locate the addresses listed on the map that I had. One thing every Israeli learns in the IDF is navigating unfamiliar territory. I memorized the map of Manhattan, which helped me greatly in finding the addresses.

As I wandered the streets, I saw a handwritten "Help Wanted" notice attached to a cafeteria window. Without hesitation, I marched inside and looked for the person in charge. A short, chubby man in a white apron arose from behind the counter. He glanced at me and said in a heavy Hispanic accent: "I need someone to wash dishes on the night shift. This restaurant is open twenty four hours a day. Do you speak English?"

"Do I need to know English in order to wash dishes?" I answered in my basic English, like a typical Jew – with a question.

The man laughed. Apparently he liked me, due to my clever answer.

"Be here at seven in the evening. I pay one dollar an hour. What's your name?" he asked.

"Sholom," I replied, and immediately added: "Sam."

"My name's Romeo, come on time," said the Hispanic in a boss's tone, and disappeared behind the counter.

I went out to the street and was overjoyed. I had a job! I searched my pants pockets; I had very little cash. Now I could finally earn some money and bring Sara to me. I crossed the street and studied the cafeteria, which was located on 44th Street, corner of Broadway, in famous Times Square – the hub of the world. Above the entrance, in stylized, bold letters, appeared the name "Dubrow's." I stood there in wonder, examining the many people coming and going. The place was filled with diners.

"Dubrow's?," shouted Zipporah over the phone as I told her the news. "That's a very well-known cafeteria. How did you manage to get work there? All of New York's celebrities go there. It's open twenty four hours a day, and famous theater actors frequent it every night. I'm proud of you!" Her voice was choked with emotion.

I ended my call with Zipporah, and thought a moment of the name I had given Romeo: "Sholom…Sam." I had blurted it out unintentionally. My name would be Sam from then on, I decided – an American name.

That very night I reported for work, one hour early. Romeo greeted me with a smile, and explained my duties. At the time, there was no dishwashing machine in the restaurant; such appliances were yet to be invented, and everything was done manually. Dirty dishes began arriving in unbelievable quantities, and I was transformed into an expert dishwasher, able to keep up with the pace. In the morning, after my shift, I looked at the palms of my hands. They were snow white and the skin was peeling – presumably because I had used so much soap. I had to buy lotion in a pharmacy in order to ease the pain and preserve the skin of my hands.

At the end of every week I received my salary. The work was not easy, but the forty dollars I earned gave me much satisfaction. I saved every penny. My first task was to fund my wife Sara's trip to New York, and I was headed in the right direction.

After two weeks of hard work, I decided to rent an apartment in Manhattan, so that Sara and I would have privacy after her arrival. For $15 a week, I found a room that answered my needs at the time. It was located in the heart of Manhattan, in a building owned by a Jewish woman who also lived there. Those were the prices in those days. The purchasing power of the dollar was high, but dollars were not easy to come by. I recall that in Dubrow's, a sandwich sold for $0.52, a coffee for $0.10, and a subway ride was $0.15.

Aside from my sister, I had one other relative in New York named Paul Gorman. His father and my father's father (whom I had never met) were brothers. Paul himself was a Holocaust survivor who had arrived in the United States years earlier. He had managed to establish himself, and now owned a clothing store on Orchard Street off Delancey, in lower Manhattan. He had heard of my arrival from Zipporah, and asked that I visit him. Accordingly, one morning after my night shift I boarded the subway in Times Square and traveled to see Paul on Delancey Street. I had no need to introduce myself – Paul identified me immediately, and embraced me warmly, mumbling, "Shulem, Shulem"…

I sat in his store and related the details of the family's life in Israel, of my military service and of my marriage to Sara. Unhesitatingly, he pulled a fifty dollar bill out of his wallet and placed it in the palm of my hand.

"Take this. It will help you in your first steps in America," he said in Yiddish, and asked one of his workers to bring me a pair of pants, two shirts and a sweater so I could try them on. I was thrilled. For the first time in my life, I was looking at a fifty dollar bill. This bill would hasten Sara's arrival in America, I thought.

I thanked my uncle from the bottom of my heart. He refused to let me go until I agreed to join him for lunch. He brought me to one of Manhattan's prominent restaurants at the time, Katz's Delicatessen, known for its special sandwiches. My uncle ordered me a jumbo sandwich, filled with slices of beef. I had never seen such a sandwich. The amount of meat in it would have sufficed to feed an entire IDF squad. By the time we returned to the store, the tailor had already altered the pants, and my uncle packed the sweater, the pants and the shirts for me. I thanked him again for his welcome, and we said good-bye.

The time came when I remembered my uncle's warmth and generosity, and offered him a partnership in a property I acquired on West 51st Street in Manhattan. We continue to be partners in this building to this very day.

After weeks of work at Dubrow's, I began to recognize many of the customers, particularly the steady ones. One of the diners was a Jew who became aware of my financial troubles. He offered me an additional job, in this case cleaning a movie theater not far from Dubrow's, on 42nd Street. I jumped at the opportunity. It wouldn't hurt to augment my savings, I reasoned, and in any case I had nothing to do during my time off.

Thus I dashed from the cafeteria to the movie theater every day. As I vacuumed the theater floor, I was delighted when I heard the sound of metal hitting the insides of the vacuum cleaner, indicating that a coin dropped by a moviegoer had been sucked into the unit. I would turn the vacuum cleaner off, insert my fingers into the dust, and remove the treasure. There were days when this hidden treasure amounted to as much as half a dollar! A gift from heaven.

I worked at both locations for a number of months. At Dubrow's I was entitled to one free meal a day – franks with beans. This was in essence my only meal during the entire day. I very much missed the sandwich my uncle had bought me during my visit on Delancey Street. Through the kitchen window I saw the plates heaped with every delicacy going to the restaurant patrons, and my eyes bulged.... I was particularly fascinated by the steaks lying in their glory on wide plates brimming with French fries and garlic bread. The aroma drove me crazy. I'm not ashamed to admit that when those plates reached the wash room, I would check to see if a small piece of meat was stuck to any of them; and if so, would swallow it surreptitiously....

One day, Romeo informed me in his gravelly voice that the cafeteria would be closing for a month for renovations. This fact troubled me. How would I pay my rent? I immediately informed my landlady that I would be late this week with my rent. She was very angry, leveled various accusations at me, and claimed that I was lazy and did not want to work. I suffered her abuse in silence. After she calmed down, she knocked on my door and asked if I knew how to paint. Although I had never held a paintbrush in my hand, I unhesitatingly answered in the affirmative.

"If so, I have work for you. You are to paint all seven rooms in the building," she said in a commanding tone and disappeared.

We bought paint and brushes, and I strenuously painted all seven rooms, finishing them that day, to her surprise. But the effort cost me my health. It seems that I became a victim of poisoning, acquired by breathing the acrid, lead-containing paint fumes for many hours (such lead-containing paint is illegal today). I went to my room and lay sprawled on the bed, trembling and vomiting. Dizziness overcame me as soon as I tried to rise, so I lay on my back and fell asleep. I was roused by knocks on the door, and again heard my landlady:

"Get up, lazybones, time to get up. Go look for work. How long have you been sleeping?"

I got up and barely made it to the door, still under the influence of the poisons in my lungs. It then dawned on my landlady that I was not feeling well, and I perceived her attitude towards me undergo a transformation for the first time. She bought me medicine, and prepared a sandwich and a hot drink for me. From that moment on, she stopped calling me lazy.

I continued to look for a job. I had no work permit, and was therefore forced to take anything that was available, at any wages offered. Employers took advantage of workers like me, and paid very low salaries.

I eventually found employment with one of Manhattan's building contractors. My job was to carry bricks from street level to the upper floors being built. In those days, the bricks were placed in a wooden apparatus that was carried on one's shoulders like a backpack, up improvised stairs to the upper floors. The weight was unbearably heavy. I went up and down dozens of times daily. I would return home exhausted, with a "broken" and aching back, and go to sleep. Most of those doing this kind of work did not have work permits.

Once, as I was carrying bricks to the fifth floor, I noticed that all the workers below were abandoning their equipment and disappearing. In response to my question, one of them explained that the immigration authorities were raiding the building, and anyone caught would face imprisonment and deportation. I immediately threw down my load and descended to the second floor. I leaped to the street from the scaffolding, and disappeared amongst the many passersby. Luckily, I was not injured when I jumped.

The contractor was arrested, so all my work was for naught. There was, of course, no one to turn to regarding the wages I was owed. With no other choice, I resumed my search for employment; experienced as I was, I explored every potential opportunity. In the end, I found a branch of a supermarket chain where I was hired to load and unload merchandise from trucks. The work was back-breaking and required considerable physical strength. But this job, too, was temporary.

I was back at square one – once again searching endlessly.

Chapter 18

A Long, Hard Road

"Hence, a man must work and labor with both hands
before the Holy One, blessed be He, will send his blessing."

Midrash Tanhuma, VaYeitzei, 13

Life in America was no bed of roses during this initial period, but it changed beyond recognition after Sara joined me. She inspired confidence in me, provided me with the warm home that I had been missing, and was both wife and friend to me. Before her arrival, I would return to my room after an exhausting day and remain confined within its walls. Now I had someone to come home to, someone waiting for me with a loving heart and an attentive ear inclined to my indecisions, my worries, my plans. I now had a true partner in life.

Aside from my immediate family, I had few acquaintances. One of my close friends was Morris Meiderman. I had met him in Berlin after the war, and we moved to the Zeilsheim DP camp together. Morris arrived in the United States after the war. He came from a family of established diamond dealers, who had managed a diamond business already back in Germany, and who owned a hotel named the Knickerbocker on 45th Street in Times Square. Morris assisted me in my first steps in New York; he took Sara and me under his wing and arranged our residence visas and work permits.

My livelihood suffered, of course, when Dubrow's closed for renovations. After stumbling from one temporary position to another, I finally showed up in my friend Morris's office and asked him to help me find work. Without hesitation he phoned another friend, Jerry Wartski, a partner in a small sweater factory whom I also knew from Zeilsheim.

Morris asked if it would be possible to also hire Sara at the factory, as she knew how to sew. Jerry answered in the affirmative. Thus we both began working at the sweater factory, I as the cleaning supervisor and Sara as a seamstress. My salary was one dollar an hour, and Sara, being a "professional," earned $1.50 an hour. The factory employed about forty workers.

Jerry eventually bought out his partner, and became sole owner of the factory. We worked there for about two and a half years, a period in which we enjoyed relative "financial security." We rented an apartment with one room and a kitchen in the Highland Park section of Brooklyn, very near Zipporah. My friend Morris gave us a television set as a present. Although we worked hard for a living, we led a happy life.

One of our happiest moments together was the birth of our oldest child Ron – Reuven in Hebrew. Ron was a delightful baby and our joy was indescribable. When I finished work, I would hurry home to enjoy another hour of bliss with him. Sara outdid herself in lavishing him with warmth and love, as only she could. The child was the center of our existence, and we wanted to provide him with all that was good in the world. During the period in which Sara worked, my sister Zipporah looked after Ron.

Sara with our oldest son Ron

One day I traveled with Sara to Delancey Street to buy clothes. The area was known for its concentration of cheap clothing stores, and customers would come from all over New York. Before we left home, we carefully calculated how much money we had. The sum in question was the exact amount needed to buy one pair of workpants for me and two blouses for Sara. But alas! We forgot to leave money for the return subway ride. Thus we found ourselves crossing the long Williamsburg Bridge and then continuing to our home in Highland Park – all on foot. Unbelievable….

After two and a half years, the sweater factory ran into difficulties, forcing Jerry to retrench and leaving us without a livelihood. In my hour of need I again turned to my friend Morris Meiderman. He owned another hotel called the Kimberly on 74th Street, corner of Broadway. I sensed Morris's discomfort as he offered me the position of cleaning supervisor at the hotel, but I reassured him; no job, I said, is an embarrassment, and I was willing to work at anything in order to support my family.

I began my job as the cleaning supervisor at the Kimberly, and also as an assistant to the painter who worked there. I arrived every day at 5 a.m. together with two African-American laborers to collect the garbage that had accumulated. I never exploited my connections with Morris in order to gain special perks. During the lunch break I would go down to the basement with the other workers, and eat the sandwich that Sara had prepared for me. Other workers in the hotel, those with higher salaries, enjoyed meals prepared and sent by one of the local restaurants. For years, I never had the means to benefit from such a service.

One day, the elevator operator failed to show up for work, and the manager asked me to replace him. All I had to do was turn the handle in order to send the elevator up or down, and see to the safety of the passengers. I was glad to have a one-day break from handling garbage. That same day, one of the hotel guests entered the elevator drunk. Handing me a ten dollar bill, he asked me to buy him cigarettes. I asked another worker to cover for me, and ran immediately to the nearby store. I brought the guest his cigarettes together with the change, $8.20. The man took the cigarettes and told me to keep the change as a tip. This was a particularly delightful day, as I had enough money to buy food for the entire week.

On our days off I would go with Sara to every Israel-related event in New York. I felt every bit the Israeli, and connected to Israel heart and soul. I followed the news from Israel, and devoured every piece of information. At home, I spoke to Sara in Hebrew. During those early years in the United States, I dreamed of buying a semi-trailer and bringing it to Israel so that I could support myself through it, but this dream was far from being realized. All my savings amounted to a few hundred dollars only, and these had to serve as insurance for my family's welfare.

In those days, returning to Israel was a very real possibility in my mind. Night and day I thought about buying a semi-trailer. Every weekend I traveled to auctions for used vehicles in New Jersey, hoping to find a bargain, something reasonably priced that I could ship to Israel. But the idea remained a pipe dream. Times were hard, and without a steady job, I was afraid to embark on any risky financial adventure.

Daily life in New York was not easy, and the constant search for a job was not simple. In America, those who do not fend for themselves end up as the wretched and the depressed of society, and there were many of those. Manhattan was filled with people who slept in the streets and rummaged through garbage, utterly neglected. I therefore charted a cautious and responsible course. I began to envision a small business that would provide a steady income and a proper future, and waited for a suitable opportunity.

My children Ron and Jay. New York, 1966

One mundane workday at the Kimberly, the hotel manager told me about a card club located in one of the upper floors of a prominent building. He said the night shift worker had gotten sick, and the club manager had asked him to send a replacement, if possible. The hotel manager asked me if I was interested in the job. I immediately said yes, and was hired there as a waiter.

The club opened in the early evening hours between seven and eight. The club members appeared to be wealthy individuals, businessmen, financially powerful. One of the club owners, a short Italian, took an instant liking to me. My income rose several levels as a result of my job at the club. My weekly salary was about $100, and included tips; here was my first exposure to the full significance of the concept of tips. My friendship with the Italian, who later discovered my managerial talents, eventually led to my promotion to the position of manager.

At the same time, Sara and I were allotted an additional, joyous blessing when our son Jay entered the world. He was given the Hebrew name Yaakov, after my grandfather Yaakov Domb who was killed in

With Sara and our son Ron

the Holocaust. He was a charming, energetic baby, with a smile on his face proclaiming "Here I am, ready to conquer the world." No one was happier on the day of his birth than Ron, who had anxiously awaited Jay's arrival. During Sara's entire pregnancy, Ron was always interested in what his mother was carrying in her womb, and couldn't wait to see the baby and play with him. There is no greater pleasure than seeing one's two children playing together. Sara and I would sit for hours enjoying every moment of the children's company.

One day my friend, the Italian, summoned me for a meeting. He told me that he was very impressed with my organizational skills and offered me the management of a building he owned on 84th Street. Extremely touched by his compliments, I went to see the building. It was in a good area but was inhabited entirely by African Americans, and was very poorly maintained, to put it mildly. A significant number of the building's inhabitants were drug dealers. That same day, I told the

Italian that I was not the person to manage that building.

A few days later he got back to me and offered to sell me the building. "Which building?" I asked.

"The one you went to see on 84th Street," he answered decisively.

I burst out laughing.

"Why are you laughing?" asked my friend.

"I'm not built for business like that, and besides I have no money," I responded.

"You don't need money to buy the building. I spoke to my partners and we are willing to have you pay us in installments over five years. This is a serious offer, think it over," he said, giving me a pat on the back.

For days I seriously considered the proposal. On the one hand, this was a good, once-in-a-lifetime business opportunity; on the other hand, it was very dangerous, because most of the building's residents were drug dealers. Sara told me: "Do what you think is best. I trust you." That entire time, I pondered what my merchant father would do in my situation. I recalled a favorite adage of his: "A wise person does not enter a place that only a clever person knows how to escape from." In any case, it was important for me to get legal advice.

I was very friendly with a Jewish lawyer by the name of Irwin Kissen, one of the many club members. During one of his visits at the club, I asked to speak to him, and told him about the offer. He indicated that it seemed like a good deal, and that he was willing to represent me. He promised to introduce me to an African-American friend of his who was familiar with the residents' mentality and would know how to deal with them. The idea was to evict the building's residents, renovate it and bring in suitable tenants who would pay a higher rent and maintain their apartments properly. Once the drug-dealer blight was eliminated, the property would be improved and appreciate in value.

Irwin's fee for representing me and preparing a contract was

$300. Even this sum was beyond my means, but I took the risk – a calculated risk with potential profit built in. In the end, the deal was finalized.

Irwin introduced me to his friend Gladys, a heavy-set black woman with a formidable personality. She had previously handled such people. It turned out that the building was much more heavily infested with drug dealers than we had thought. Gladys handled this too, and went armed at all times. By dint of great effort and force, in the face of constant life-threatening danger, I succeeded, together with Gladys, in clearing the building. In view of the dangers involved, Gladys supplied me with a weapon as well, and I carried it with me for a long time.

Investors offered me $150,000 for the vacant building. I had bought the property for $100,000, and thus in a few months made a profit of $50,000, a considerable sum in those days. I was proud of myself; but I decided not to sell, and instead to stick to the original plan of renovating the building. But how to renovate without any money? Once again I was in need of Irwin Kissen's connections.

Irwin called a few of his clients and asked them to supply me with construction equipment and materials on credit. One of those clients was a Holocaust survivor by the name of Harry Domansky, who owned a building supplies store. When I asked him for flooring material sufficient for 135 rooms, he asked me how I intended to pay for the merchandise when I could not even give him a down payment. I replied that I would work hard to pay him, and that he would get his money before I used any to buy food for myself. My entire savings at the time amounted to $1,500.

He was very impressed with my frank response, and sent me a semi-trailer full of grade B flooring the next morning, as I had requested. I hired a Peruvian laborer named Antonio to help me with the renovations and painting. I personally took an active role in all the construction work. I mixed and poured cement, and even painted, and thus became an expert in renovations. Each room that was renovated was immediately rented to good tenants with sufficient financial means.

After the renovations were completed and the rooms rented, the resultant income sufficed to pay back my debts and support my family respectably. To this very day, I own the property, and it now contains apartments instead of rooms for rent. Antonio, the Peruvian laborer, is still one of my six hundred employees.

After this first successful transaction, the Italian group again contacted me and offered to sell me another building located on the corner of 14th Street and Third Avenue. Experienced now, I bought the property at terms similar to those of my first acquisition. The purchase price was $700,000, but this time I made a down payment of $60,000. The building contained six stores and 150 hotel rooms, and I renovated it as well. My experience in renovating the previous building on 84th Street helped me to become more efficient and reduce costs this time around.

One day, a woman carrying several suitcases appeared at the 14th Street hotel and requested a room for several nights. She looked familiar to me: she sold jewelry, occasionally setting up a stand at Union Square on 14th Street. I gave her a room, and she asked me to send the bellhop to carry her suitcases. I explained that I was replacing him since he was sick; I carried her bags and she thanked me. She showed up again a week later. I gave her a room, and she again asked for the bellhop. When she saw me carrying her suitcases, she asked me if he was sick today as well. I replied that from now on I was the bellhop....

This was the beginning of my hotel career. I have since expanded, and the hotel business remains my primary commercial activity to this very day.

Throughout all my years in America, I followed events in Israel closely, and made every effort to remain up to date regarding the news. Sara and I rejoiced over every positive development, and were distressed whenever we heard about security operations with military casualties. As a result of my participation in the 1956 Sinai Campaign, I possessed a certain ability to estimate the IDF's strength relative to the challenges it faced from Israel's enemies. I was nevertheless alarmed when I heard of the Arab League's January 1964 decision to divert the waters of the Jordan River, an important artery for Israel. The establishment of a joint Arab command and of the PLO (Palestine Liberation Organization) threatened the security of Israel. One did not need to be a strategic expert to realize that the creation of such a terrorist organization, supported and funded by the Arab states, would seriously disturb life in Israel.

Ever since the Sinai campaign, concluding with the utter defeat of the Egyptian forces, the security situation in Israel had deteriorated steadily. After intense American and Russian pressure, the IDF had withdrawn from the Sinai and the Gaza Strip. I well remember Ben-Gurion's statement at the time that any future closing of the Straits of Tiran would be tantamount to a declaration of war. An international emergency force was stationed at the Egyptian border and at Sharm el-Sheikh, guaranteeing Israel the freedom of the sea between the Gulf of Eilat and the Far East. Some of the Arab states were in conflict with each other; others had unstable regimes. Sizable Egyptian forces were involved in and immobilized by the civil war in Yemen. These factors led to the perception that the southern border would remain quiet at that time, and that Egypt would not entangle itself in another war with Israel after its humiliation in the Sinai Campaign.

Furthermore, the Cold War between the United States and Russia had spilled over to the Middle East. We were worried by the position of the Soviet leadership, which always supported the Arabs, supplying Egypt and Syria with considerable weaponry: planes, tanks, military equipment and accelerated financial assistance. In addition, we were deeply concerned by the Soviet naval bases established in Egypt and Syria.

In 1966 and 1967 I was up to my neck in debt as a result of two significant investments involving major financial commitments. These investments bore serious risk and necessitated constant and intensive efforts on my part. I was determined to succeed at all costs and not to allow my commitments to plunge me and my family into financial ruin. My childhood home had been destroyed, and I would do everything in my power to prevent the life of distress I had known from befalling the family I had just begun to raise.

Nonetheless, while working very hard, I tried to take an active role in the Jewish community's efforts on behalf of Israel. I befriended Israelis arriving in the United States and received updates from them on events in Israel. This is how I learned that the "Arab Joint Chiefs of Staff" had met in Damascus and begun coordinating an attack on Israel.

Israel's security began to deteriorate seriously in those years. When the Syrians started diverting the Jordan River, the Israel Air Force (IAF) destroyed the equipment being used for that purpose. A Syrian MIG-21 was downed in a dogfight, and in August 1966, the IAF downed two additional MIGs. The Egyptians announced that they would react harshly to the Israeli belligerence toward Syria. In early November, a Syrian-Egyptian defense treaty was signed. The Jordanian border was not quiet either. Mines planted by the Jordanians killed three IDF soldiers close to the Green Line, and the IDF retaliated by launching Operation Samu. The Jordanian forces incurred heavy losses in that action.

In April 1967 I was in my office on 14th Street, busy with renovation plans for one of the floors in a building I had acquired. The radio on my desk was tuned to an all-news station. The broadcast was suddenly interrupted by the story that the IAF had shot down six Syrian MIGs in aerial combat over Damascus. The phones did not stop ringing. Everyone called to tell me the news and express their delight. I was extremely worried that day. Being somewhat familiar with Middle Eastern mentality, I was afraid that the incident, in spite of its successful outcome, would deeply offend the national honor of the Syrians and of the Arabs in general, and result in escalation.

The Syrians indeed began subjecting communities in the Galilee to artillery barrages, and the IDF again responded by downing enemy aircraft. In May, heavy Egyptian forces crossed the Suez Canal and deployed in the Sinai. At the same time, Egyptian President Gamal Abdel Nasser demanded the removal of the 4,000-man strong United Nations Emergency Force from Egypt. Following their withdrawal, Nasser declared the Straits of Tiran closed to Israeli shipping.

During this tense period, I was constantly on the alert for news from Israel. My ears were glued to the radio, and I maintained continuous telephone contact with my friends in the consulate. I reminded my friends of Ben-Gurion's declaration after the Sinai campaign, that closing the Straits of Tiran would be a *casus belli*. The level of concern was high.

Israel called up its Reserves and a waiting period ensued. The pace of events increased, as did the worry and tension. Iraq joined the fray as well. Egypt, Jordan and Iraq established a joint military command, and Iraq's ruler, Abdul Rahman Arif, agreed to supply military forces via the Kingdom of Jordan for a war against Israel. The incitement coming from Arab countries, and Egypt in particular, reached new highs. Calls for the destruction of Israel were heard everywhere. In Israel, a National Unity Government led by Levi Eshkol was formed: joining the government were Moshe Dayan as Defense Minister, and also Menachem Begin (for the first time in history!) and Tommy Lapid as Ministers Without Portfolio.

Israel completed the call up of its Reserves and prepared for this fateful war. As the reader will recall, Moshe Dayan was Chief of Staff during my military service. His personality inspired confidence in us all. As Chief of Staff during the Sinai Campaign, Dayan had won many medals and enjoyed great fame. His appointment as Defense Minister and the establishment of the National Unity Government intensified the public's sense of security. History had taught us that as long as we were united, nothing could break us – our strength was in our unity. Like everyone else, we were glad to hear of Dayan's appointment and of the National Unity government's establishment.

On 5 June 1967 we awoke to the news of the war's outbreak. We were worried. Little news had trickled through, due to the communication blackout that Dayan had insisted on imposing. The reports indicated that the Israel Air Force, in a brilliant and surprising stroke, had destroyed the air forces of Egypt, Syria, Jordan and Iraq, both on the ground and in aerial combat. The lightning-fast action lasted three hours. It provided aerial superiority and created an aerial umbrella for IDF ground forces on all fronts. The radio and television networks interrupted regular broadcasts in order to report on the war, and analysts began to dissect the situation. Newspaper headlines informed the world of events in the Middle East, and television newscasts publicized maps that detailed battlefield developments.

After a few tense days the picture became clear, and we breathed a sigh of relief. We understood that Israel had the upper hand, and that IDF forces were advancing on every front. I followed the movements of the forces in the Sinai closely. I was very familiar with the maps being publicized, and with the names of the sites and settlements captured by the IDF. I tried to compare the moves in the current war to those of the Sinai campaign in which I had taken part.

With the war's end, the magnitude of the defeat suffered by the Arab states became evident. At the same time, the Israeli casualty lists were being publicized. Like Jews the world over, we sat bowed over the lists, and our hearts ached at the mention of every name; we tried to ascertain if friends or family members were among the dead.

The war ended with Israel in control of extensive territories, among them the Sinai Peninsula and the Gaza Strip, the Golan Heights and the Hermon Range, the entire West Bank, the Old City of Jerusalem and the Western Wall area. Like many Jewish communities throughout the world, we in the United States were engulfed by a wave of joy and identification with Israel. Tourists and volunteers flocked to Israel from every corner of the globe. We could not stand idly by, and after a short time I took Sara and the children on a visit to Israel, the first since I had arrived in America.

We toured the length and breadth of the country. The tours were organized by my brother-in-law Yitzhak Zippori, husband to Ora, Sara's sister. He was the most veteran Master Sergeant in the IDF. My good friend, Major General Uzi Narkiss, arranged our tour of Jerusalem. He accompanied us personally and gave an account of the fighting at every site we visited. I was particularly moved by our visit to the Old City and to the Western Wall, accompanied as we were by Major General Narkiss, commander of the forces that liberated the Old City.

From Uzi Narkiss himself, I learned that he experienced many difficult periods in his childhood. In the 1929 riots, when the Arabs mercilessly slaughtered Jews in Israel, he was four years old, and hid during one of the attacks in the basement of his house. This incident influenced him greatly. After the birth of the state, he became one of the senior commanders in the IDF. He served in a variety of positions, among them Deputy Head of the Intelligence Corps, and led the team that established the National Defense College. In the Six Day War he was Officer Commanding (OC) Central Command, which comprised seven brigades, including, as stated, the brigade that liberated the Old City. Uzi was one of those who pressured Dayan to take advantage of the Jordanian shelling in order to liberate the Old City and the Western Wall. He was immortalized in the famous photograph together with Dayan and Chief of Staff Yitzhak Rabin at the entrance to the Old City. The photograph graced every war album of that period.

I first met Uzi Narkiss at an IDF conference during my military service, prior to my national mission abroad. We stayed in touch, and met many times during his frequent official visits to the United States.

At every gathering, Uzi made sure to inform those present about my activities on behalf of, and my contribution to, the State of Israel. I tried to stay in touch with other friends as well, both from my military service and from my service abroad.

I considered it a great privilege to tour the "city bound firmly together" (as Psalms 122:3 refers to it) guided by the very man who was in command of its liberation. I was extremely moved, and this later influenced me to join Ariel Sharon's initiative to expand Jewish settlement in the Old City, in order to "restore it to its former glory."

Of course we also took advantage of our trip to visit family and friends. We visited Sara's parents, who were delighted to meet their grandchildren Ron and Jay for the first time, as well as Father and Leah, and Ita and her husband. The visits were very emotional. Neither did I neglect my many friends – from the army, from the Kfar Saba soccer team and from Hanitah.

Unfortunately, the visit was short. I had to return to New York and continue to manage my new business. Although throughout my stay in Israel I had maintained continuous contact with the managers of my hotel and my residential building, my presence in New York was imperative.

Years later, when the Yom Kippur war broke out in October 1973, we were filled with concern over the news that reached us in the United States. The photographs of the Israeli prisoners of war broke my heart, and I was ready to do everything in order to help.

When I heard that many Israeli reservists were stuck in the United States, unable to fly to Israel and join the ranks, my friends and I organized a mission to fly them urgently to Israel. We advertised on the radio, and many who were interested in returning to Israel turned to me. To further this initiative, we reduced the prices on El Al and subsidized

the airfares. The project was a success. After the war, I received a letter
of thanks from the Israeli Consul in New York, and later Arik Sharon
thanked me too, during one of the events he attended in the United
States.

With Sara, Ron and Jay. New York, September 1967

Chapter **19**

For the Sake of My Home,
For the Sake of My Brethren and Friends

"For the sake of my brethren and friends,
I pray for your well-being."

Psalms, 122:8

I went through many ups and downs during my first decade in America, but eventually achieved financial stability. This was definitely a period of favorable commercial opportunities and, to the extent that my monetary situation allowed, I took advantage of every one of them. The dollar was very strong and served as the dominant currency in the post-World War Two world economy.

Exercising utmost caution, I expanded my business, thoroughly examining every deal that came my way: its real market value, its economic benefit and, of course, funding possibilities and future development.

My experience in renovating residential buildings and sometimes converting them to hotels or office buildings helped me set profitable purchase prices for the various proposals I received. This is how I ultimately decided that real estate would be my primary occupation. Learning to work more efficiently over the years, I quickly saw the results: lower costs and greater profits.

In the course of my work, I tried to avoid unnecessary risks. For investments that required major funding, I was helped by partners from among my many friends in Manhattan. One of my chief partners was Ulo Barad, a Holocaust survivor, with whom I acquired and developed a hotel chain in the city. Ulo was a very pleasant person and a generous philanthropist. He was well-known as an enthusiastic supporter of Israel and a benefactor of Jewish educational and welfare institutions in the United States and Israel. For me, he was not just a friend and business partner, but a fellow supporter of many charitable organizations.

In 1970, my family and I moved away from the bustling city to Jamaica Estates, Queens, a mixed Jewish-Italian neighborhood. It was a quiet area, bathed in green, and Sara and I thought it would be a wonderful place to raise our children. On property that I purchased, we built a charming house that answered all our needs. Sara and the children designed the house and made it comfortable, filling it with happiness and love. Indeed, we were ecstatic when Michal (Michelle), sister to Ron and Jay, was born. The arrival of this enchanting, smiling baby made our family unit complete.

Our foremost concern was the children's education. Here, I implicitly trusted Sara, who wasted no time in applying herself to the matter with her usual talent and energy. I wanted to give my children

Sara hugging our daughter Michelle. New York, February 1972

the best, everything that had been denied me during World War Two. Sara made this a reality with her full heart and soul, being involved in every stage of the children's development. Before our move to Jamaica Estates, she registered them in the best Jewish schools in the area. Along with their general, formal education, we also made sure to foster in our children Jewish, traditional and Zionist values.

Holding Michelle in my arms. New York, February, 1972

My intensive commercial involvement did not prevent me from also devoting time and energy to activities on behalf of Israel and the Jewish people. I did this out of the firm belief that as a Jew who had experienced the Holocaust, I was obligated to do everything to prevent another tragedy from befalling our people. Many organizations were established in the United States to support Israel and to provide aid to suffering Jews in various countries throughout the world. I felt I should become active in some of them and provide as much assistance as possible.

This was during the tension-filled years of the Cold War between the United States and the Soviet Union. Missiles with deadly warheads were aimed at major American cities, accompanied by threatening declarations. No one could guess the intentions of the Kremlin leaders at that time, for everything was conducted in secrecy over there behind the sealed, inflexible Iron Curtain. We had already witnessed the harm that one predator, sweeping an entire leadership with him, could cause in the world. The wounds inflicted by Hitler and his cohorts had not healed and were evident everywhere.

In this difficult atmosphere, reports from the Soviet Union were leaked to the West about a wave of arrests of Jews – Zionist activists who wanted to immigrate to Israel – and their exile. The messages from Russia betrayed tremendous hardship and were reminiscent of the dark days in Europe not too many years earlier, when Jews were persecuted and murdered because of their religion. News of the denial of Jews' requests to immigrate to their homeland only intensified. Many of the refuseniks, who actively and openly protested the intentional delay in processing their requests, were arrested and sentenced to prison terms.

On December 16, 1970, the trial of eleven people accused of hijacking an airplane began in Russia. All they had wanted to do was to draw world attention to the closing of Soviet gates against Jews who wished to immigrate to Israel. Their arrest and trial received wide media coverage throughout the world.

Protest organizations for the release of these Prisoners of Zion, who were rotting in Soviet jails, were established in Israel, the United States, England and other European countries. In addition, senior government officials in America, a country sensitive to human rights, also lent their support to these organizations, taking part in demonstrations and allowing their names to feature prominently in large newspaper advertisements. They were joined by artists and intellectuals, who considered these prisoners freedom fighters and prisoners of conscience. I felt obligated to help and exert as much of my influence as possible on the decision-makers in Washington.

American elections have always been characterized by the drive for the Jewish vote and funding. As a result, I was invited to interesting meetings with politicians from both the Republican and Democrat parties, in which I met many senators and members of Congress and their aides, as well as other government officials who provided me with an opening for my requests on behalf of Israel and the Jewish people. I met with them more than once and demanded unconditional support for Israel, their influence in opening Soviet gates for immigration to Israel and the immediate release of Prisoners of Zion. The pressure created by Jewish organizations and private individuals like myself led to both America's active involvement and also an international outcry against the powers that be in the Kremlin.

Consequently, I made up my mind to travel alone to Moscow, in order to get a close look at the situation of the Jews there. I arrived at my decision after consulting with my friends in the Israeli consulate in New York, and in full coordination with key activists in Soviet Jewry organizations in the United States and England.

With the assistance of American government officials, my friends in these organizations helped me obtain a visa to Russia. It turned out that an American passport could open doors that would undoubtedly remain closed to an Israeli citizen. My primary meetings in Moscow were arranged by friends in England – Soviet Jewry activists who maintained contact with members of the Soviet government. Newspaper mogul Robert Maxwell, who lived in England, had offices in Moscow and the organizational activists utilized his good connections there.

One morning in 1974, I found myself on an American plane destined for London, where I would board a British Airways flight to Moscow. During the flight to the Soviet Union, I did not cease pondering the odd situation I found myself in right then, during those moments of tension. Here I was, returning to the country I had left twenty-five years earlier in a refugee-packed train that crossed the ruins of Europe after that terrible war. Then I had been a thin, starving, homeless, penniless boy, weary of wandering, on my way to Warsaw, to a hazy, unknown future. Now I was an established American businessman, with a family, returning to that same country on a visit whose results were impossible to predict.

This contrast gnawed at me throughout the flight to Moscow, together with the stress I felt concerning the possible response of the Soviet authorities to my visit. Question marks floated in the air, as if a cloud of mystery filled the plane. Would I be arrested? If so, where would I be taken? Would I be deported? In every analysis we conducted prior to my trip, my friends and I had concluded that the Russians would not want to open another diplomatic front, especially

With Alexander Lebed in Moscow

since I had received a legal visa. They were already under a great deal of international pressure. Still, anything could happen behind the Iron Curtain.

During the flight, I met a young African student from Ghana, who was studying medicine in Moscow. He enthused about my American origin and did not leave me alone for a minute, asking about life in the United States and the possibility of obtaining a work visa there. Well-acquainted with Moscow, he promised to take me around the city and show me its famous sites, and I was happy to have so easily found a guide to the city.

Waiting for me at the Moscow airport was a young Russian, a representative of the contact person I was to meet. He tended to border control matters and then took me to the Metropol Hotel near the Kremlin, where I had a reservation. After giving me details regarding my meeting with Alexander Lebed, my contact person left. Lebed was

In Red Square. Moscow, 1974

a young Russian officer (eventually a general), who lived in Moscow and who had served in the past as an officer in the Russian paratrooper corps.

As he had promised, the Ghanaian student came to my hotel the next morning. I invited him for a meal and afterwards, we left to tour the city. He was absolutely familiar with every corner of Moscow, and this is how I first laid eyes on the Soviet capital about which I had only heard and read. I again recalled the stories I had heard from Father about the terrible war that had been fought here while I had wandered in the forests, and about the casualties among the city's residents during the German siege. My personal tale intrigued the young African, who escorted me throughout my stay in Moscow, and he requested more and more information about what had transpired during those terror-filled days.

The meeting with Alexander Lebed was fascinating. Before me stood a tall young man, strong and broad-shouldered, with a heavy Russian accent. His animated tone of voice, fluent speech and way of expressing himself testified to an obvious natural leadership ability. This was our first meeting. Our second was held in 1987 during my second visit to Moscow, as I will recount in upcoming chapters.

Lebed was eventually awarded two medals of distinction for the courage he demonstrated in the fighting in Afghanistan and years later, for defeating the Moldavian army in the battle over the Transnistria region. He was active in the Soviet political elite after the upheaval in the Soviet Union and ran for president of the country. He was killed in a plane crash on April 28, 2002.

During our meeting, we discussed the general political situation, and when I raised the request to release the prisoners, he promised to investigate the matter. He said he would check if the charges against them could be changed and thus, lighten their punishment. At the same time, he inquired about the political situation in the United States.

Without a doubt, one of the inspiring experiences I had in

Moscow was the visit to the city's main synagogue where I was received by the chief rabbi, Rabbi Avraham Shayevich, and his assistants. At that hour the synagogue was filled with many worshippers. They were happy to receive live greetings from their American brethren, but it was difficult to have a discussion with them.

When I asked to speak with the rabbi, I was told to go to his office; only there would he be willing to listen to what I had to say. At first he was suspicious and refused to cooperate in the conversation; then, realizing that I was not hostile, he gradually softened and agreed to talk about the community. The rabbi informed me that the Jews were living well, had freedom of worship and were not prevented from practicing their religion. He treated me to a cup of tea and some cookies. I offered him my address and telephone number in case he needed any assistance.

I also visited the cultural center for Jewish soldiers who had fought in World War Two. This was a veterans' center whose members wore many military ribbons and medals on their lapels. Our meeting was extremely interesting: I related my personal history of childhood wanderings in Russia during the war, and they told me about the battles in which they had fought during that same war.

I did not miss the opportunity to visit Robert Maxwell's Moscow office. There, I felt more freedom to speak. His staff inquired as to the purpose of my visit, and I explained that I was acting to release the Prisoners of Zion, jailed because they were Jews. I also told them about the many organizations operating throughout the world with the same goal.

On my last day in Moscow, moments before I left the hotel, I noticed a tiny light, a kind of electric eye, hung above the light on the ceiling. I understood that I had not been alone throughout my stay there....

Before leaving, I wanted to go buy a souvenir of Moscow accompanied by the African student. I purchased a set of crystal glasses in one of the stores, but unfortunately, I later discovered that the Russian saleswoman who wrapped the merchandise had not done a good job. When I opened the package upon my return to the United States, I found nothing but shattered glass.

I said good-bye to my friend from Ghana, boarded a plane to Tehran, and from there continued to Israel on an El Al flight. In those days, during the regime of the pro-Western Shah who maintained close ties with Israel, it was safe to land in Tehran.

I utilized my time in Israel to visit my family and meet with my friends in Raanana. Father, Leah and my sister Ita and her husband were happy to hear about Sara and the children, and were glad that I had established myself in America. Of course, I also visited Sara's parents and family, who were thrilled to receive direct regards from her. I parted from all of them and returned to my daily routine in New York.

The many conversations I had in Moscow left me with the feeling that it was somehow possible to "ransom" the freedom of the Jewish prisoners in the Soviet Union in exchange for an appropriate monetary "investment"….

The thought that there were Jews in the world living in distress would not leave me in peace. I therefore undertook to provide assistance for the mass demonstration being organized outside the Russian embassy in New York for the release of the Prisoners of Zion. Among the organizers were my friends Rabbi Arthur Schneier and Rabbi Haskel Lookstein. With 100,000 participants, the demonstration received wide media coverage in the United States and throughout the world. American political leaders from both major parties united in expressing their unconditional support for the demonstration's objectives. They called for the release of the prisoners and for the opening of the Soviet gates for those seeking immigration to Israel.

My business activities had expanded in that period and I had a large staff at my disposal operating the hotels I owned and supervising the renovations and ongoing maintenance of the buildings I had purchased. I located my office in the Belvedere Hotel on 48th Street, west of Broadway.

One of the tourists who regularly stayed at the hotel was an Arab Moroccan citizen who seemed to represent his country in some kind of economic activity in the United States. He made sure to meet with me and exchange pleasantries during every one of his visits. I understood from his comments that he had strong ties to the royal family in Morocco. His brother served in a key position in the palace and was close to King Hassan II. My conversations with him turned to the topic of the relationship between Jews and Arabs. More than once, I expressed my opinion about the need to make peace between Israel and its neighbors, and the well-being and prosperity it would bring to the nations of the region. He agreed with me. It seemed as if he had been educated in the West; he was open to new ideas and did not share the fanaticism typical of many Arabs at that time.

One day, the Moroccan guest suggested that I join him on a trip to Morocco. He promised me a visit to the royal palace and a meeting with his brother. I told him I would consider the matter in a positive light. I consulted with my Israeli friends in the consulate in New York, and those in the American government. When informed that there was nothing to prevent my traveling there, provided that I could obtain a visa, I responded in the affirmative and my Moroccan friend immediately arranged for a visa. Israel and Morocco did not have diplomatic ties in those days, again proving the advantage of an American passport.

I flew from New York to London and from there on a British Airways flight to Casablanca, where I was welcomed by my Moroccan friend and received VIP treatment. This is what happens when one is connected to the ruling power.

I stayed at the new, luxurious Hyatt hotel in the center of

Casablanca. My host took me around the city and introduced me to his family. With a population of about six million, the city is located in western Morocco on the Atlantic coast, and most of the country's commercial activity is conducted there. There are new, modern buildings and the beaches boast an eight mile-long promenade with hotels, restaurants and cafés. We also toured the walled old city and walked through its narrow alleyways.

I met my host's brother during my visit and, as promised, was invited to the royal palace. The visit to the palace was fascinating – my hosts were aware that I was a Jew and Holocaust survivor, and this did not present a problem. Of no less interest was my conversation with the brother. We spoke a great deal about Arab-Israeli relations and I finally raised the question: why are we killing each other? I noted that even this visit could bring an end to the bloodshed; after all, not all international agreements are arranged by politicians. Some are known to have been initiated by common people like myself, since most people are peace lovers.

The response of my host was definitely on the positive side. I gave the brother my address and the means of contacting me in the United States, and before saying good-bye, requested that they maintain contact with me.

During my conversations with my Moroccan friend, he made it clear to me that Egypt was the key to making peace with Israel. He noted that he had many friends who were connected to the Egyptian administration and was willing to arrange for me to meet with them. I picked up the gauntlet, expressing immediate interest in going there; incredibly, my friend used his contacts to obtain an Egyptian visa for me that same day.

The flight to Cairo was short, and waiting for me at the airport was a guide, arranged for me by the Moroccan, who took me to the Hilton hotel in the center of the city. Cairo is a large city, the largest in Egypt and, apparently, in all of the Middle East. With a population of

17 million, it is overcrowded and its infrastructure cannot cope with the enormous human burden.

Accompanied by the guide, I toured the marketplaces and tourist attractions of the city, which was divided by the Nile River into the old city and the new. The domes of many mosques stood out among the city's buildings. We, of course, did not omit a visit to the pyramids and famous museums.

During my stay, a meeting was scheduled to take place with a senior Egyptian political personality. Unfortunately, I waited in my hotel for naught. The man never showed up, but at least I got to know the Egyptian capital.

I flew to Cyprus and then on to Israel for a much-needed family visit.

Chapter 20

New York, New York

"If I can make it there, I can make it anywhere
It's up to you. New York, New York."

From the lyrics of "New York, New York,"
John Kander and Fred Ebb

New York is a huge city. It is difficult to describe its size and power; a tourist exposed to the city for the first time would find it hard to truly appreciate its potency immediately. It took me years to recognize the tremendous power secreted within this city. It has everything. Undoubtedly, New York is the world's primary artery, and through it flow the globe's business and financial dealings.

"The Big Apple" – that is the nickname that has stuck to the city. Everyone wants to take a bite out of it, smell it, experience its taste. It is big enough to satisfy the appetites of the millions who descend upon this most populous city in the United States. New York boasts more than eight million residents, speaking more than 170 languages. The largest commercial and financial enterprises in the world are concentrated here. The city's influence is felt in every sphere – in communications and finance, insurance and real estate, education and culture, fashion, the arts and more.

The eyes of the world are focused on a daily basis on Wall Street, the world's financial hub. About one and a half million workers arrive in Manhattan alone every day. This is the unfathomable power of the city, whose Gross Domestic Product approaches $950 billion a year.

New York serves as the country's primary aerial gateway, through which upwards of 100 million passengers pass annually. This is a city that never sleeps, whose skyscrapers dominate its airspace, and whose tremendous network of giant bridges, tunnels, roads, and subways connect it with its surroundings.

New York is not an easy place in which to do business; every step must be carefully considered. Everything here is large-scale. Businesses can flourish and grow into behemoths, but can also fail spectacularly, toppling many individuals in the process. The greater the growth, the harder the fall. Accordingly, caution must be exercised daily, and the finger must always be kept on the commercial pulse.

By its nature, a city like New York serves as a breeding ground for graft and corruption. At the end of the 1970s, New York stood on the brink of bankruptcy, its debts estimated to exceed $1 billion. This negatively impacted the city's maintenance and the level of municipal services, and of course led to the decline of the local economy.

As stated, my office was located in the Belvedere hotel, which I owned. While holding a discussion with the hotel staff one day, the phone rang, and I heard a familiar voice on the line. There was no need to guess; I identified the caller at once. It was Congressman Ed Koch, requesting a meeting.

With New York City Mayor Ed Koch, in his Manhattan office

Our meeting was riveting in every respect. I was charmed by Koch's personality – he was pleasant, energetic and matter-of-fact, full of motivation to change the city. He described the city's bleak situation as well as his plans to boost it onto a path of renewed growth and development. He also had ideas about improving the efficiency of City Hall and fighting crime. Ed Koch captivated me, not only because he did not hide his Jewishness, but because he was determined to attain every goal he set for himself. A wonderful friendship was born that day, one that continues even as these words are being written.

Koch outlined what he needed to do in order to get elected as mayor. Firstly, he needed to defeat his opponents in the Democratic primaries. There were seven other candidates, among them Mario Cuomo, a strong rival, who would stop at nothing to overcome him. Secondly, he would need to run against the Republican candidate in the mayoralty election.

Ed explained the importance of having my support and assistance, due to my influence and the respect in which I was held by many in the Jewish community. I consented, and joined Ed Koch's team to elect him mayor of New York City.

From that moment on, I had direct phone access to him. I prepared an aggressive campaign for the Jewish vote, presented it to him and then toured all the boroughs with him. I raised significant sums of money, and these assisted in his victory; but it was no easy ride. During primaries, his Democratic rivals leveled various accusations at him, including hints about his sexual orientation. One of them outdid himself with an election poster that declared: "Vote for Cuomo, not the Homo." Despite this, Koch achieved a landslide victory, receiving 713,000 votes to Cuomo's 587,000.

On my advice, Koch conducted a largely issues-oriented campaign. He spoke about cutting crime and about his plans to rescue the city from its heavy burden of massive debt. In the end, he indeed attained the longed-for position and entered City Hall, from where he successfully and decisively conducted the city's affairs until his retirement in 1989.

Koch was a special breed of politician. He held liberal views, worked on behalf of human rights and was an enthusiastic supporter of Israel. He succeeded relatively quickly in saving the city from financial disaster, in creating a more efficient bureaucracy and in reducing the inflated salaries customary at the time. He did not hesitate to cut expenses he thought unnecessary. In 1983, he managed to create a budgetary surplus of half a billion dollars. He enjoyed tremendous popularity in the 1985 elections and gained a landslide victory of over 75% of the votes.

Mayor Koch's door was open to me. Every so often I would receive a phone call from him or a request to consult with me. His staff maintained continuous contact with me until his retirement. Koch was a regular guest in my home during his tenure as mayor and afterwards.

During these years my children grew up, completing their academic studies. My two sons received degrees in business administration, Ron at the University of Miami and Jay at Adelphi University on Long Island. Both joined me and assisted me with the management of my expanding business, bringing with them a fresh, youthful, energetic and efficient outlook. I was able to rely on them and their decisions. The cooperation between them was practical and productive; every step was undertaken with good judgment and after joint consultation with me. Without a doubt, they reduced my work load, leaving me time for my growing public and political activities.

After hearing some of my speeches to the Jewish community, my friend Gershon Jacobson, editor of *Der Algemeiner Journal*, asked me to write a weekly column in his newspaper. I accepted the offer and my article on events of the day appeared every week. The paper was

With the Lubavitcher Rebbe, Rabbi Menachem Mendel Schneerson, zt"l, at his Beit
Midrash in Brooklyn

supported by the Lubavitcher Rebbe. Some of his followers, aware of my activities, wanted to arrange for me to meet with him.

It was a fascinating and very moving meeting. The Rebbe's very presence and the meeting venue were infused with an atmosphere of holiness. I felt I was standing before a unique figure who radiated holiness. His sharp look and penetrating eyes reached the depths of my soul; they had a tremendously powerful effect, inexplicably so.

My conversation with him was short and to-the-point. He spoke about preserving the "chain of generations" by transmitting Jewish heritage values to youth at an age when their personalities are still developing. His voice was calm and each word that he uttered bore weighty significance.

The Rebbe had heard of my political connections with Israeli and American leaders, and it became evident that he himself was well-versed in the intricate politics of both countries. I was very impressed with his wise and accurate analyses of the situation. It is no wonder that many politicians and leaders came from around the world to partake of his knowledge and wisdom.

In general, it was customary for those visiting the Rebbe to request his blessing. At one of my meetings with him I told him that, in contrast to others, I wished to impart a blessing to him. He said that I myself was blessed and he would be happy to receive my blessing. I grasped his hand and recited: "May God bless you and protect you. May God cause His face to shine upon you and be gracious to you. May God raise his face to you and establish peace for you and for the Jewish people." The Rebbe was very moved by my words and by the fact that I had included the Jewish nation in my blessing.

The Rebbe was aware of my support for his educational projects and asked to hear details of my activities. He pointed out that I had fulfilled a commandment of unparalleled significance: "He who saves one Jewish life, saves the entire world." I was able to participate in several of his Torah lessons. His amazing expertise in the mysteries of the various texts, *midrashim* and commentaries astounded all those attending. He recited from memory sentences and even whole chapters from the Bible and the Talmud.

The Rebbe's genius was also evident in his analytical ability and expert knowledge of his various lecture topics. The Jewish nation has produced well-known geniuses throughout the generations. I have no doubt that the Lubavitcher Rebbe will join their ranks, not only due to his special talents and personality, but because of his widespread efforts to bring the Torah and its legacy to Jews throughout the world.

One day, Rabbi Jacob Hecht, a close associate of the Rebbe, called to tell me that the Rebbe wanted to invite Arik Sharon and me to be the guests of honor at Chabad's annual dinner. I transmitted the request to Ariel Sharon, who accepted the invitation.

About a thousand people participated in the festive event. Arik's and my speeches received wide media coverage. Since then, I have been invited to speak at the annual conference of Chabad emissaries. At one of them, I told those present that although I do not resemble them externally – I have no beard and do not dress as they do – deep inside, I feel like two "Lubavitchers." My comments were warmly and enthusiastically applauded. I admired the Rebbe and his community. His emissaries are scattered in every corner of the earth and, in their pleasant manner and without coercion, they try to preserve Jewish heritage throughout the world.

This was during Ronald Reagan's tenure in the White House. Given that I was doing my utmost to help him get re-elected to a second term, I was appointed to the Republican National Committee. In appreciation for all my assistance and activities on his behalf, I was invited, together with a small group, to meet the president in the White House in September 1983.

The president welcomed us warmly and thanked us for our aid and cooperation. Since we were permitted to ask questions, I raised the point that, according to newspaper sources, the president had great influence in the Arab world. Therefore, I asked, why did he not act with determination to stop the terrorists operating against Israel and the United States?

Several days later came the news report of the explosion in Beirut in which dozens of American soldiers were killed. I received a phone call the following day from one of President Reagan's assistants, who took the trouble to call and tell me that my question to the president had come at the right time and to the right person.

In 1985 newspaper headlines announced the arrest of a Jewish American citizen. He had served in the Intelligence branch of the United States Navy in Washington and was caught spying on behalf of Israel. His name was Jonathan Pollard, and publication of his arrest and alleged crimes shocked many people and caused great embarrassment for the State of Israel. Pollard was tried, convicted and sentenced to life in prison, where he has sat ever since 1985.

It came to light that during his work, Pollard was exposed to classified information relating to Israel. He maintained that American defense officials intentionally withheld this information from Israel, thus endangering the lives of its citizens. He therefore relayed this intelligence to Israel, as was the norm between the two countries. During the course of his trial, he claimed that he had acted out of good conscience and for moral reasons.

For years, Israel refused to recognize him as an Israeli agent. However, at a later stage, the Israeli government granted him citizenship and began to exert pressure on the American administration to release him from prison, with no results so far.

Minister Ariel Sharon telephoned me one day, asking that I utilize my personal connections with American politicians and administration personnel to influence them to free Jonathan Pollard. Without hesitation, I turned to several politicians and senior government officials with this request. At a later point, I also met with Vice President Al Gore whom I also asked about freeing Pollard. He promised to look into this, but until now nothing has been done. Pollard has been rotting in his jail cell for twenty-seven years.

Jonathan is aware of my lobbying on his behalf and has sent me several thank-you notes. In the last one, he expressed the hope of meeting me outside the prison on the longed-for day of his release. Would that this be so.

"Regards" I received from prisoner Jonathan Pollard

Chapter 21
With Israeli Leaders and Personalities

"Every manifestation of Jewish vitality, of Jewish activity,
knowingly or unknowingly leads to Zionism."

Ze'ev Jabotinsky, Fourth Russian Zionist Congress,
The Hague, August 1907

Only someone who had survived the inferno of the Holocaust and witnessed the helplessness of a nation led like sheep to the slaughter, unable to fight or defend itself, could understand my great admiration for the military leaders of Israel's founding generation. From the early days of Zionism, through the establishment of the state and until today, our nation has produced heroes and military leaders who have written spectacular chapters of our history. One of these great leaders, in my opinion, is Ariel Sharon.

Many books, and even more articles, in Israel and throughout the world have been, and will be, written about Arik; but due to the wonderful friendship that grew between us over the years, I am able to tell you about the other Arik. I will describe him from a personal perspective, stemming from my experience in the course of the many days we spent together, at times accompanied also by his beloved wife, Lily, of blessed memory.

In February 1983, Time magazine published a long, accusatory article about Ariel Sharon. The article claimed that Sharon had spoken with the family of Bashir Gemayel, the assassinated Christian Phalangist leader in Beirut, about the possibility of revenge, even before the Phalangists had entered the Sabra and Shatila refugee camps and prior to the massacre that took place there. Sharon sued the magazine for libel, in a trial that lasted about two years. The irritating absurdity in this case was that here Christians had slaughtered Moslems and yet – once again – the Jews were being accused….

It was painful for me to observe such terrible injustice accorded to a hero of Israel, to the IDF and to the State of Israel. From a practical point of view, Arik's trial cost a great deal of money and I tried to help him as much as possible. The jury cleared him, but also acquitted Time of libel, stating that "there is no reason to believe that the facts are incorrect."

I first met Arik at a military conference held in Israel in 1974, to which I had been invited by Major General Rafael Eitan (Raful), who had been a guest in my New York home. He introduced me to Arik as a former IDF soldier currently living in New York. However, the actual friendship with Arik began in 1988.

That year, I spent my summer vacation at the Tel Aviv Hilton. While I stood in the lobby, Ariel Sharon came in through the main entrance, surrounded, as usual, by security guards, and accompanied by Ehud Olmert. This was in the stormy days before the elections, at the height of the campaigning. There, standing right before me, was the man I had admired for so long. Without a second thought, I approached him, shook his hand, greeted him and mentioned that I would be happy to help him as much as I could. I handed Olmert my business card and departed. Who would believe that a wonderful friendship would grow from such a chance encounter, a friendship that continued until the tragic stroke on January 4, 2006 that has left him in a coma to this day.

Upon my return to New York, I was contacted by a fellow named Gershon Stav, who presented himself as an educator, a representative of the Beitar youth movement and an adviser to Prime Minister Yitzhak Shamir. He requested to meet with me. Attending this meeting in my Manhattan office was a pleasant man, well-connected to Israel's political elite and privy to its political secrets. From our very first conversation we formed a strong friendship, one that continues to this day.

Gershon Stav organized the visits of Likud members to the United States and their contacts with local Jewish communities; and my close relationship with him would lead to my eventual introduction to many of Israel's leaders. Foremost among them were Mr. Yitzhak Shamir, then prime minister of Israel; Moshe Arens, Minister of Defense at the time; Ariel Sharon; Binyamin Netanyahu, the "media star" of that period who was then at one of the heights of his popularity; Ehud Olmert; Uzi Landau; Dan Meridor; Benny Begin and many others. I hosted all these personalities during their visits to the United States.

In that first meeting with Gershon Stav, he informed me that he was planning several events and meetings for Arik Sharon, who was coming to New York. He asked if I could arrange a support rally in which Arik would be the main speaker. I immediately answered in the affirmative.

The date for the rally was set and I quickly began to organize it. Word got around among my friends, many of whom volunteered to help. My friend Murray Alon offered to hold the rally at no cost in a large hall in a hotel he owned. Another friend donated money for the food. The phones in my office rang off the hook, and enthusiasm was sky high.

The rally in Queens honoring Arik was successful in every respect. The crowds that had amassed expressed their support and willingness to contribute and assist. In my speech, I stressed the importance of a strong Israel and the need for tough leadership, as exemplified by Yitzhak Shamir and Ariel Sharon. Speaking after me, Arik reviewed the situation in Israel and the social, economic and security challenges facing the government that would be elected.

The day after the rally, Arik asked for a private meeting with me. I went to his hotel, the Park Lane on Central Park South, one block from my apartment. We sat and talked at length. He again emphasized that my speech of the previous day had left him highly impressed, particularly the mention of my family's suffering during the Holocaust, and he requested further details on this subject. I explained that many of those present at the rally were Holocaust survivors and that this topic resonated with them too.

I then recounted to Arik all I had been through as a Jewish boy in Nazi Europe. Until my meeting with him, I had never spoken about this to anyone. My story mesmerized him and he listened to every word – I actually noticed tears in the eyes of this "tough" man. By the time I had ended my tale, he had become speechless. We sat wordlessly facing each other for a long time until finally Arik's voice broke the silence. He declared, in a tone full of resolve, that such horrors could never transpire in our days because now we had our own country and our own army! He emphasized that we would never allow the atrocities of the Holocaust to be repeated.

Arik explained the importance of a strong, reliable leadership in Israel, one possessing life experience. Hence, he explained, the Likud's victory in the upcoming elections was imperative. He felt that the party's leadership was worthy and capable of meeting the challenges facing the country. He pointed out that since the current issue of debate concerned the status of Jerusalem, as many Jews as possible should settle in the Old City. He expanded on this topic and presented his plans to me. He then thanked me for the assistance I had given him and invited me to be his guest on my next visit to Israel.

After Arik's return to Israel, we exchanged several phone calls in which he updated me on political developments. Our friendship subsequently deepened, and during his visits to the United States and mine to Israel, we would meet together with our families either in my New York home or at his Sycamore Ranch near Sderot.

The elections for the twelfth Knesset took place on November 1, 1988, following the outbreak of the first Intifada. Prior to that, a National Unity government had been in power, with Yitzhak Shamir and Shimon Peres in rotation as its head, Yitzhak Rabin as Minister of Defense and Ariel Sharon as Minister of Trade and Industry.

It was a stormy election campaign. Yitzhak Shamir was the head of the Likud party and Shimon Peres led the Alignment. Shamir presented an attractive group of young politicians, among them Binyamin Netanyahu, Ehud Olmert, Dan Meridor, Roni Milo, Benny Begin, Limor Livnat, Uzi Landau and others. The top tier of candidates included Moshe Arens, Ariel Sharon, David Levy, Moshe Nissim and others. Without a doubt, this was an impressive and promising list.

In all their election campaigns Israeli politicians could not ignore us American Jews, and this time was no exception. Candidates needed the public backing of American Jewry and, in particular, their financial assistance to sustain the activities of the organizations supporting these politicians. Following the rally for Sharon, Prime Minister Yitzhak Shamir also paid us a visit. On this occasion, too, I was recruited by Gershon Stav to arrange the rallies. Indeed, the halls were filled to capacity and public support only grew. I spoke at every event and repeatedly stressed the importance of the strong group led by Yitzhak Shamir.

The prime minister also invited me to a private meeting. He presented the Likud platform and the list of front-running candidates, which incorporated talented and promising newcomers alongside veterans highly experienced in military, diplomatic and political matters. Shamir thanked me for my help and commended my speeches.

During the 1988 elections, I met many Israeli politicians who would eventually become prime ministers and senior cabinet ministers. At one point or another I hosted most of them in my home, and I've maintained contact with them to this day. One of the most impressive figures in the gallery of politicians was, without a doubt, Binyamin Netanyahu. He had, several months previously, completed his position as Israel's Ambassador to the United Nations and had gained wide popularity in Israel and the world as the State's advocate.

In the elections, the Likud, led by Shamir, won forty Knesset seats, and the Alignment thirty-nine. Had the *Haredi* parties joined him, Shamir could have formed a government with a majority of sixty-five Knesset members; but since the *Haredi* demands were too extreme, he preferred a National Unity government without any rotation. In this government, Peres served as Minister of Finance and Yitzhak Rabin as Minister of Defense. This government collapsed one and a half years later after what Rabin termed "the dirty trick," in which Peres tried, and failed, to establish a narrow government composed of the Left and the religious parties.

During this period of major political events, I hosted many ministers and Knesset members, both in Israel and in the United States. Through my intensive activities on behalf of Shamir and of Arik, many in the New York Jewish community became aware of me. American politicians who sought informal ties with Israeli leaders also contacted me to make introductions.

Prime Minister Yitzhak Shamir invited me to attend a conference in Jerusalem in support of global Jewish leaders. During this visit, I held many personal meetings with the prime minister, Netanyahu, Arens, Fuad Ben-Eliezer and others, and it also represented an opportunity to meet with world Jewish leaders.

My family and I were greatly honored when I was granted the Crown of Jerusalem award by Prime Minister Yitzhak Shamir. This is a prestigious award, on par with the Israel Prize, conferred on individuals and organizations for their work on behalf of the State of Israel and the Jewish people. The list of its ten recipients includes Dr. Henry Kissinger. The award ceremony took place in the presence of the prime minister during an impressive, festive event in New York, organized by Eric Spektor of the Jabotinsky movement.

The threats facing Israel, both domestic and regional, did not cease. Israel was in the midst of the first Intifada, whose accompanying terror attacks took a heavy toll in human life, while radical leaders in the Arab world called for the state's destruction. Iraqi dictator Saddam Hussein posed one of the most brutal threats to Israel. He was unable to get over the humiliation of the Israel Air Force attack ordered by Menachem Begin on Iraq's nuclear reactor.

On August 2, 1990, Saddam Hussein's forces invaded Kuwait, conquering it within two days. Saddam's unrestrained appetite and the threat he posed to Saudi Arabia was of great concern to the West, particularly the United States. The tyrant's aggression knew no bounds. He had ended his war with Iran two years before the Kuwait invasion, a war that caused over one million casualties. He had not hesitated to launch missiles on Tehran, and to use poison gas weapons prohibited by international law.

The ultimatum set by United Nations Resolution 678 for Iraqi forces to retreat from Kuwait by January 15, 1991 fell on the Iraqi ruler's deaf ears. President George Bush Sr. headed an international coalition established to enforce the ultimatum. Coalition forces led by General Norman Schwarzkopf were concentrated in the Gulf area around Iraq.

Operation Desert Storm was launched, during which many strategic military installations were destroyed throughout Iraq. Saddam Hussein carried out his threat and attacked Israeli cities and population centers with Scud missiles, causing great damage, injuring dozens of citizens and leading to the deaths of two people. When the invasion of coalition forces was complete and Kuwait was liberated, President Bush declared an end to the war.

I publicized many articles and placed full-page ads in the American press supporting President Bush and his determination to confront the attacker. The president sent me a moving thank you letter accompanied by an invitation to a personal meeting at the White House. Together with his wife Barbara, he received my wife Sara and me very warmly, and explained how touched he had been at what I had written and that he had wanted to thank me in person. At his request, I told him a little bit about myself – that I was a young Holocaust survivor who had immigrated to Israel, served in the IDF and even now, in America, continue to help my people. I pointed out that I had come to the United States to have a "second chance" at life and was grateful to the country for the opportunity I was given. The president and his wife were moved by my words and heartily thanked me for my support.

Throughout the Gulf War period I remained in touch with my friend Gershon Stav in Israel, receiving ongoing updates from him on events there. Arik occasionally contacted me and enlightened me as to the course of the war through his "general's analyses." He expressed disappointment with how the war had ended: in his opinion, the goal should have been the total defeat and collapse of Saddam Hussein's regime.

I maintained an insatiable interest in events in Israel. Though I read every bit of information and followed, on an almost daily basis, the news from Israel that flooded the American television networks, I was also privy to "behind-the-scenes" commentary provided by my friends in Israel – political or military leaders. One of them was Danny Yatom, a close friend – an IDF major-general, head of the Mossad, Knesset member from the Labor party and, today, a businessman. I meet with him frequently in Israel and abroad and am always interested in his interpretation and evaluation of ongoing events.

One of my close friends is Dr. Uzi Landau, with whom I meet during his visits to New York. Uzi, the son of the late Chaim, a commander of the Irgun, continued in his father's footsteps and became part of the Likud's young leadership. Recognizing his talents, Ariel Sharon appointed him Minister of Internal Security. His honesty and reliability became well known in Israel and abroad and placed him at the top of the list of highly valued Israeli politicians. Today, he serves as Minister of National Infrastructures in Netanyahu's government, representing the *Yisra'el Beiteinu* party. In our meetings, I came to appreciate his clear and honest analyses of Israel's diplomatic and security situation. His wise words are always filled with a sense of mission and love of Israel.

Another close friend of mine – despite our ideological differences – is Fuad Ben-Eliezer, a senior member of the Labor party with whom I meet often. Fuad made sure to see me on every one of my visits to Israel and I hosted him in my home whenever he came to New York. Our close relationship has always been based on mutual trust. On several occasions, I mediated between political leaders, carrying messages Fuad asked me to transmit, none of which were ever leaked to the press.

With Fuad I had many discussions regarding the Labor party's situation, during the height of the internecine struggle between its Rabin and Peres supporters. This struggle seriously harmed the party's overall functioning and it began to lose voters. Fuad and I spoke at length about Peres's attempts to bring down the government; and he explained that as head of the party, Peres bore sole responsibility for the process that Rabin later dubbed "the dirty trick."

One day, Arik phoned me and asked me to help organize Ateret Cohanim's annual event. He explained that this institution was engaged in holy work – redeeming Old City buildings by purchasing them and populating them with Jews. I agreed and proceeded to recruit many friends to the event, in order to help the organization achieve its objectives. Arik was the guest of honor and keynote speaker; and it was on this occasion that I learned about the important activities of Ateret Cohanim and met Mati Dan, the driving force behind this important enterprise. I will relate more about him later.

Ehud Olmert, Binyamin Netanyahu, Moshe Arens, Uzi Landau and others would meet with me during their frequent visits to the United States. Considering me a Likud representative in the United States, they tended to consult with me about various topics, particularly about arranging pro-Israel events in the New York community. I spoke at each such event and quickly became a sought-after speaker among various Jewish organizations. Eventually, these, too, began to request my assistance in organizing their annual affairs.

In the course of my life I have met many people, including fascinating figures who made history – Jewish heroes and intellectuals. Without a doubt, one of the most intriguing personalities I came to know in New York was Peter (Zvi) Malkin. Meeting him marked the closing of a circle in my life.

I first met Peter at one of the receptions I held for my friend Ariel Sharon in my West Hampton home. Arik did not have to introduce us, as Peter recognized me from the period of my national service abroad. At the reception, he told Arik about my important mission on behalf of the Jewish people during this hidden chapter in my life, a period with which Peter was well familiar, as he was with its key players. Since then a wonderful friendship developed between us,, continuing until his death in March 2005.

Peter was born in Poland in 1927 to an observant, Zionist family. Due to the rising anti-Semitism, some of the family members, Peter among them, decided to immigrate to Eretz Israel. The remaining relatives were all killed in the Holocaust, including his sister, Fruma, and her three children. Peter served first in the Haganah, and then in the IDF, as an expert in sabotage and explosives. In 1950, he was recruited to the Mossad, where he served for twenty-seven years. On May 11,

1960, Peter played an active role in the capture of Adolf Eichmann in Argentina, together with a team led by Rafi Eitan. The Eichmann trial was held in 1961 and the evil oppressor was convicted and put to death by hanging on May 31, 1962.

After retiring in 1976, Peter devoted his time to his beloved hobby, painting. He moved to New York in the last years of his life and wrote five books. He also served as an international consultant in the war against terror.

After we met, Peter was a regular guest in my house and became aware of my close friendship with Arik. During one of Arik's trips to New York, Peter phoned me and asked if Arik would be visiting me this time, too. Upon hearing my affirmative response, he showed up at my door bearing a piece of his own artwork – a portrait of Arik and me. Arik very much admired the wonderful accuracy of the portrayal. Peter gave me the painting as a present and wrote a personal dedication.

My conversations with Peter were compelling. He was familiar with the problems facing Israel and had ideas for solutions. He had served the state at one of its main junctures and had acquired a great deal of knowledge and experience. The journalist Uri Dan defined him as a "wonderful combination of Ariel Sharon, Meir Har-Zion, the General Security Service *(Shin Bet)* and the Mossad."

Every so often, in my discussions with him, he complained about Israel's helplessness in its war against suicide bombing incidents and claimed that there was a solution to the problem. According to him, Israel, as a sovereign state, should act decisively on the matter; this would be possible only if a courageous leadership was in place, willing to assume responsibility.

He indeed was a wonderful example of a brave-hearted man with a fertile imagination, and this is how I will always remember him.

Chapter 22
Giuliani

"Managers motivate workers with the carrot and the stick;
leaders do this with the help of vision and inspiration."

Anonymous

My involvement in New York political life enabled me to meet many candidates for key positions in the city. Such candidacies required significant financial resources and wide media exposure, without which a contender had no chance of gaining the desired position. Another crucial element was the massive support of the Jewish community, the absence of which would make it difficult to win elections.

Towards the end of 1988, President Bush (Sr.)'s headquarters asked me to help the Republican candidate for mayor of New York City, Rudolph (Rudy) William Giuliani III, who had served as United States Attorney for the Southern District of New York. Rudy became widely known for his courageous war against drug dealers and against both organized and white-collar crime. Stressing Giuliani's enthusiastic support for Israel, the Bush activists wanted me to work in the Jewish community on his behalf.

My first meeting with Rudy was arranged by people from the Bush headquarters. He came to my office in the Travel Inn hotel, introduced himself to me and announced his decision to run for mayor. Research he had conducted along with many discussions, he said, had revealed that I was an individual who was essential for the success of his race, due to my connections and influence in the Jewish community. Indeed, this conversation took place at a time when I was speaking at many events throughout the city in which Israeli leaders, including

With Mayor Giuliani at my New York home

the prime minister, took part. When Giuliani requested my assistance and suggested my joining his campaign headquarters staff, I agreed and became one of his main supporters.

This was a difficult period in New York. During David Dinkins' tenure as mayor, the city suffered from poor quality of life. The public lived in the frightening shadow of street crime and a high murder rate. Manhattan was filled with homeless people milling about and giving the city a negative image.

New York City consists of five boroughs, one of them being Brooklyn, with a population of 2.5 million. This is a dynamic borough with many neighborhoods, whose residents have maintained their ethnic character. Borough Park is populated mostly by Jews, Bedford Stuyvesant by African-Americans, and Bensonhurst by Italians. Brooklyn has the largest concentration of Jews in the world (except for Israel) – approximately three quarters of a million. Most live in places like Borough Park, Flatbush, Gravesend and Crown Heights.

Up until the 1960s, Crown Heights was primarily Jewish and

housed hundreds of synagogues, *yeshivot* and Jewish institutions. *Hassidic* rabbis lived in the neighborhood, surrounded by their followers. The 1960s saw an influx of African-Americans into the neighborhood, which changed its character and caused many Jews to leave. The Lubavitcher Rebbe was decisive about not abandoning Crown Heights, which remains until this day the bastion of Chabad *Hassidim*. 20,000 of them live side by side with 130,000 African-Americans. The many Jewish institutions in the neighborhood include Chabad World Headquarters at 770 Eastern Parkway, schools, *yeshivot* and synagogues.

August 1991 saw the outbreak of heavy rioting in the area between the *Hassidim* and the African-Americans. The Rebbe's driver crossed one of the local intersections and crashed into a car whose driver lost control and hit two African-American boys, killing one of them. Crowds gathered at the scene and began to shout insults at the *Hassidim* and the police, and the situation quickly developed into a major, uncontrollable riot. The enraged masses shouted anti-Semitic remarks and attacked many Jews. During the course of the riots, a Jewish student from Australia, Yankel Rosenbaum, was stabbed to death. A non-Jewish motorcyclist, who accidentally drove into the neighborhood, was also attacked and stabbed to death by rioters who mistook him for a Jew because of his beard and clothing. Stores owned by Jews were broken into, looted and set on fire. The scenes were extremely hard to watch.

Crown Heights did not look like a neighborhood in America. What happened reminded me of anti-Semitic events in Poland and I saw no distinction between the pogroms in Europe, in which Jews were murdered and their property abandoned, and what had transpired here. The only difference was that there it was Europe of the 1930s and 1940s, and here it was the enlightened and democratic America of 1991. Mayor Dinkins had not succeeded in bridging the ethnic gaps in the city and the police had difficulty dealing with the situation.

I could not bear to witness what was going on. But it was

precisely here that I was able to observe Giuliani's behavior – as a person and as a leader. I went with him to Crown Heights. Our car was stoned on the way by the masses, who vented their wrath on every vehicle that drove into the area. We had no choice but to immediately begin organizing young Jews for self-defense. We set up a base in the office of Rabbi Hecht, a close associate of the Rebbe, and instructions were issued from there. We collected money to purchase equipment for communication and protection and recruited security guards who acted in coordination with the authorities.

During the course of the events, my friends put me in touch with Jesse Jackson, one of the leaders of the African-American community. I thought that his visit to the neighborhood could calm things down. Unfortunately, Jackson said that he was unable to get involved because he was recuperating from a severe accident. He relayed that he would be happy to honor my request at a later date.

At the same time, I turned to the authorities via the written and electronic media, calling upon them to take immediate action to arrest the rioters and bring them to justice forthwith. I also wrote and called key people in Washington, requesting their intervention to help relieve the tension. Many people reacted positively to my actions, which were widely covered in the media. One response came from S. Drimmer on behalf of the Crown Heights Emergency Fund, who warmly praised my behavior during the riots.

Many responses came from Washington. One was from Congressman Charles Schumer, who expressed his deep concern regarding the Crown Heights riots and his sorrow at the murder of Yankel Rosenbaum. In his letter to me of September 17, 1991, he promised to continue pressuring the police to bolster their resources as necessary in order to achieve calm in the neighborhood. He conveyed the hope that the police and the authorities would learn their lessons and be better able to deal with such events in the future.

The riots in Crown Heights strengthened my resolve to support

Giuliani's run for mayor, as he had definitively proven his leadership during this difficult period. Thus, I sprang into action and thoroughly canvassed the entire city together with him during the campaign. I gave speeches before voters in Brooklyn, the Bronx, Manhattan and in remote neighborhoods, introducing him as the mayor for all, regardless of religion, race or gender.

One way to expose Giuliani to the Jewish community was to include him in the rallies I organized for Israeli Prime Minister Yitzhak Shamir and other Israeli ministers and public personalities. Giuliani received good media coverage at these events and his picture appeared in newspapers alongside those of Yitzhak Shamir, Moshe Arens, Ariel Sharon and others.

On the night of the elections, we gathered – all the key activists – in Giuliani's personal headquarters in the Roosevelt Hotel. At 11pm the television network commentators reported that Giuliani had won

At the opening of the Salute to Israel Parade with my wife Sara, Robert Maxwell, Tel Aviv Mayor Shlomo Lahat, New York City Mayor David Dinkins and Minister Yitzhak Moda'i

the mayoral election. There was great joy and I felt much gratification, believing I had done my share in electing one of the best mayors the city had ever seen. In his televised victory speech, Giuliani remembered to thank me for my part in the success of the campaign.

The new mayor began forming his team and offered me a senior political position, which I politely declined. In my view, my place was in the world of business and in offering assistance – as much as possible, behind the scenes – to the State of Israel and the Jewish people.

Under Giuliani's leadership, the crime rate in New York City dropped drastically – by 57%! Murders decreased by 65%. Quality of life improved; homeless were taken off the streets; many streets were thoroughly cleaned and upgraded; and porn shops and other hotbeds of crime were removed. Times Square underwent a facelift and was restored to its former glory.

During the mega-terror attack on 9/11, Rudy became a highly admired figure as a result of the strong leadership and level-headed thinking he demonstrated during the unprecedented tragedy that struck New York. When I asked him in one of our many meetings what the secret of his success was, he answered: "Be yourself, surround yourself with an excellent, trustworthy staff, take care to be loyal to your people, set goals, promise less and deliver more." When I eventually read his book, *Leadership*, I saw that these and other principles had guided him throughout his life and on his political path.

Giuliani became a friend and one of the regular visitors to my home. He also did not hesitate to pick up the phone and consult with me during the various crises that plagued the city. He refers to me in his book as one of the close friends who enriched his political life.

He was replaced as mayor by my friend, Michael Bloomberg, in 2001.

Years later, I undertook to help Giuliani when he wanted to run for president of the United States on the Republican ticket. In July

2009, I hosted a large event in his honor in my West Hampton home, and invited many of my friends and community leaders. During the evening, Giuliani suggested that I present myself as a candidate for Congress, claiming that I was very well-suited for the job and had a good chance of winning. I immediately responded that I saw my mission in life as serving the Jewish people, which I had been doing for years without the title "Congressman."

During that entire period, I spared no effort in my work on behalf of the Jewish community. From 1991 onward, for five consecutive years, I headed the team that arranged the Salute to Israel parade, held each year in honor of Israel's Independence Day and organized by the American Zionist Youth Federation. To this day, tens of thousands of New York's Jews take part in it, along with the mayor, members of Congress, prominent politicians and Jewish leaders from Israel and the United States – all coming to identify with the State of Israel on its holiday. The parade proceeds up Fifth Avenue in Manhattan and includes Jewish day school students and Jewish institutions and organizations, accompanied by marching bands, dance troupes and floats highlighting Israel's achievements in various sectors.

It all began with a phone call I received from the Israel Consul in New York, Mr. Uri Savir, who asked me to head the organizing team of the 1991 Salute to Israel parade. After some deliberation I agreed to his request; I viewed the parade as something that would unite the American Jewish community with that of Israel. I had always advocated unity among our people, and in my speeches had stressed that "when we are united, God smiles down on us." The time had come now, I thought, when I could do my small part for the smile of the Almighty.

In my first meeting with the organizers, I laid out my ideas. I thought we should change directions, and try to instill a different character into the parade by widening the circle and inviting representatives of Jewish communities throughout the world. Indeed, that year the parade participants ended up including Jews from Russia, France and other countries. I also invited my friend Robert Maxwell from London to serve as the parade's Grand Marshal, and my friend Binyamin Netanyahu accepted my request to speak in the name of the State of Israel. (On a tangential note: I maintained contact with Robert Maxwell and his family until his tragic death; and after he died, I tried to help his wife Elizabeth and his son Kevin to extricate themselves from their financial troubles. The family was very grateful and kept up contact with me, and I was recently invited to London to celebrate Elizabeth's 90th birthday with her and the family.)

The "parade of parades" succeeded beyond anyone's expectations. Producing an event of such grand proportions required precise planning, a talented and reliable staff, good organization, coordination with many people and fundraising. I felt that we had met all of our goals. Many staff members mentioned that the spirit of action and dedication that I exhibited throughout the production stage influenced and guided them in their work.

I received many thank you letters from people and institutions who took part in the parade:

Mayor David Dinkins wrote: *I assure you that my commitment to Israel and a united Jerusalem will always remain firm and that I echo your parade theme – "For Zion's sake I will not be silent".*

President Bush (Sr.) wrote: *. . . we rejoice at the success that Israel has enjoyed. I am glad that we were able to contribute to that success. In the past year alone, we defeated Iraqi aggression and repealed the awful resolution that wrongly equated Zionism with racism.*

The United States is especially proud of the role that it has played in helping to bring about Jewish immigration from the former Soviet Union and Ethiopia and in working with Israel in the pursuit of lasting peace in the Middle East. Our commitment to Israel and is security, based on a mutual commitment to democratic values, is fundamental.

The period during which I headed the organizing team of the Salute to Israel parade was unforgettable. I was happy to see our people united at such a joyous occasion, celebrating with Israel. Over the years I received letters in honor of the event from Israeli Prime Ministers Yitzhak Rabin and Yitzhak Shamir. They thanked me for my work and stressed the importance of the bond between Israel and the Jews of the Diaspora.

One of the American organizations I helped found, together with Dov Hikind, was the United Jewish Coalition, whose activities received wide media coverage in the United States. Its goal was to fight the anti-Semitism that had reared its head in the United States, as well as to initiate events and take part in the work of other entities that condemned anti-Semitism. The Jewish Coalition was established in response to the lessons learned from the violent anti-Semitic riots in Crown Heights. It attracted many activists who participated in the various demonstrations that were organized for, among others, the Jews in the Soviet Union who were at the time imprisoned behind bars.

Chapter 23

Return to Pultusk

"Let us not forget that which should not be forgotten
Let us not forgive that which should not be forgiven."

Simhat Ani'im (Joy of the Poor), Natan Alterman

During my years in the United States, between the mad race for personal rehabilitation, establishing a family and establishing myself financially, the question of my family roots would often trouble me. I was, for the most part, not privileged to know my mother and did not even own a photograph of her as a memento. Every so often, during moments of solitude and reflection, those visions I so wanted to erase from my memory would surface anew.

In addition, my desire to impart to my children the meaning of our lives as Jews, as a nation that suffered through many generations of wandering and destruction, eventually led to a decision of utmost significance – to take them on a "roots trip." I knew that such a journey would not be easy but, hard as it might be, embarking upon it was imperative – the experience of actually seeing something with one's own eyes is significant and the memory lasts forever. But in order to take my children on such a journey, proper preparation was essential. I awaited an appropriate opportunity.

Just such an opportunity presented itself in 1987. Through my public activities in New York, I became acquainted with City Councilman Noach Dear, a Jewish politician involved in human rights issues who devoted much time and energy to the cause of Soviet Jewry. Having closely followed my activities in this area, he suggested that I join him on a visit to the Kremlin for a meeting with then Soviet Foreign

Minister Eduard Shevardnadze. Dear intended to discuss the Prisoners of Zion issue with Shevardnadze and other government officials, and raise the possibility of opening the gates of the Soviet Union for Jewish immigration to Israel. Recalling my previous, unsuccessful, visit, I decided that it was worth another attempt, particularly if this would be conducted openly and officially, with the participation of a publicly elected American such as Noach Dear.

This time, I decided to include my wife Sara in the Moscow visit. In the course of preparations for the trip, I came to the conclusion that this was the perfect time to add Poland to the itinerary and return to my native Pultusk, the city from which my family had been expelled forty-eight years earlier.

We were ready for the journey and our passports were stamped with visas to Poland and Russia. We had agreed to meet Noach Dear in Moscow, and from there I intended to continue with Sara to Poland. We flew from New York to London, where I visited my friend Robert Maxwell, who invited Sara and me for dinner at his house.

At our host's home, we discussed at length our planned visit to Moscow and Poland. Maxwell told us that he had just finished writing his book, in which he describes his history and that of his family in Europe during World War Two. In recent years, he had begun to discover his Jewish roots. It turned out that he had been a member of the Zionist movement Beitar, which was active at the time in his native city Solotvino, in what was then Czechoslovakia. Maxwell also informed us of his decision to cultivate his ties with Israel and invest in the country.

In addition to the meeting he had arranged with Foreign Minister Shevardnadze, the tycoon asked his representatives in Moscow to arrange for me to visit Alexander Lebed, the military man whom I had met during my first Moscow visit. Maxwell pointed out that Lebed would certainly be happy to see me, as he had been very impressed with me when we first met in 1974.

We left London on a British Airways flight and, upon landing, were transferred to a passenger terminal for passport control. This was the same old terminal I had encountered in 1974, but this time, unlike my previous visit, I was subject to strict interrogation. I was asked why I had traveled to Moscow and who had arranged the visa. I responded that I had come with my wife to visit the city, and had gotten my visa lawfully from the Russian consulate in New York. Fearing that this would complicate things, I did not mention the planned visit with Shevardnadze. After prolonged questioning, I was finally allowed to leave for the city.

We stayed at the Savoy Hotel in the center of Moscow. I took Sara on a tour of the city's famous sites, and the next day went to visit the Chief Rabbi of Moscow, Rabbi Avraham Shayevich. The rabbi welcomed me warmly at the Great Synagogue and recalled our 1974 meeting.

While talking with the rabbi, I noticed that it was freezing cold in the synagogue. I asked why they hadn't turned on the heat, and the rabbi explained that they lacked the funds to replace the main boiler, which was out of service. I offered to donate the money to purchase a new one, and the rabbi was very happy to accept. A new heating system was installed that same day.

Rabbi Shayevich inquired as to the reason for my visit. I answered that I was interested in getting a list of all the Jewish prisoners in order to work towards their release. My host was afraid to do this for reasons that were understandable at the time, but in the end, he agreed to cooperate. This time, I felt that my visit to the synagogue had accomplished something for the local Jews.

When the time came to meet with Foreign Minister Shevardnadze, I went to the Kremlin with City Councilman Noach Dear. After undergoing a brief interrogation, we were taken to the guest room, where we awaited our host. The minister arrived after a few minutes, shook our hands and welcomed us. I spoke with him in Russian.

The foreign minister took an interest in my origins. I gave him a brief account of my experiences during World War Two – my many wanderings throughout Russia until I reached Kutaisi. Shevardnadze interrupted me and exclaimed that he was from Kutaisi! He asked what years we were there and how long we had stayed. I replied that, in my estimation, we had been there for several months until the end of the war in May 1945. I mentioned that I had positive memories of that period because we were treated so warmly by the Jewish community there, as well as by the authorities and the military stationed there at the time.

For the remainder of the meeting, though, we were the ones who asked the questions. I bluntly asked the minister why the Jewish prisoners were not being released. He responded that the government was currently working on a plan to free them very soon, and that President Gorbachev himself was monitoring the situation.

With Foreign Minister Shevardnadze and Councilman Noach Dear in Moscow

After the meeting with Shevardnadze, I analyzed his comments with Noach Dear. We concluded that the prisoner issue was, indeed, on the Soviets' agenda. It seemed that the demonstrations and the international pressure had been effective, and we were sure that we would hear further developments soon.

We left Moscow and flew to Warsaw on a Russian airline. Sensing my emotions, Sara tried to distract me with other topics. On the way, I tried to search my memory for every bit of information about Pultusk and about my family. I wanted to recall things I had heard from Father and my sisters over the years and add them to the puzzle I had constructed in my imagination. Unfortunately, many details were missing and the picture was incomplete. Various documents, letters and photographs that would generally be preserved from one generation to the next had been destroyed, eradicated as if they had never existed. I tried to remain calm, organize my thoughts and focus on the little that I knew.

My father had told me that he had been born in Pultusk to a family of cattle traders, as had been my grandfather, Chaim Yankel Domb. From what I understood from my conversations with Father, our family had always lived in Pultusk. Grandfather Yaakov, a forward-thinking person with broad horizons, had married Hinda Leah née Luschitz, my grandmother. They had six children, four boys and two girls, all born in Pultusk. From my father, Avraham Domb, I had heard little about his father's family. It was a completely Jewish household, whose family had integrated well with Jewish life in the city.

Cultural life was advanced in the Pultusk community, and the community produced famous authors, poets and rabbis who published well-known *halachic* (religious legal) decisions and essays of great Jewish significance. Accounts I have read recently indeed confirm that the community boasted a rich Jewish culture. Local Jews co-existed fully with the Poles; Jewish merchants lived peacefully and undisturbed alongside Polish farmers.

My father grew up in the town and married my mother, Rivka née Mermelstein, who, to the best of my knowledge, had been born in Ukraine. Father had related that Mother had nine siblings. Her parents, Gittel and Yankel Mermelstein, lived in Ukraine. Mother was murdered in cold blood, and almost her entire family was also killed in the Holocaust – no one survived except for her brother, my uncle Aryeh Mermelstein, who immigrated to Israel after the Holocaust. It is difficult to put into writing the hell that Ukrainian Jews went through; although the horror stories of persecution, torture, slaughter and destruction wrought by the Germans, with the active cooperation of the Ukrainians themselves, have been recorded in thousands of documents.

The liquidation of Ukrainian Jewry was an extremely savage process. It commenced with Nazi-encouraged pogroms carried out by Ukrainians in collaboration with the Germans immediately after the Russians retreated. The Nazis stormed into Ukraine and conquered it in 1941, bringing about the extermination of all its Jewish communities. All the history I know of my mother's family is summarized in the above lines. It will be recalled that the Germans murdered my mother right in front of me, during the deportation from Pultusk in September 1939.

Father lived with Mother in Pultusk, in our house on Warszawska Street, where my three sisters – Ita, Sara and Zipporah – and I were born. Father worked as a grain merchant, and maintained close ties with many farmers in the area, for he traded with merchants in towns near Pultusk. He traveled a lot for business to Warsaw, Bialystok and other distant cities. My grandparents did not survive the Holocaust, dying, as mentioned in an earlier chapter, from hunger and cold in Arkhangelsk. My father's other brothers, who had been expelled from Pultusk, endured the same saga of wandering as we did. Some survived and immigrated to Israel after the Holocaust.

Throughout the flight, visions of events I had experienced as a child kept coming to mind. A rising wave of incidents passed before my eyes, chief among them the images of my sisters in their youth, SS-uniformed Nazis, Russian soldiers, trains, lines of refugees, planes spitting fire and dismembered bodies. I was unable to bring this flood of memories to a halt....

The pilot's voice informing us of our imminent landing interrupted my thoughts, jolting me back to reality. After we were done with passport control, we took a taxi to the hotel. I hired a local guide, Pultusk born and bred, to take us around my native city. On the way, we passed the Warsaw train station and I asked the driver to stop. The place had not changed much.

"Father met Leah here. I remember this place. The station was jam-packed with tens of thousands of refugees. All the buildings around us had been totally demolished and Russian tanks surrounded the place," I explained to Sara, pointing to a corner of the station building.

The guide added details of Warsaw's post-war recovery and we continued on our trip to Pultusk. The city appeared astounding in its beauty: as in days gone by, one of the tributaries of the Narew River bisected the city, and bridges spanned its banks. Steeped in green, the city was surrounded by forests and pasture lands. I asked the guide to take us to Warszawska Street. I was overcome with emotion. Sara was by my side the whole time, making sure that I kept drinking water.

"Here is the house!" I shouted, pointing to a two-storied building. "Here is where I was born. From here we were deported in September 1939."

I stood with Sara in front of the house for a long time. I tried to reconstruct the route of the terror-filled march to the public park, where, not far away, near the bridge, my mother had been murdered. I asked the guide to take us to that park. Fortunately, he was an expert in the area's history. On the way to the park near the bridge that led to Wyszków, he showed us where the city's Jews had lived, where the synagogue – of which there was now no remnant – had been located. I stood there, overcome with emotion. In my eyes as a child, the park had seemed back then like a huge soccer field….

"Here, thousands of the town's residents were packed together before deportation. Here we endured a thorough search by the Germans, who beat us and humiliated us. In this area, they murdered my mother in cold blood," I told Sara.

My account moved Sara very much. For long minutes, we stood in the park facing the bridge on which we had marched into the hell of war. The guide showed us the memorial that the Poles had erected in memory of the Jews murdered here.

I asked the guide if he was familiar with the spot in the forest where the Germans had murdered the Jews of Pultusk and he immediately replied in the affirmative. He informed us that the location was well-known; dozens of Jews were buried there and a memorial had been set up in their memory.

We drove to the edge of the forest and the guide pointed to the place where the slaughter had occurred.

"Here is where I stood among the rows of the murdered. From here I fled with another boy, and it is thanks to him that I am alive today," I told Sara, translating my comments for the Polish guide.

We returned to the center of Pultusk. The city had undergone many changes during the fifty-plus years since the deportation. The picture I had painted in my imagination differed totally from what I now witnessed. The spirit of the vibrant Jewish town had disappeared as if it never was, and had been replaced by a secular atmosphere. Streets that had once bustled with masses of Jews were empty and seemed desolate, as if the city had eroded. But its current tranquil appearance could not banish from memory the volcano that had erupted in 1939, spewing its molten lava of hatred and evil into the heart of the city.

I asked the guide to take us to the municipality, where I intended to ask for a copy of my birth certificate. I owned no document that even testified to my birth, let alone to details of date and place. In the building, I presented myself to a clerk as a Jew who had been born in the town, and requested a copy of the birth certificate. I spoke to her in English. To my surprise, she treated me rudely and raised her voice at me. Then I reprimanded her in Polish: "There are no Jews here anymore, but your behavior indicates that anti-Semitism apparently still exists!"

One of the clerks who heard me – apparently a senior staff member, perhaps the mayor himself – emerged from his office to see what was going on. I explained:

"I am an American citizen, a tourist with a valid visa. I met the Polish consul in New York, who promised to help me obtain my birth certificate. If I am not taken care of properly, I will complain to the Polish ambassador in the United States."

The clerk apologized for the behavior of his colleague, calmed me down and said that my request would be honored. He referred me to another clerk to whom I gave my New York address, along with a $10 tip, equal to a month's salary at that time. She winked at me and promised to tend to my application immediately.

Upon my return to New York, I received a letter from the Pultusk municipality with the birth certificate.

I returned to Pultusk several times after that first visit with Sara. One of those trips was in 1988, with my sons Ron and Jay who had asked to go on a "roots trip." They were very moved by this journey, which exposed them to an important chapter in the history of the family and of the Jewish nation. This time, I was familiar with the place and all its sites.

My third visit was in 2008, with my life partner Orly Gal.

Chapter 24

In the Depths of American Politics
(Encounters with Leaders and Heads of State)

"Ask not what your country can do for you,
Ask what you can do for your country."

John F. Kennedy

My daily routine in New York encompassed many areas. Above and beyond the expanding world of my business, I became more deeply involved in pro-Israel politics in America. I sought every means of reaching the decision-makers in Washington in order to influence them to assist Israel and our people, in the United States and worldwide.

The telephones in my office did not stop ringing and my desk was piled with numerous invitations to events, both of a local political nature and also those organized by Jewish and Israeli institutions. One particularly intriguing call came from an old friend, a famous New York lawyer. He asked me to participate in a private meeting in his office with an old friend of his who was running for the presidency of the United States. This was in 1992, when Republican President George Bush (Sr.) was in the White House.

I had a very full agenda that day, with many business meetings scheduled. However, not wanting to disappoint my friend, I showed up at his office as requested. A young man named William Jefferson Clinton was present. He introduced himself as the governor of Arkansas and a candidate for the presidency of the United States. Speaking freely and with a great deal of charm, he demonstrated vast expertise with respect to many issues – both domestic and foreign. He also elaborated on his commitment to the security of the State of Israel, and said that he would act vigorously to advance the peace process.

My friend referred to his guest as "Bill" and posed several questions to him. Afterwards, he introduced me to him, emphasizing my involvement in the New York Jewish community and my close ties with leaders in Israel.

In a long discussion with Clinton, I made it clear that I would support anyone who acted in the interests of Israel's security and would assist the Jewish people. Clinton promised that he could be relied on, adding emphatically that he was a good and loyal friend of Israel and the Jewish people, and that his commitment stemmed from a profound recognition of Israel's right to exist in peace and security. In this context, he recounted the promise he had made to the clergyman of his church, that he would never abandon Israel and would look after its security. It was obvious to me that the next president of the United States stood before me.

I indeed ended up contributing significant sums to Clinton's campaign and recruiting many of my friends to help him. After winning the Democratic nomination, he campaigned hard for the national vote. Running against him were the incumbent George Bush and the independent candidate Ross Perot. In what turned out to be a particularly stormy election, Clinton succeeded in defeating his rivals and winning the presidency. His election ended twelve consecutive years of Republican rule in the White House.

The new president did not forget my active efforts to secure his election. Besides thanking me, he invited me to attend his inauguration ceremony in Washington, where I was seated in the VIP section, along with many leaders from throughout the United States. Politicians keenly on the alert introduced themselves to me and asked for my business card, aware that my seat among the notables testified to my close ties with the president and that a connection with me would prove worth their while.

In my first meeting with him as president, Clinton reiterated his commitment to Israel's security, emphasizing that the issue was at the top of his agenda. During this period I arranged many meetings for friends who wanted to contribute to the Democratic Party, and obtained invitations for them to White House events. These friends included, among others: the late businessman Manfred Lehmann; Jack Avital, president of the Syrian community in the United States; and Jewish community activist Jack Kassin. Another interesting meeting I coordinated was for the head of the Belarus parliament.

Clinton was very well-liked in Israel. His popularity and warmth towards Israel were evident not only in his speeches, but in practice, too, in his policies and his intensive involvement in the peace process. He was the force that drove King Hussein to sign a peace agreement with Israel, and, together with Prime Minister Yitzhak Rabin and Jordanian King Hussein bin Talal, was present at the signing ceremony in the Aravah on October 26, 1994.

The assassination of Prime Minister Rabin shocked the entire world. Everyone wondered how such a terrible crime could be committed by a Jewish murderer. I had been introduced to Yitzhak Rabin by my friend Fuad Ben-Eliezer during one of my trips to Israel, when Rabin was Minister of Defense. In previous chapters I have already described my admiration for military people. For me, Rabin was "Mr. Security," the architect of the victory in the Six Day War. While I did not always agree with his policies as prime minister, from the moment he was elected he was my prime minister and that of my country, the State of Israel. The despicable act that caused the death of a prime minister in Israel cannot be forgiven and cannot be atoned for. As a Jew, I felt obligated to publicize these sentiments and I published obituaries that expressed my feelings in American and Israeli newspapers, receiving many supportive responses.

One day, Maxwell's oldest son Kevin, with whom I had become friendly after his father's tragic death, phoned me from England. He told me about a Russian businessman named Gregory Luchansky, who had great political influence in Russia, Ukraine and Kazakhstan. Kevin requested that I try to obtain an invitation to the White House for Luchansky. I was indeed able to arrange for him to be invited to a White House event during one of his trips to the United States.

Luchansky introduced himself to President Clinton as a businessman from Russia and my personal friend. He explained that he was in the United States in order to buy $200 million worth of advanced agricultural equipment for Ukraine. The president commended his guest's investment in the United States, adding that such a transaction stimulated industry and employment in America while simultaneously assisting agricultural development in Ukraine.

At this opportunity, President Clinton mentioned to Luchansky that the United States had encountered difficulties in persuading Ukraine to participate in the nuclear disarmament program that was being formed. Luchansky commented that the Ukrainian president, Leonid Kravchuk, was his long-time personal friend with whom he frequently met. The short conversation ended with a cordial handshake.

Several weeks after the meeting with President Clinton, I received a phone call from Gregory Luchansky, who was in Vienna. He asked me meet with him and Ukrainian President Kravchuk regarding the issue of nuclear disarmament. I responded that since I held no official position, I was not authorized to discuss national issues on behalf of the United States. He explained that this would not be an official meeting, and that President Kravchuk was his personal friend and would be happy to meet me. After deliberating and consulting with various people, I decided to accept the invitation.

I flew to Vienna and from there, we continued to the Ukrainian city of Kiev in Luchansky's private plane. Kevin Maxwell also joined us on this trip. In our meeting with the president, Luchansky relayed President Clinton's complaint about being unable to come to an arrangement with Ukraine on the subject of nuclear disarmament. Smiling, President Kravchuk remarked that the problem could be resolved, but that it depended on the compensation offered his country in exchange for signing this agreement. He asked if I could transmit this message to President Clinton. My response was a resounding "no." I explained that my capacity on this visit was that of a tourist and that no one had authorized me to deliver formal messages to government officials.

The president smiled again and suggested that we sit down to lunch. After the meal, he repeated: "I will give you a letter, which I request that you give to President Clinton." I asked him why he chose not to utilize the accepted official channels, namely via the ambassador. The president explained that the most successful diplomatic messages he knew of were relayed via private individuals like myself, not through formal diplomacy.

We continued in Luchansky's private plane from Kiev to Kazakhstan, landing in a town called Kostanay near Siberia, a city that led the Soviet Union in iron production. It was freezing there, with temperatures reaching -4°F, and I was not dressed properly for this weather. A military convoy awaited us near the plane and took us to a meeting with President Nursultan Nazarbayev of Kazakhstan.

Luchansky once again raised the same issues as he had with President Kravchuk. Here, too, the president invited us to a meal, after which he handed me a letter for President Clinton. I repeated my reservations to him too, pointing out that such a mission should be conducted through formal channels, since I definitely do not represent the United States or its president. Again, my objections were to no avail.

Our return flight to Vienna took seven and a half hours; from there I flew back to the United States. Upon landing in New York, I contacted a government official in Washington, informing him that I had two letters in my possession for the American president – from the presidents of Ukraine and of Kazakhstan. I received a phone call that same day from a woman in the White House named Nancy Sutherland, who informed me that two FBI agents were on their way to pick up the letters from me.

After several months, the agreement between the United States and Ukraine on the nuclear issue was signed. I was eventually told that President Kravchuk's letter mentioned that the assistance of a New York Jewish community leader was more useful than the activities of experienced diplomats.

Shortly afterwards, reports flooded the American media saying that President Clinton had hosted Gregory Luchansky, a well-known arms dealer and KGB agent, at the White House. A photograph including Luchansky, Clinton and me appeared in the newspapers and on television.

The next day, when I left my apartment building on Central Park West, awaiting me were vehicles from the television networks, replete with reporters and cameramen clamoring for an interview. I refused and continued to my office at the Travel Inn hotel on 42nd Street, where I found CBS journalist Mike Wallace with his crew, also wishing to talk with me. Although I declined, they insisted on remaining there. Their presence disturbed the hotel staff and I was forced to call the police to evict them.

My conclusion from these events was that diplomatic practices in Eastern Europe were far from the norm. Furthermore, even if it was true that Luchansky was a major arms dealer, no one could deny that he helped the president of the United States sign a nuclear disarmament agreement with Kazakhstan and Ukraine.

Eventually I was also able to establish ties between Luchansky and the State of Israel via Minister Fuad Ben-Eliezer, who invited him to visit. I did not participate in his meetings there and have no information about their outcome.

My business and political activities brought me to visit many countries throughout the world, and to fascinating meetings with leaders, prime ministers and presidents. Some of these took place as part of my work in the Conference of Presidents of Major American Jewish Organizations (a Jewish-Zionist organization based in New York). The Conference of Presidents represents about fifty key Jewish organizations that work to coordinate positions vis à vis the American administration, the Israeli government and other government institutions.

Heading this umbrella organization until his death in 1986 was Yehuda Hellman. Since then, it has been led by my friend Malcom Hoenlein as Executive Vice Chairman. Every so often, the organization convenes in Israel and holds political meetings with presidents and prime ministers in various countries.

One interesting meeting took place in Cairo, in a visit to Egyptian President Hosni Mubarak's palace. It was fascinating to

With Egyptian President Hosni Mubarak and members of the Conference of Presidents at the Cairo palace

observe the functioning of the president's team of staff and how he managed them, as well as the security and hosting arrangements.

President Mubarak received us in a special guest hall and gave a speech about the importance of peace in the Middle East. He stressed the need to advance the negotiations with the Palestinians and pointed out that a peace arrangement would bring calm to the entire Middle East. When he concluded, he agreed to respond to two questions, one of them mine.

I told the president that I had read an article in New York about the ancient synagogue in Cairo that served the few Jews left in the city. The article mentioned that the synagogue's roof was falling apart and that rainwater leaked into the building in the winter. I asked: Why does His Honor, the President, not issue an order to repair the facility? The president responded that there was nothing to prevent this, and suggested that I fix the building with my own money.

With Jordan's King Hussein bin Talal at a New York event in his honor

In 1995, I participated in a visit arranged by the Conference of Presidents in Qatar. In this emirate, "supreme power" is granted to the ruling Emir, who answers to no one. There are no elections in Qatar and political parties are prohibited. At the time of our visit, Qatar was ruled by Sheikh Hamad bin Khalifa, who had deposed his father several months earlier in a quiet, bloodless coup.

We met Emir bin Khalifa in his magnificent palace. He addressed us, citing the openness in his country, emphasizing the commitment to a solution to the conflict with the Palestinians and expressing hope that peace would reign throughout the Middle East.

We toured Qatar and observed the wealth and prosperity enjoyed by its residents. What struck me most was the contrast between the poor living conditions of millions in Egypt and the abundant riches the Arabs of Qatar. The revolution led by Emir bin Khalifa broadened the freedom of the press; the Al-Jazeera television station operating there has gained a world-wide reputation.

I visited the royal palace in Amman twice, meeting King Hussein bin Talal during my first visit. The bond between us began in October 1995, during a festive dinner hosted in his honor by New York Mayor Rudolf Giuliani. The event took place during a period in which Giuliani refused to invite Yasser Arafat, claiming that he did not host terrorists.

Giuliani seated me during the dinner at the same table as King Hussein and his wife. During the course of the event, the mayor praised me and introduced me to the king as a Jewish activist in New York and as a successful businessman. At the evening's close, King Hussein invited me to Jordan and asked his aide to get my address. Several days later, I received a formal invitation from the king, via the Jordanian Ambassador to the United Nations, Hasan Abu Nimah.

On a particularly hot morning, I flew to Amman. Royal staff waited for me at the airport. I was treated with the respect accorded important guests of the king, and was taken to my meeting with him at the palace. The king was in good health then, showing no signs of the disease from which he later was to suffer. He was in an excellent mood and inquired about Giuliani, apparently aware of our close relationship.

The king took an interest in my businesses, and inquired as to which was the primary one. I explained that I specialized mainly in the hotel industry and owned several hotels in New York. He mentioned that tourism was an important issue for him and that peace between Israel and Jordan could advance tourism in his country. He told me about Aqaba and its development, suggesting that I build a hotel there.

During our conversation, the king asked me where I was born. I told him that I was a Holocaust survivor, and related to him briefly my childhood history under Nazi occupation. He sat open-mouthed as he listened to my story. I added that I had served as a soldier in the IDF when it fought against his army. I commented that now, however, I was happy to be sitting next to a wise, courageous king who had signed a peace agreement with Israel. The king smiled and, extending his hand in parting, said that he was happy to have met such a good and interesting man as myself, and asked me to give his regards to Mayor Giuliani.

My second visit to the Jordanian royal palace was with members of the Conference of Presidents. This time, we met with Hussein's son, King Abdullah II. He addressed us, saying that he was continuing his late father's policy on the issue of peace. He spoke about the Palestinian problem, pointing out that it was important to accelerate the peace process and find a solution to the conflict.

Refreshments were offered after the speech, and we were permitted to ask two questions. I raised my hand and the king nodded his head and pointed to me. I got up and asked the king:

"His Majesty spoke a great deal about the importance of peace and the need to resolve the Israeli-Palestinian conflict. Therefore, how does His Highness explain the fact that in geography classes at the Palestinian school in Abu Dis, teachers show pupils a map on which Israel does not appear at all?"

Unprepared for my question, the king replied in his fluent English:

"This is a tough one!"

He explained that this was, indeed, a tricky question, and that it would require many years of education and public diplomacy until the Palestinians might understand that Israel is a *fait accompli*. My question and the king's response were broadcast on television and radio news programs in both Jordan and Israel, and a longer article also appeared in *The Jerusalem Post*.

My long-time friend Jack Avital works tirelessly on many volunteer projects. His concern for those in need knows no bounds. He has supported the Syrian-Jewish and Moroccan-Jewish communities and their affiliated organizations in New York for many years. Among his other public positions, he heads the New York committee of activists of Moroccan descent, through which many meetings take place with public leaders and personalities visiting the city.

Jack Avital invited me, together with the committee of activists of Moroccan descent, to meet Moroccan King Hassan II during one of his visits to New York. The king proudly noted that Jews under his leadership enjoyed a peaceful and good life. Like other Arab rulers I had met, he also spoke about the importance of achieving peace in the Middle East, for the benefit of all countries in the region.

I must admit that every meeting with a king from the Arab world – certainly not the norm for an Israeli – was a moving and special experience for me. The ceremonies, the royal etiquette and manner together with the unique atmosphere always left me with an unforgettable feeling.

Another interesting visit, also with the Conference of Presidents, was to Tashkent in early March 1997, to meet with president of Uzbekistan Islam Karimov. The purpose of the trip was to encourage and strengthen commercial and diplomatic ties between Israel and Uzbekistan. I was asked to speak at the meeting, which was held at the American embassy, with the participation of President Karimov. I thanked the president and the American ambassador for hosting us, and also expressed gratitude to President Karimov's – and my – friend, Boris David Kandow, an Uzbek native now living in Vienna, for his valued assistance to the Jews of Uzbekistan. In my remarks, I also singled out Boris's father, who had

With members of the Conference of Presidents. To my right, Boris Kandow; to my left, Ron Lauder. March 1997

helped incoming Jewish refugees during the Holocaust.

In January 2000, I was appointed observer-monitor of the elections in Uzbekistan. My life partner, Orly Gal, also joined me during this visit. After it became clear that President Karimov had been reelected, I was invited to a celebratory toast at the president's residence together with our mutual friend Boris David Kandow. My friend Boris was received with well-deserved honor.

In light of Boris's contributions, his ceaseless activities on behalf of the Jews of Uzbekistan and his vigorous efforts to advance the community's interests with the authorities, he was viewed by everyone as a prominent Jewish leader. As mentioned, community activism had long characterized the Kandow family. Boris's father, Hananel Kandow, had already earned public admiration during World War Two, when Jewish refugees began to stream into Uzbekistan after escaping the claws of the Nazis. It was the Kandow family that opened its heart and harnessed the resources to absorb the penniless Jews arriving in the host country.

In 2005, a large conference was held in Vienna, attended by representatives of Jewish communities from all over Europe. Rabbi Yisrael Meir Lau, who, like me, was a child survivor of the Holocaust, honored us with his presence and delivered a moving speech. Also participating in the event were members of the ZAKA organization in Israel, known for its sacred work in identifying victims of terror attacks. I addressed the forum, emphasizing the importance of memorializing the events of the Holocaust as a lesson for the Jewish people and for all of humanity.

Chapter 25

Sara

*"Many women have done well,
but you surpass them all."*

Proverbs, 31:29

My life saga has been filled with quite a few painful partings, but the most painful of all was my parting from the love of my life, my wife and the mother of my children, Sara.

Her untimely departure from our lives was unbearable. Sara was an inseparable part of my very being and essence. Our children had a particularly difficult time dealing with their heavy loss, because the relationship they had with their mother was much deeper than that of most mothers and children.

Sara's life story began in the Yemenite city of Sana'a, where she was born to her parents, Shalom and Yonah Siri. She was the scion of a respected rabbinical dynasty: her maternal grandfather was the Chief Rabbi of Yemen. Born in 1937, Sara immigrated to Israel with her parents in 1944. The family covered a significant part of the journey from Yemen to the Holy Land by foot, in an exhausting trek.

Upon arrival in Israel, the family lived in temporary housing on the edge of Raanana. They eventually built their house in the "Yemenite neighborhood" established in the city. Sara's father, Rabbi Shalom Siri, was devoted to his Torah studies and at the same time earned a living doing agricultural work. Together with her siblings – Avraham, Zechariah, Danny, Moshe, Orah and Zion – she grew up in a household that strictly observed Jewish tradition, while integrating into the developing life of the State of Israel.

I have related the story of my chance encounter with Sara in earlier chapters. I was strongly attracted to her gentle shyness. Beginning with that meeting on the main road in Raanana, between our respective homes in Ahuzah Street and the Yemenite neighborhood, our relationship strengthened and deepened. The flames of love ignited between us continued to burn without flickering until the day Sara ascended to Heaven.

Throughout all my periods of absence – in my army service and while on my national mission abroad – my thoughts were with Sara. In those days, means of communication were few and almost impossible. We exchanged numerous letters –whenever we had the opportunity. Unfortunately, the letters were not saved.

Later, after we were married and were building our home in the United States, I sought every possible way to provide Sara and our children with the happiness they deserved. Like every married life, ours had its ups and downs, particularly as a result of the difficulties in adjusting to, and earning a living in, a new country. However, we always found our way to overcome obstacles and were careful to ensure that these would not negatively impact our lives together or the children's education.

Together we raised our three children Ron, Jay and Michelle. Sara was in their lives on a day-to-day basis, showering them with endless warmth and love. For them, she was not only a devoted mother, but a true friend. Her ears were open to every request and every problem, and even after the children matured and became independent, they still asked her advice and listened to her wise words.

Sara will be remembered as a beautiful woman with green eyes, wise, diligent, dedicated and loving. She had a charming and dominant personality, evident both in our extended family circle as well as in community activities. She made sure to fill her life with positive and creative activity dedicated to both our local community and also our beloved country, Israel. She was an active volunteer for various groups in numerous fields. I particularly remember her attending countless meetings of the Association for the Wellbeing of Israel's Soldiers, and utilizing all her energy and talents to collect donations for the welfare of IDF soldiers in times of war and peace alike.

Sara gave utmost priority to the subject of education. She was a full partner, in terms of responsibility and influence, in all our children's schooling. It was only natural to see her as a member of the schools' PTA, as president of the Solomon Schechter school, as well as taking her place on that school's boards of directors. In this, she served as an excellent role model for many, while at the same time being an outstanding mother and wife.

Her external beauty testified to her inner sensitivity and mirrored her talents. We valued her wisdom, her honesty and her loyalty. She knew how to navigate our family's life even during stormy times, demonstrating profound personal strength and an ability to "proceed as normal" despite the emotional burden. She always appeared energetic, full of life and imbued with faith.

I was blessed with a talented wife, devoted to me, our family, her friends and her fellow Jews. In our life together, Sara proved to be a noble-minded and generous partner, with qualities that words cannot encompass. Above all, she taught me to see the world from her point of view.

One of Sara's fundamental and prominent characteristics was helping others. She knew how to listen and be a true friend, lending a shoulder to her friends and displaying rare magnanimity to anyone in need. Sara had many friends who always wanted to be close to her due to the kindheartedness, warmth and serenity she exuded. They saw her as a *Kotel*, a "Wailing Wall", where they could pour out their troubles and receive advice.

Among Sara's many friends were Shoshana Damari and Lily Sharon, who made a point of visiting her when they came to the United States. Leah Rabin also became friendly with her during Yitzhak Rabin's tenure as ambassador in Washington, in the former's frequent visits to New York. Moreover, Sara participated in activities at the Israeli Consulate in New York, and was a member of its cultural committee.

Sara enveloped our house in joy and happiness. She remembered every birthday, turning each into a real occasion. The house took on a festive air during Shabbat and holidays, and the unique atmosphere she created led to an unforgettably pleasant experience. Her culinary skills were known far and wide. Various VIP guests also dined at our table – Israeli prime ministers, ministers, Knesset members, chief rabbis, American Congress members and mayors.

Sara was fortunate enough to know her oldest granddaughter, Morielle, our son Jay's daughter, upon whom she showered all good things. None was more delighted than she when we had Morielle over at our house. Sadly, however, she did not live to see her other three grandchildren – Michelle's children Adam and Sara, and Jay's son Tomer.

From the moment when she first took sick in 1991, Sara fought her illness valiantly, until she passed away. Throughout her illness and all of the treatments, she radiated optimism and "business as usual," as only she knew how. The concept of defeat did not exist in her lexicon. She struggled fiercely against her disease, coped with the day-to-day difficulties that were part and parcel of the heavy treatments she had to endure and, deep in her heart, hoped to recover.

Even in the last days of her life, Sara appeared poised and well-groomed, exhibiting grace, charm and dignity. The permanent smile never left her face, even during those difficult hours. But in the end the disease conquered her, and she left us in the early morning hours of July 29, 1992.

We brought Sara to Israel for burial. Waiting for her at the aircraft's ramp were Arik Sharon and Gershon Stav. She was buried in the "Yemenite section" of *Har HaMenuhot* in Jerusalem. It was a stately funeral.

Numerous friends and relatives came to take leave of her, as well as many members of the upper political echelons in Israel, including Arik Sharon, Ehud Olmert, Binyamin Netanyahu and Fuad Ben-Eliezer.

The unveiling was conducted by then Chief Rabbi of Israel, Rabbi Yisrael Meir Lau. Aside from family members, countless others came to pay their last respects to Sara.

Just as she entered my life with serenity and grace, so did she part from the family and me to the next world. We were left bearing deep pain, utter sadness and endless yearning.

Sara Domb

Chapter 26

Arik – Leadership and Friendship

"Lo, a people that rises like a lion,
leaps up like the king of beasts."

Numbers 23:24

"Come, let us sit down on a rock and reflect on our memories of Sara," suggested Ariel Sharon. We were visiting my wife Sara's grave at the end of the seven-day mourning period, and we were alone. His faithful chauffer, Gilbért, awaited him in his car, while Arik and I sat silently on the slope of a hill in *Har HaMenuhot*, not far from Sara's grave. We took in the Jerusalem scenery and soaked up its clear air.

It was early evening, with the sun beginning to set in the West. A light breeze slightly cooled the *Tammuz* heat. We sat on that rock for quite a while. Suddenly, Arik broke the silence:

"She was a very special and noble woman. Lily loved her friend dearly. Her absence will be deeply felt, she will be sorely missed. You've endured many tragedies in your life, and this is a particularly difficult loss for you and the children; but you will overcome this, you're a strong man. Life has toughened you."

Such was Arik the friend: sharing your sorrow and with you in your difficult moments. Not in a closed room, not in a bustling office, but here, in the heart of nature, surrounded by hills and pine trees, overlooking the spectacular Jerusalem scenery. I reflected for a moment on how different the true Arik was from the image generated by the media: full of warmth and love, a nature lover, and expressing, in his unique way, true friendship.

These were unforgettable moments that shall remain locked

within my heart forever.

Eight years later, I found myself led by Arik up to "Anemones Hill" and standing together with him at the fresh grave of his beloved wife Lily. She had been buried there just a few days earlier.

Again, that same twilight hour in the heart of nature, on a lovely hill. Arik was heartbroken from the pain of his heavy loss. Inwardly, I comprehended, how difficult was his parting from Lily. To him, she was far more than a wife. We stood by her grave in contemplation for a long time, surrounded by a sea of flowers. And again, that same ongoing silence. This time, I broke it, whispering to Arik:

"I want to remind you of what you told me in our conversation on that rock, at the foot of Sara's grave. 'You are a strong man and will overcome this.' "

Arik did not utter a word. On the way back to the ranch, we passed by the giant tent in which he had received the tens of thousands of condolence callers from all over the country and the far ends of the

Sharing a confidence with Ariel Sharon

Sara with Lily and Arik Sharon at a Jerusalem meeting

world. Upon entering his house, we sat down in the area where we usually sat during my visits to the ranch. I recalled the many hours we had spent together, with Lily serving us her delicacies.

Before I left, Arik came over to me and with his hand on my shoulder, said:

"Thank you. I wanted you to know – I remember every minute of that conversation of ours."

I sensed a deep sadness in his voice. We had maintained phone contact throughout the period of Lily's illness, and I had detected the sorrow in his voice at her suffering; though in his media appearances, which I followed, I had noticed no outward indication of his inner torment. He functioned well as the head of the Likud, as the unmistakable opposition leader to then Prime Minister Ehud Barak. Apart from his close friends, no one had an inkling of the rough time he was having.

In early April 2000, I returned to my routine in New York. In the following months, leading up to Arik's September visit to New York, our phone conversations became more and more frequent and took on a personal character. In every conversation, he mentioned his disappointment with Barak's performance as Prime Minister. Arik traveled a lot throughout Israel in this period, appearing wherever possible. His position as head of the Likud and as its prime ministerial candidate occupied his every free moment.

In July 2000, Israel Prime Minister Ehud Barak and Yasser Arafat held summit talks at Camp David, under the watchful eye of United States President Bill Clinton. Arik felt a great deal of concern regarding Barak's numerous concessions to Arafat for the sake of reaching a quick peace agreement "at any cost." Particularly disturbing to him was the Israeli Prime Minister's willingness to surrender sovereignty on the Temple Mount in exchange for sovereignty over the Western Wall. In general, Arik considered any topic related to Jerusalem to be off limits. On more than one occasion, he had publicly and explicitly stated his firm position on the unification of Jerusalem; and he practiced what he preached, establishing his own residence within the walls of the Old City. He worked vigorously to settle as many Jews as possible in the Old City, recruiting me for this purpose as well.

In his letter to me dated March 1989, while serving as Minister of Trade and Industry in the Shamir government, Arik had already thanked me for my activities toward the reclamation of homes in the Old City quarter and populating them with Jews. He also pleaded with me to make every possible effort to house Jews in every room and apartment in the Old City, especially during this difficult period when our enemies had designs on East Jerusalem.

At the summit talks in Camp David, Arafat refused to accept Barak's offer regarding Jerusalem, claiming that no Jewish temple ever stood there. The talks ended in failure. Undeterred, Barak continued talks and communications on the topic of our national holy sites, without approval from the government of Israel and the Knesset.

Barak's willingness to cede the Temple Mount and Arafat's foolish claim led Arik to conclude that some action had to be taken. He searched for a viable way to arouse public opinion in Israel and in the Diaspora concerning the severity of what Barak was about to carry out – to concede what had always been the holiest site for the Jewish nation, throughout its thousands of years in exile and in perpetuity.

During his trip to New York in September 2000, Arik visited me as usual in my home on Central Park South, right near his Park Lane hotel. That same week, he had appeared before the Conference of Presidents and before our friends in the New York Syrian Jewish community. Raising the issue of the Temple Mount, he maintained that surrendering sovereignty there was tantamount to giving up the Old City itself.

We spoke at length in my house. Arik brought up the idea that he himself ascend the Temple Mount and asked what I thought. Recognizing the significance of this issue for the Jewish nation, I immediately answered in the affirmative. I said that he had the right, even the obligation, to take this step, even as a citizen and certainly as a leader of the Jewish people. He needed to stir up public opinion in Israel and abroad with regard to the willingness of a Jewish-Israeli government to relinquish sovereignty on the Temple Mount.

Contrary to what most people believe, Arik did consult with his friends; but the ultimate decision of what action to take was one he made himself. From my house, he phoned several of his friends in Israel and elsewhere, and it became apparent that he had formulated his decision. Before parting, I told him not to hesitate; his going up to the Temple Mount would prove to Arafat that there was no national consensus for Barak's proposals.

On September 28, 2000, Arik ascended the Temple Mount and the next day, Arafat launched the Al-Aqsa Intifada. According to newspapers and other sources, Arafat had made the decision to begin the Intifada many months before Arik stepped foot on the Temple Mount.

Several months later, Arik could be found vigorously preparing for the early February 2001 elections. He surrounded himself with a headquarters team, advisers and public relations people, and also took on Arthur Finkelstein, an American expert on elections. Analysis of polls conducted several weeks prior to the elections indicated that Arik was leading the prime ministerial race against Barak. It turned out that the Israeli public was refusing to buy the slander leveled against him by his Labor party rivals.

Arik sounded optimistic in our phone conversations. I received ongoing updates about the campaign from my friend Gershon Stav. Gershon, too, indicated the presence of a highly positive atmosphere; from his experience, he estimated that there was a good chance that Arik would win. Not wanting to miss this historical moment, I flew to Israel several days before the elections. With the campaign at its peak, the atmosphere in the country was tempestuous and stormy. Posters of Barak and Arik appeared prominently in central locations in the cities.

Accompanied by Gershon, I toured several cities in central Israel and in Tel Aviv's environs in order to receive for myself a direct impression of the atmosphere. Every taxi driver we rode with supported Arik unhesitatingly and we found this encouraging, since taxi drivers are usually a reasonable gauge of the public's state of mind.

On election night, I was invited by Arik to his Tel Aviv hotel to watch the exit polls. A small group of friends was in attendance. At ten o'clock, the television news anchor announced that according to one of the polls, Arik had won by an impressive majority and would apparently become Israel's next Prime Minister. The outbursts of joy among Arik's close friends at that moment were indescribable. Arik, however, did not leave his seat and continued to watch the polling results on the other networks. Observing him, I whispered to Gershon, who was also present: "How sad that Lily did not live to see these moments. I'm sure Arik is having the exact same thought right now."

We all shook hands with the next Prime Minister and happily congratulated him. Phone calls started streaming in from all over the world. Arik, however, refused to get carried away and began already that night the work of forming a coalition. The following day, he paid a visit to his wife Lily's grave and to the Western Wall.

The year 2001, Arik's first as Prime Minister, was accompanied by horrendous terror incidents that took many lives. I recall the night of the slaughter at the Tel Aviv Dolphinarium in early June 2001. It was midnight in Israel when the reports reached America. The pictures broadcast from the scene of the massacre were shocking: twenty-one young people, mostly Russian, were slaughtered. Everyone was certain that Israel would respond to this beastly attack, especially with Ariel Sharon as Prime Minister. But his response was: "Restraint is also strength." I received irate phone calls from friends who knew of my special connection with Arik, asking in fury for the meaning of this non-reaction. Sharon was waiting with a leader's patience for the right moment to take action.

In August, about two months after the Dolphinarium attack, a suicide bomber blew himself up in the Sbarro restaurant, this time in Jerusalem, the Israeli capital. This, too, was a shocking massacre, leaving fifteen dead and many wounded.

Several days later, Arik took the necessary actions. He expelled Arafat's representatives from Orient House and our forces took control of the building, which Palestinians viewed as their bastion of government in Jerusalem. At the same time, Arafat's office in Abu Dis was closed; all archives, containing minutes and other secret material, were confiscated, and all activists expelled. This was a heavy blow to Arafat's prestige and he strove to have the decree annulled. Although Israel was censured by some several European countries, the PLO infrastructure had been removed from Israel's capital.

Arik's second year as Prime Minister was also a bloody one. Arafat violated the Oslo Accords and fanned the flames of the Intifada. American envoys George Tenet and Anthony Zinni tried in vain to find a formula to halt the blood bath. One after another, suicide bombers blew themselves up throughout Israel, causing heavy casualties. After closing down Orient House, Arik decided to isolate and confine Arafat. In December 2001 he initiated a siege of the Muqata (the "Rais's" government building) in Ramallah, from which Arafat did not emerge for about three years.

The capture of the *Karine A* weapons ship, and the proven link between the ship and Arafat and his associates, convinced the Americans that Arafat was no longer a reliable partner and in every respect was "not relevant."

In late March 2002, the Israeli government decided to launch Operation Defensive Shield, a large-scale offensive in Judea and Samaria whose goal was to eliminate terror nests and to capture terrorists and those who dispatch them, including those funding their crimes. During the operation, which lasted until May, the IDF succeeded in curbing the wave of terror and in unequivocally crushing the Palestinian Authority and the terror organizations on the West Bank. Many terrorists were killed or captured. The IDF also succeeded in collecting many documents linking Arafat to terrorism and its funding.

Arik devoted all his time to eradicating terrorism, working tirelessly to capture and kill terrorist leaders. Under the shared threat of terror, his relationship with President Bush was strengthened particularly following the mega-terror attack on the Twin Towers in New York.

I spent the *Succot* holiday of 5763 (late September 2002) in Israel. On *Hol HaMo'ed* (the Intermediate Days), Arik invited me to breakfast in the Prime Minister's Residence in Jerusalem. I was staying at the David Citadel hotel in Mamilla. As usual, I woke up early for *Shaharit* (morning) services at the Western Wall, and from there, with my friend Gershon Stav, hurried to reach the 8:30 am meeting with the Prime Minister. His bureau staff was expecting us and asked that we wait in the living room for the Prime Minister to return from his rounds. I very much appreciated the fact that Arik found time to meet with me despite his full schedule. Arriving after forty-five minutes, he greeted us very warmly, apologized for his lateness and requested that the breakfast table be set for three. He had not eaten anything since he had left in early morning.

Arik asked how I was and recounted his efforts to vanquish terrorism. Between courses, he answered the many phone calls that he received. He spoke about his last meeting with United States President George Bush, who saw eye to eye with him on the war against terrorism; and about isolating Arafat and effectively destroying the Palestinian leadership. The task facing him at the time was to succeed in the Likud primaries and the general elections, scheduled for late January 2003.

I congratulated Arik on his efforts to strengthen Israel's security, and asked him to take care of his health. I related to him that I had fended off complaints by friends who had claimed that he was not doing enough to stop the blood bath in Israel – I had urged them all to trust the Prime Minister who, in his own courageous and steadfast way, would achieve this goal. And so it happened. On the other hand, many others had, in fact, contacted me in order to express support for Sharon in Operation Defensive Shield.

Arik asked Gershon Stav about the situation in the "field." Gershon provided him with a report about the organizations and activists who maintained contact with him, describing their activities geared towards success in the primaries. He also explained that from his conversations with many friends, including mayors and heads of local branches, Arik's position in the "field" appeared to be strong. Gershon suggested investing effort in efficiently organizing the Primary Day itself, including proper distribution of staff in order to assure victory.

The meeting lasted about an hour. We parted cordially, and I wished Arik good luck in the primaries and in the general elections. This was my last meeting with him in Israel.

As expected, Arik defeated Binyamin Netanyahu in the internal elections, becoming the Likud candidate for Prime Minister in the elections to the sixteenth Knesset. I called to congratulate him. He thanked me, saying that the important battle was yet to be waged, against the Labor party. After Barak's retirement, this party was immersed in many internecine struggles. The results of the Labor primaries were unclear, and there were suspicions of forgeries. Ultimately, Haifa Mayor Amram Mitzna succeeded in becoming Labor's prime ministerial candidate.

I followed the results on the night of the elections, January 28, 2003, and received ongoing updates from Gershon Stav. The results came in without much delay. Arik had won an impressive victory, doubling the Likud's power from nineteen Knesset seats to thirty-eight. This constituted the Israeli public's vote of confidence in Arik and his policy. That evening, notwithstanding the insults and accusations of alleged corruption leveled against him and his family, Arik was crowned as leader. His political and military approaches were endorsed by the nation. That very evening, I congratulated him on his remarkable success.

That entire day, the telephones in my office did not stop ringing throughout . Friends and politicians, rabbis and community leaders – everyone wanted to congratulate me on Arik's victory, as if I myself had been the candidate. Deep down, they knew that only a very few had believed Arik would reach this moment; and since I had been among those few, they viewed Arik's success as a kind of personal victory for me. I was happy for him; but most of all for the State of Israel, which had gained a fitting leader for this difficult period.

The following years were stormy, just like Arik's entire life, and he neither rested nor let up. I will try now to reconstruct the period leading up to the stroke he suffered led to the coma he has been in for eighty-three months as of this writing.

In the short period before that terrible event, Arik managed to accomplish a lot and revolutionize many things in the life of the state. I cannot recall a leader who achieved so much in such a brief time. Nevertheless, during this period, it was if everyone was "attempting" to shorten his life: the State Attorney and the police with their investigations; the media and its defamations; the right-wing parties and their demonstrations; politicians and the various plot-hatchers; and, of course, aggressive opponents within the Likud. Arik told me that he was unconcerned about the police investigations, certain as he was of his innocence. He joked that according to the methods of the State Attorney and the police, only a premature baby could serve as Prime Minister in Israel…

Nonetheless, Arik held his ground. He galloped full steam ahead as usual, defining a policy that he thought was best for Israel at that time. He justified his method with his well-known saying: "Things look different from there than they do from here."

In a relatively short term of office, Ariel Sharon managed to remove Arafat from the political map; demolish the terror infrastructure in Judea and Samaria; pursue to the death the terrorist leaders and their agitators; and liquidate Hamas leaders, among them Rantissi and their spiritual head Sheikh Ahmed Yassin, something no one had dared to do previously. He shook up the Mossad, reestablishing it as a serious operational entity; strengthened the alliance with the Americans; evacuated the Gaza Strip in an astounding operation, avoiding both civil war and bloodshed; left the Likud and founded the Kadimah party; and much, much more. All this, until his health deteriorated.

During Arik's visit to New York in May 2005, I hosted a warm reception for him in my new Manhattan home. In his honor, I invited New York City Mayor Michael Bloomberg, legendary former mayor Ed Koch, Executive Vice Chairman of the Conference of Presidents Malcolm Hoenlein, and several leaders of the New York Jewish community. Before the reception began, the American security services spread out throughout my house, checking every corner. They closed off the street and inspected everyone who came and went.

The event took place on Sunday, May 22nd. My friends and I were enormously excited. Apart from those who opposed the Disengagement, many had begun to recognize Ariel Sharon's leadership, and he had already been treated sympathetically by the media during this period.

Dinner was served during the first part of the evening; I made sure the menu included Arik's favorite foods, the nature of which I had learned from meals we had shared in the past. Afterwards, everyone was invited to the fifth floor of my house to hear the guest of honor.

There was a wonderful atmosphere. Although Arik appeared fatigued, he acted normally, spoke with his friends and, as always, peppered his comments with humorous remarks. As I usually did at these functions, I opened the evening and introduced Arik. Turning to him, I said:

"Mr. Prime Minister, have no fear of public opinion. When the boy Mohammed Dura was killed in Gaza – and not by our forces – his photograph was publicized on the front page of *The New York Times* and in media throughout the United States and the world. The story occupied the media for many weeks. But when the Nazis murdered my mother, her picture did not appear in any newspaper. When Jewish blood is spilled, there is no public opinion."

Arik spoke for about fifteen minutes and answered questions briefly. He discussed the problems facing Israel and mentioned the disengagement from Gaza. He pointed out that, in his opinion, the disengagement would make it clear to the world that Israel was interested in true peace. He emphasized the special relationship with the United States and with President George Bush.

In his greetings, Mayor Bloomberg thanked Arik for visiting New York and for his activities on behalf of the State of Israel and the Jewish people. Bloomberg thanked me for my hospitality, stressing my important contribution to the Jewish community in New York.

Arik was in my home that night for approximately two and a half hours. When we said farewell at the door, I thanked him for the visit and wished him success and good health. He entered his car and left. It never occurred to me that this would be his last visit to my house.

Several months later, I saw him lying unconscious at Jerusalem's Hadassah Hospital. No one was permitted to approach him. These were very sad moments for me; I never imagined that the man I so admired would end his life's work in this fashion. Beyond all the titles as military commander and political leader, he was a true friend. I have never stopped missing him and, it seems, I never will.

Chapter 27

In the Tent of Torah

"Open to me the gates of righteousness;
I will enter them, I will give thanks unto the Lord."

Psalms, 118:19

As a result of my meetings with the Lubavitcher Rebbe, I moved closer
to Judaism, and my lifestyle started to change. The truth is that I had not
been all that far from it previously. Sara had kept a strictly kosher home
– her parents were observant and, as related earlier, she was descended
from a rabbinical dynasty. I had made sure to attend synagogue on
holidays and we made *kiddush* every Friday evening.

Many of my Holocaust survivor friends had strayed from
religion. After their horrific experiences, some even doubted the
existence of God. Penetrating questions were asked, and remained
unanswered: How is it possible that great, God-fearing rabbis, who
devoted their lives to the Jewish religion and community, were burned
alive with no one to their rescue? And what sins did tiny infants commit
to deserve having their heads crushed in front of their parents? Where
was God during the Holocaust? Everyone asked, over and over again,
yet no explanations were forthcoming.

To be frank, I also experienced discomfort upon hearing these
complaints. But an inner voice instructed me not to abandon the faith of
our forefathers. After all, throughout our lives we are confronted with
phenomena that defy our understanding, and not everything can be
explained or understood logically. The human brain is not sufficiently
developed to understand each event or act of nature.

If someone had claimed five hundred years ago that a fifty-ton vessel would float in the sky, that person would have been considered crazy, or at least ignorant. Even in contemporary times, no one could have imagined fifty years ago that it would be possible to transmit documents or pictures to the other side of the world at the mere press of a button. The human brain has developed and is now capable of deciphering and understanding phenomena that years ago no one would have believed could transpire. We can assume that the human brain will continue to develop and will, in the future, be able to absorb and understand experiences and events that are today incomprehensible.

Against this background, my support for religious institutions and organizations striving to spread Torah and Jewish heritage slowly intensified. Over the years, I established synagogues and educational institutions throughout the city, and, with the encouragement of Israel's Chief Rabbis, I expanded my assistance to *yeshivot* and charitable causes in Israel.

One of the organizations I have aided in recent years is Rabbi Ephraim Buchwald's National Jewish Outreach Program (NJOP). An important American organization, it works tirelessly to help Jews return to Judaism. In a country where assimilation has reached worrying proportions and threatens our future as a nation, particularly in these modern times, everything must be done to bring this dangerous process to a halt. Rabbi Buchwald's organization has met with great success in doing so.

I first became familiar with NJOP's activities through my friend Aviva Levinson. The daughter of my late lawyer, Harry Levinson, a dear and modest God-fearing man and philanthropist, she introduced me to the founder and spiritual father of the organization, Rabbi Ephraim Buchwald. From the moment I was exposed to the work of the NJOP, I was immediately impressed with it and with the Rabbi's leadership. I decided to devote time and financial resources to help further its mission. I undertook to raise funds and over the years, millions of dollars have been collected. These funds were invested in heritage events held throughout the United States.

Since the NJOP's founding in 1987, it has provided an urgent response to the ever-growing problem of assimilation among our youth, a result of the failure of Jewish education. Through attractive educational programs provided free of charge, this enterprise has succeeded in reaching unaffiliated Jewish youth and offering them meaningful, positive and enjoyable Jewish experiences. Using unique and innovative methods and specially developed marketing tools, the NJOP has managed to deliver a Jewish message these young people have never heard before.

The NJOP offers a variety of free programs, including crash courses in Hebrew language, and interesting heritage projects such as: "Turn Friday Night into Shabbat"; "Shabbat Across America"; "Beginners' Services," and more. The programs are offered in 3,300 locations throughout North America and in twenty-seven countries all over the world, reaching and enriching the lives of over 600,000 Jews. One particularly moving experience, from which I learned the significance of these efforts, took place during my 1990 visit to Tashkent in Uzbekistan (see Chapter 24), accompanied by my life partner Orly Gal. Orly had brought, for our own personal use, the same "Shabbat Kit" which we had frequently distributed on behalf of Rabbi Buchwald's educational programs. The kit contained Shabbat candles, a small bottle of *kiddush* wine, matches and a decorated card bearing the blessing for the candles.

She placed the kit on the dresser in the hotel room in Tashkent while the chambermaid – a woman in her forties who only spoke Bukharian – was cleaning the room. The chambermaid got excited and pointed to the "Shabbat Kit." We thought that she was interested in the wine, but we suddenly heard her say:

"Juden?"

Orly answered her with a question in English:

"Jewish?"

Without a word, the chambermaid covered her eyes with her hands and murmured the blessing. We understood that she was Jewish and was essentially asking if she could have the candles, which she had no opportunity to purchase. Barely able to contain her emotions, Orly gave her the entire kit, along with a tip, and wished her a "Shabbat Shalom."

Impressed with the wide-ranging National Jewish Outreach Program, I continued to support Rabbi Buchwald. The door to my house was always – and still is – open to the needs of the NJOP. At times, I also gave of my organizational experience to help it become more efficient and to strengthen the fund-raising activities critical to its existence. Over the course of my life, I learned that education costs money. Our Sages expressed this nicely in the well-known saying: *"Im Ein Kemach, Ein Torah"* (without flour i.e. bread, there is no Torah). As the People of the Book, we must ensure that our offspring, and indeed all Jewish children, receive a proper Jewish education. In this way, we will protect them from spiritual destruction and guarantee the nation's continued existence.

After my father passed away, I founded the Young Israel of Jamaica Estates synagogue in memory of my parents – Avraham and Rivkah Domb, of blessed memory – and of my father's wife Leah. The synagogue was built in my neighborhood, and I made it a habit of attending. Each time I was there, the images of my parents rose before me. The death of my father had left a hole in my heart that could not be filled. I will always miss his wisdom and life experience and, especially, the humanity and sensitivity with which he was blessed.

My children Ron and Jay decided to preserve their mother's tradition and established Tifereth Yisrael, a Yemenite synagogue located on 76th Street between Amsterdam and Columbus. Services there are conducted according to the generations-old format and style of Yemenite Jewry, including reading the Torah accompanied by Onkelos's translation. My two sons also cover the synagogue's expenses and manage it on a day-to-day basis. They sponsor a proper Kiddush on Shabbat, followed by lunch. The congregation established a project to deliver food to families in need before holidays and special occasions. In the same building, next door to the Yemenite synagogue, is the West Side Institutional Synagogue, with a 1,000 person capacity. Since the building was in such poor condition, I undertook to restore it in coordination with synagogue management, for the benefit of the worshippers.

One of the active synagogues on the West Side of Manhattan is Ohav Sholom, which has a daily *minyan* (prayer quorum). It is located on 84th Street, west of Broadway. I renovated the synagogue in honor and in memory of my father's wife Leah Domb, of blessed memory.

Another synagogue I renovated is The Carlebach Shul on 79th Street. The uplifting services there resonate with the well-known melodies of "The Dancing Rabbi," Rabbi Shlomo Carlebach, of blessed memory.

The Ramath Orah synagogue, located on 110th Street in Manhattan near Columbia University, hosts about four hundred students for *Kabbalat Shabbat* services every Friday evening. This synagogue, too, underwent extensive restoration.

I carried out all these renovations out of a deep belief that Jewish life must be preserved for generations. In this context, an unusual article was published one day in *The New York Times*, entitled: "Hotel Developer Recasts Himself as an Angel for Old Synagogues," detailing all the prayer sites in Manhattan I had rebuilt. Someone viewed this as significant. For me, it is the outcome that is important.

After Sara passed away, we looked for a suitable way to perpetuate her memory. We did not deliberate much. It was clear that it would involve Jewish education, which she had advocated throughout her brief life. After a round of discussions, we decided to establish an educational youth center named after her – The Sara Domb Youth Center. It was set up in Jamaica Estates and run by a professional staff, which runs daily educational activities for Jewish youth.

We celebrated the dedication of the center in an impressive ceremony attended by family members and many guests from Israel and throughout the United States. The Chief Rabbi of Israel, Rabbi Yonah Metzger, also honored us with his presence. He mentioned some of Sara's personal characteristics as a mother, wife and educator. Many letters of greeting were read aloud, including that of Israeli President Shimon Peres. The president emphasized the importance of educating the young generation in the Diaspora and bringing it closer to its Jewish heritage.

Another significant educational project in Sara's memory is the Sara Domb Scholarship Fund, directed by my daughter Michal (Michelle). The fund distributes scholarships for Jewish studies and general education to children in need. Over the years, it has granted hundreds of scholarships valued at thousands of dollars.

One of the causes close to my heart is the Or Yakar yeshivah located in the kabbalistic city of Safed and led by Rabbi Yirmiyahu HaCohen. I learned about the yeshivah from my life partner Orly Gal.

I met Orly in 1999. She looks after me and works to keep my family close. She took it upon herself to promote various welfare and charity projects and has channeled many of my contributions to those in need and to people with incurable diseases in Israel and the United States.

Orly was born in Israel to a large family, served in the air force and became a holistic healer. Her parents, Penina and Nissim Gal, immigrated to Israel from Libya in 1949 and experienced the absorption process in the early days of the state. All members of her family acclimatized and established themselves in the country. When I was told of her family history, I learned that the long arm of the Nazi oppressor had reached Libya. The head of the family, Nissim, was incarcerated in the Jado concentration camp in North Africa, where Libyan Jews were brought before being taken to forced labor. Due to Rommel's defeat by Montgomery's forces and to logistical difficulties, the Nazis succeeded in transporting "only" two groups of people from Jado to the crematoria in Europe. Part of the first group reached its destination, and the second was halted when Rommel was defeated.

In my first visit to Or Yakar in Safed, I was deeply impressed by the personality and leadership of Rabbi Yirmiyahu HaCohen – a

The Beit Midrash in Safed named after Nissim and Penina Gal, z"l

modest, humble rabbi, Torah and Talmud expert and author of the work *Ashqecha MiYayin*. Orly's nephew studied at this yeshivah. The fact that its students work for a living in addition to their studies greatly appealed to me, and I decided to fund the establishment of a welding shop in order to provide the students with a source of employment. When I learned that the yeshivah needed a *beit midrash* (study hall) for its daily activities, I donated the funds for its establishment, commemorating Orly's parents, Penina and Nissim Gal, of blessed memory.

The dedication ceremony was held in full glory at a festive event in the courtyard of the yeshivah facing Mount Meron, Rabbi Shimon bar Yochai's burial place. In attendance were Orly's family members from throughout Israel as well as various city rabbis, the Chief Rabbi of Safed and many other guests. Warm greetings from the honorable Rabbi Ovadiah Yosef were read at the ceremony and were emotionally received.

Through my friendship with Jack Avital, I met well-known rabbis with whom I became friendly over the years. One of them is the honorable Chief Sephardi Rabbi, Rabbi Ovadiah Yosef. I was privileged to visit him and receive his blessing in his home on several occasions. Each meeting with the rabbi was an unforgettable experience. Spending time in his company always imbued me with a sense of holiness.

The walls of Rabbi Ovadiah's house are lined with sacred texts, many authored by him, and it was astounding to see the abundant works of Torah on which he labored so hard. I often ask myself when he had the time to write all these books. It was, without a doubt, the result of his genius. His expertise in *halachah* (religious law) has earned him a reputation as a major *posek* (religious legal decisor) and won him many admirers. The rabbi's exquisitely beautiful and precise handwriting also impressed me tremendously.

Seeing the many books in the rabbi's house reminded me of a passage in the fascinating memoir written by my long-time friend Rabbi Yisrael Meir Lau, *Out of the Depths: The Story of a Child of Buchenwald Who Returned Home At Last,* which tells of a Jewish bookstore in Mea Shearim in Jerusalem frequented by a young Torah scholar named Ovadiah Yosef. The father of a large family, he did not have enough money to purchase books. He would therefore visit this store, read a book from beginning to end, storing its contents in his brain as onto a hard disk. Our sages would certainly apply the words of *Pirkei Avot* (The Ethics of the Fathers), 2:11 to describe him: "A cemented cistern which loses not a drop."

I first met the Sephardi Chief Rabbi, the honorable Rabbi Shlomo Amar, through my friend Jack Avital in Jerusalem. I enjoyed listening to his lectures, relating as they did to all aspects of life. His words were always peppered with passages from sacred texts and quotes from sources which he knew by heart. Conversing with him gave the impression that a biblical concordance was etched into his brain. He cited the exact source of each of his quotes – the name of the book, its chapter and its verse. In his rulings on religious law, the rabbi, in his genius, knew to consider the needs and set of circumstances of the particular occasion. When visiting his home, I always enjoyed his wonderful hospitality and the warmth showered upon me by his wife.

I developed an especially warm friendship with the Ashkenazi Chief Rabbi of Israel and head of Israel's Chief Rabbinical Council, Rabbi Yonah Yechiel Metzger. He has a very impressive personality and was chosen for this esteemed position when he was a mere forty-nine years old. Born in Haifa, he served in the IDF as a tank gunner in the armored corps and fought in the Golan Heights during the Yom Kippur War, taking part in the battles that checked the Syrian army's advance.

Since taking on the position in 2003, he has worked tirelessly to establish contacts with spiritual leaders of other faiths for the purposes of dialogue, outreach and emphasis on common positions. He has participated in various international events and in his remarks has represented Israel and the Jewish people most honorably.

When Rabbi Metzger heard of my contributions to various educational institutions and my synagogue restoration work, a deep friendship, born of mutual respect and appreciation, developed between us. In our conversations, the rabbi showed particular interest in my activities to prevent assimilation among Jewish youth. Every meeting with him enriched me anew spiritually. We also spoke a great deal about his role as Chief Rabbi. He explained that the position is not merely ceremonial, but requires work around the clock, alongside heavy public and *halachic* responsibility.

I have attended many events in which Rabbi Metzger was the guest of honor. His erudite lectures fascinated me and indeed the entire audience. His lectures, delivered in a pleasant and eloquent fashion, never fail to exhibit a profound expertise in Talmud and responsa. He personifies our Sages' saying: "The words of the wise are spoken quietly."

One of my sons accurately expressed my feelings after Rabbi Metzger visited our home. He said: "I felt honored and proud to be in the rabbi's company." Indeed, it was an honor to host this impressive personality. We are all likewise proud that a clergyman of Rabbi Metzger's stature represents the Jewish People.

Chapter 28

Jerusalem – A City Bound Firmly Together

"Ten measures of beauty descended to the world;
nine were taken by Jerusalem,
and one by the rest of the world."

Babylonian Talmud, Kiddushin 49b

I have noted my special relationship with Jerusalem in earlier chapters. The very name "Jerusalem" electrifies and excites my entire being; every time I go up to the city, my heart is filled with feelings of holiness and splendor.

Several years ago, festivities were held marking 3,000 years since King David established Jerusalem as the capital of Israel. One swells with pride at the sight of the developed Holy City. There is no precedent in Jerusalem's history for all that the State of Israel has wrought in the holy city since its liberation and unification.

Ever since my tour of the Old City after the Six Day War with Major-General Uzi Narkiss, I have made sure to visit Jerusalem and the Western Wall during every trip to Israel. I experienced a particularly moving visit to the capital on the day after Arik's election victory in February 2001. As usual, I used the opportunity to pray the *Shaharit* morning service at the Western Wall. I always feel strengthened after praying there. This time, I added a prayer for Arik's success and the prayer for the welfare of the State of Israel.

After the services I had breakfast at the home of Matityahu HaCohen Dan, who is the driving force behind Ateret Cohanim, the organization dedicated to reclaiming buildings and reestablishing a Jewish presence in the Old City. I met Matityahu HaCohen in 1989 at

Ateret Cohanim's annual event in New York. This was the same event that Arik Sharon had asked me to help organize, and to which I recall recruiting many of my New York friends. Arik was the guest of honor and I had succeeded in also involving my friend, New York City Mayor Ed Koch.

In my speech, I applied all my skills to convincing those present to contribute to the organization's important objective. In one of the highlights, I stated clearly in English: *"The Jews have the will to live in the Old City, but not the wallet."* My remarks received enthusiastic applause. At this event, we succeeded in raising more than one million dollars and recruiting many supporters for the idea of settling Jews within the perimeters of the Old City walls. I, too, personally joined that cause.

In my late 1989 visit to Israel right after this event, Arik took me on a tour of the Old City's quarters, where I became aware of the important and holy work of Ateret Cohanim. Matityahu HaCohen Dan and Rabbi Shlomo Aviner also joined the tour, which was accompanied by security guards.

With Mati Dan and Gershon Stav on the roof of Beit HaTzalam in the Old City

During the tour, Matityahu HaCohen (Mati) took us to a building called *Beit HaTzalam* (Photographer's House) in the heart of the Moslem Quarter. The building has a unique location: its roof provides a panoramic view of the whole city in its full glory, with the spectacular scenery of Jerusalem spread out below.

Why was it called *Beit HaTzalam?* Mati explained this in the following story in which I played a role:

During Yitzhak Shamir's tenure as prime minister in the mid-1980s, Michael Dekel, Shamir's adviser on settlements, visited the Moslem Quarter. Mati hastened to find a photographer to record the event. After the visit, he called the photographer and asked for the pictures; but apparently, he had dialed the wrong number and a young Arab man answered: "What do you want?" Not knowing with whom he was speaking, Mati did not hesitate to answer: "Your house in the Old City." The two arranged to meet and to Mati's surprise, the seller of the house showed up with all the deeds of ownership.

But as it turned out, the forces of "coincidence" had brought another building for sale into the organization's hands; and these forces had also brought *me* to the place at the right time, for I had immediately agreed to purchase it. For lack of a better name, *"Beit HaTzalam"* (Photographer's House) had been decided upon.

Several months after we stood on the rooftop, Mati informed me that the sale had been completed. I dedicated the building in honor and memory of my late wife Sara Domb.

Ateret Cohanim's work in the Old City was fraught with difficulties. Various leftist groups and Moslem PLO members threatened anyone who dared to sell property to Jews. False legal claims were often made regarding transactions that had been carried out. As a result, Ateret Cohanim activists made sure to check the legality of every pending sale, assisted by a battery of well-known legal experts who cared deeply about Jerusalem.

Ateret Cohanim's activities in the Old City were a thorn in the

The memorial plaque for Sara Domb z"l in Beit HaTzalam in the Old City

side of terror organizations. Attempts were sometimes made on the lives of residents in the acquired buildings. Families moved into buildings as soon as they were purchased and their children ran around in the courtyards. The Israeli government was compelled to make security arrangements for the new residents, in order to provide safety, freedom of movement and a normal routine. The leftists who in 1993 were entrusted with the government funding of these arrangements thought otherwise, and worked to revoke them.

In my opinion, canceling the security arrangements right then, during the Intifada, was completely irresponsible. It meant abandoning the Jewish residents of the Old City to the hostile population in their midst and endangering their lives. When I learned of this, I urgently phoned my friend Fuad Ben-Eliezer. I pleaded with him to discuss the topic with then Minister of Defense Yitzhak Rabin, and ask him to rescind the evil decree. The conversation resulted in the cancellation of the order and security arrangements were renewed with inter-ministerial funding.

In a letter dated January 1993, Rabbi Shlomo Aviner and Matityahu HaCohen Dan warmly thanked me for my assistance in assuring the safety of 600 Jewish residents within the walls of the Old City.

In a similar occurrence, the residents of *Avnei Hefetz*, a small settlement twenty-five minutes from Kfar Sava, found themselves in an impossible situation in June of that same year. In this case, authorities had refused to fund the installation of a pipe that would bring drinking water into the community. Here, too, I spoke with Fuad and the problem was resolved. In his thank you letter to me, Uri Ariel added a quote from Isaiah (12:3) that made me very happy:

"Joyfully shall you draw water from the fountains of triumph."

Today, this community, which commands a breathtaking view, is home to 270 families and continues to grow at a rapid pace.

These and other incidents proved to me that internal strife is superfluous. With a little goodwill, even difficult problems may be solved.

I became a regular visitor to the Old City over the years, touring newly purchased buildings during each visit and inspecting seeing their renovations up close. I also stayed at Matityahu HaCohen Dan's house during one of the holidays. Whenever I am in Jerusalem, I am filled with inspiration, energy and renewed admiration of the city's beauty, its unique charm and the divine spirit that envelops it – and simultaneously, to some degree, the viewer, too.

During my last visit, I was happy to see that the Ohel Yitzhak synagogue had been restored. I learned that the plot had been purchased in 1867 from the Khalidi family by the local Hungarian community.

Viewing the Jerusalem skyline from Mayor Ehud Olmert's office

The purchase deed was found with the Kadi's legal signature and bore the date 1875. The unique location of the property – a short distance from the site of the Holy Temple, and less than eighty meters from the Temple Mount's Western Wall – imbued it with a spirit of holiness. Construction of Ohel Yitzhak was completed in 1904, and it is no less unique than the Hurva and Tiferet Yisrael synagogues.

At that time, Ohel Yitzhak was part of a 5,000-strong Jewish neighborhood. Although they lived in abject poverty, these Jews were blessed with a rich spiritual life thanks to the ten synagogues in their midst. Under Jordanian rule, the building was looted and destroyed. Matityahu HaCohen succeeded in recruiting my friend Irving Moskowitz and the American Friends of Everest Foundation, and they enabled the reconstruction of the Ohel Yitzhak building.

During one of my visits to Israel, I was invited to be a guest speaker at a Shas party event, which was attended by Rabbi Ovadiah Yosef, Rabbi Aryeh Deri, Prime Minister Binyamin Netanyahu and various government ministers. I did not speak about politics; it was not my place. I spoke of Jerusalem and its unification.

I pointed out that anyone who denies the Jewish people's link to Jerusalem should remember that when Jesus made the long trek from Bethlehem to Jerusalem, he lifted his eyes and saw the Temple Mount and the Holy Temple in front of him. He saw no mosque and certainly no churches adorned with crosses. He heard no muezzin calls. The only sounds in his ears were those of the *shofar* and the music of the *kohanim* (Jewish priests). I added that the words "Jerusalem" and "Zion" appear 821 times in the Book of Books, the Bible. In contrast, there is not even one mention in the Koran. Despite this, the Moslems speak of their "Holy City," al-Quds. On what basis?

Eighty years ago, there were those who wished to send us, the Jews, to Uganda. The Russians shipped us to Siberia, the Germans to Auschwitz.

"Where will we go today?!" I demanded, and summed up as follows: "Israel is our land and there is no other. Everything must be done to make peace between us and our neighbors. But under no circumstances can this be a peace that will lead to loss and ruin."

For me, the Land of Zion and Jerusalem comprise one complete unit. This unity can never be sundered because Zion and Jerusalem are bound together. Forever.

Epilogue
The Chain of the Generations

Arik Sharon's illness dampened my mood considerably. Besides the fact that he was a true friend to me, I also viewed him as a leader who left behind unfinished business. After he suffered his stroke, I visited him in Israel at the beginning of 2006, and returned to New York greatly depressed. I found it difficult to accept the new reality of Arik's existence.

I decided, therefore, to redouble my efforts and carry out, if only in part, the Zionist and political missions that Arik had not succeeded in completing. With this agenda in mind, I embarked upon a personal speaking tour. In my appearances around the United States, I stressed the importance of strengthening the State of Israel, and the necessity of our unity as a people. At every possible opportunity, I spoke of the internal and external dangers threatening us, and of the ceaseless war we must wage against assimilation.

I explained that the "Hitlers" of the twenty-first century are no different from their predecessors –,but the tools at their disposal are much more destructive, and are liable to drive humanity back to the Stone Age. This danger threatens all peoples, not only the Jews. The leaders of the free and enlightened world must wake up quickly and act; they must crush the snake's head before it strikes. This is the simple truth, and there is no other.

And, I added, many hold the State of Israel responsible for the world's ills. An alien landing on Earth would not understand what all the fuss was about. All lay blame on a small, Jewish state whose area is

that of New Jersey and whose breadth is one third the length of Sunset
Boulevard in Los Angeles. Israel does not threaten any country, and
wishes only to live in peace as a Jewish, democratic state. Opposing her
are the Palestinians. All the surveys carried among the Palestinians point
to their desire to destroy Israel. Even the fact that Israel has withdrawn
from territories it liberated, in a war it did not start, has not altered their
mindset in the least.

In retrospect, as I scan the pages of our people's history, I am astounded:
How did a small nation that suffered exile, expulsion, persecution and
attempted genocide in almost every corner of the globe succeed in
surviving, in fulfilling its desires, in establishing a sovereign Hebrew
state in the Land of Israel? As I reflect on this, I recall the idea the
Lubavitcher Rebbe shared with me when we first met, on the chain of
generations.

I had always wondered: What is the marvelous secret of this
eternal chain, linking *"the wondrous thunder of Sinai"* with the *"Song
of Tel Hai"* (to quote "The Vow" by Ze'ev Jabotinsky)? This is an
eternal chain in which the blood of Maccabees is intermingled with
the blood of partisans in the forests of Europe, with the blood of ghetto
fighters, with the blood of resistance fighters, with the blood of those
hung by the British during the Mandate and with the blood of Israel
Defense Forces soldiers. In my prayers, I thank the Almighty for the
privilege of living in the last generation of enslavement and the first of
redemption: a generation swept by winds of change yet nurtured still by
thousands of years of Jewish tradition.

I personally view Jewish education as a key factor in our nation's struggle for survival. I have accordingly established a one-man enterprise in which I invest all my energies in supporting educational institutions and Jewish schools. Jewish education is the best guarantee of Jewish survival and of the continuity of Jewish life, and it is that which will protect us from assimilation.

I have witnessed the fruits of a Jewish, Zionist education in my own family, with my granddaughter Morielle's induction into the Israel Defense Forces.

Beautiful, charming Morielle made the decision to volunteer for IDF service on her own, but her decision was undoubtedly the result of the education she imbibed at home. Israel was always the backdrop of her life at home, with the Hebrew language reigning in the house and spoken by her parents. Her frequent visits to Israel, several times a year, bound her soul to the country. Her Jewish studies, the emphasis on preserving Jewish tradition – these too undoubtedly contributed to her decision to serve in the IDF.

Receiving the news of Morielle's induction into the IDF was one of the happiest moments in my life. To me it was symbolic, and brought me full circle. I, who experienced the terrors of the Holocaust as a boy because our nation lacked the strength to defend itself and foil the evil intent of our oppressors, am now privileged to see my granddaughter join the ranks of the Israel Defense Forces, in our sovereign land.

Thus is another link added to that miraculous, eternal chain connecting our glorious past to our current rebirth. To my mind, the addition of this small link to that chain of generations is another tangible expression of the State of Israel's adamant determination since its inception:

"Never Again!"
Am Yisrael Hai!
The People of Israel Live!

BIBLIOGRAPHY

Bachi Kolodny, Ruth. *I Am Joseph Thy Brother* (Hebrew). Hemed, Modan, 2010.

Dan, Uri. Ariel Sharon: *An Intimate Portrait.* New York: Palgrave Macmillan, 2006.

Eck, Nathan. *The Holocaust of the Jewish People in Europe* (Hebrew). 1975.

Goren, Marta. *Silent Cries from the Black Forest* (Hebrew). 2009

Iwry, Itzchak (editor). *Pultusk Memorial Book* (translation of Pultusk: Sefer Zikaron). Tel Aviv, 1971.

Meirowitz, Aharon (editor). *Scroll of Kornitz* (Hebrew). Israel: Organization of Immigrants from Kornitz in Israel and the United States, 1956.

Padfield, Peter. Himmler – *A Full Scale Biography of One of Hitler's Most Ruthless Executioners.* Mjf Books, 1990.

Raviv, Isaac. *Through the Clearing Smoke* (Hebrew). Tel Aviv: Ze'ev Jabotinsky Center for Jerusalem Heritage, 2009.

From the
Family Album

With President George Bush

With Prime Minister Yitzhak Shamir during his visit to New York

With President Bill Clinton in Washington, D.C.

With Vice President Al Gore and President Bill Clinton in New York

At a private dinner in the Tel Aviv Hilton with Lily and Ariel Sharon. To Sara's right, Lily and my daughter Michelle; to her left, Edit Stav and Efrat Benvenisti

With Vice President Dick Cheney

At the home of the Rishon Lezion, Rabbi Ovadia Yosef, shlita, in Jerusalem

Receiving a blessing from the Kabbalist Rabbi Yitzchak Kadouri, zt"l

With Ariel Sharon and Rudy Giuliani at a gala event in New York

At a meeting with Binyamin Netanyahu in New York

With Israel Consul General Shmuel Sisso, Mayor Giuliani, and Israel Ambassador to the United Nations Dore Gold, at the Salute to Israel Parade

Visiting Mayor Giuliani together with Jerusalem mayor Ehud Olmert and Dov Hikind

With Republican presidential candidate John McCain

With President Clinton and Gregory Luchansky at a White House reception

With Henry Kissinger and Barbara Walters

With Israeli Prime Minister Binyamin Netanyahu

With UN Secretary-General Ban Ki-moon

Meeting New York City Mayor David Dinkins in his office

With Israel Defense Minister Fuad Ben-Eliezer

With Israel Chief Rabbi Yona Metzger and my son Jay, at my home in New York

With Prime Minister Yitzhak Shamir, at his Jerusalem office

With Vice President Al Gore

With Secretary of State Hillary Clinton

A dinner in honor of Prime Minister Ariel Sharon, at my Manhattan home

With Prime Minister Ariel Sharon and New York's mayor, at a reception in my home

Ariel Sharon's last visit in my home. In the photo: Ed Koch, Ulo Barad, Michael Bloomberg and Jack Avital

My children Ron, Jay and Michelle

With my grandchildren Morielle, Tomer, Adam and Sara

My granddaughter Morielle, an Israeli soldier, at her swearing-in ceremony

With my life partner Orly Gal

With my business partner Ulo Barad

With Prime Minister Ehud Olmert

With Orly and my friend Boris Kandow, his wife Nina and his daughter Lena

With Giuliani at a reception in my West Hampton home. In the photo: my life partner Orly and my business partner Ulo Barad

Speaking at a dinner in honor of Prime Minister Yitzhak Shamir. New York

At a private meal in New York with my wife Sara and Binyamin Netanyahu

With Rafael Eitan at a New York event in his honor

At dinner with Ehud Barak

With King Abdullah at his palace in Jordan

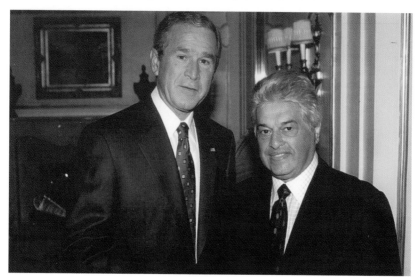

With President George Bush at the White House

With the Rishon Lezion (Chief Rabbi) Rabbi Shlomo Amar

With Mortimer Zuckerman and Rabbi Buchwald at my West Hampton home

With Prime Minister Shimon Peres

With Israel National Soccer Team coaches Shlomo Scharf and Emanuel Sheffer, and my friend Gershon Stav

With the singer Eyal Golan

With Shlomo Scharf and Yitzhak Shum

With Sara at our son Jay's bar mitzvah celebration

Speaking at a family event

My granddaughters Morielle and Sara

Michelle's children, my grandchildren Adam and Sara

With my sister Zipporah

My son Jay and my grandson Tomer

My three children Ron, Jay and Michelle

With my children Ron, Jay and Michelle, and my grandchildren Morielle, Tomer, Adam and Sara

Ravit, Tomer, Morielle and Jay at Morielle's high school graduation

Georgia 2012

I was deeply touched by the surprise organized for me by my friend Boris Kandow after he read my book. Utilizing his social and business contacts, he arranged for me to make an official visit to Kutaisi in April 2012. This emotional trip included a visit to (among other sites): the blown-up bridge, the Kutaisi synagogue, the abandoned military hospital and a meeting with the Georgian president, Mr. Mikheil Saakashvili. (The story concerning the bridge is recounted in Chapter 11.)

Accompanying me on this trip were Boris Kandow; his wife, Nina; their children, Jacob and Lena; and my life partner, Orly Gal.

I am deeply grateful to my friend Boris for organizing this moving and unforgettable journey, and I thank those who assisted him – in particular the mayor of Batumi, Mr. Robert Chkhaidze; district ruler, Mr. Aslan Abashidze; and the president of Georgia, Mr. Mikheil Saakashvili.

Photographs of the trip follow.

In front of the Kutaisi synagogue, built in 1886

Praying with my friend Boris in the Kutaisi synagogue

Photograph of the Kutaisi bridge after it was blown up by the Germans, from city archives

The Kutaisi synagogue in all its glory

In front of the synagogue in Batumi with Orly, Boris, his wife and daughter

In front of the Holy Ark in the synagogue in Batumi, built in 1800, whose renovations I am funding in honor of my friend Boris Kandow's parents

In front of the abandoned military hospital with Boris, his son Jacob and a Tourism Ministry representative

With Orly, Boris and his wife, Nina, on the bridge from which I jumped when it was blown up by the Germans in World War Two

Abandoned military hospital at the entrance to Kutaisi where I had surgery on my hand after I was injured in the explosion on the bridge

On the bridge that was blown up

Documents

(מ)

מכתב פתוח לעמי!

אני הוא בוגר המחזור של המאה ה-20. כשהייתי בן ארבע נידונתי למוות, גזר דיני נגזר בשל היותי יהודי.

לפני כ-55 שנה, הטרגדיה השחורה של האנושות קרתה לעם היהודי. הם רצחו מיליונים מאתנו והעולם שתק, תפקידנו הוא לזכור את הטרגדיה הזו, מתוך רחמים ולא מתוך שנאה, בנדיבות ולא בכעס. המטרה היא לחיות עם האחרים בשלום.

לפני 55 שנה, אחד מקורבנות אושוויץ כתב כי זוהי תקופה בה השמש אינה זורחת על ראשנו אבל היא קיימת, זהו זמן בו השם אינו מגיב לעמו אבל הוא קיים, זהו הזמן בו אנשים הם שטנים אבל לא כולם כאלה.

אני שואל את עצמי מהו טבעו של הזמן הנוכחי בחיינו. לעיתים, בעיקר בלילות, אני חסר מנוחה, בגלל שכחמישים שנה אחרי השואה של העם היהודי, כאן באמריקה, באוניברסיטאות המקומיות, צלבי קרס נחרטים על דלתות חדריהם של סטודנטים יהודים. סטודנטים כותבים עבודות אקדמאיות וטוענים כי השואה היהודית מעולם לא התרחשה. אנשים מפנים את ראשם הלאה מהכאב, אנשים שוכחים. כאשר הם שוכחים, שישה מיליון מתים שוב.

בפסח, כאשר אנו חוגגים את חרות מצרים, נהוג לומר "אנו מודים לאדוני שהוציאנו ממצרים". המורשת התרבותית הזו, האחריות והאחוה הללו, הודעתי מאז ומתמיד בתרבותי. מריתי בן גולדתי. הרי הייתי שם, במצרים. הייתי גם כבשתי המקדש נחרב פעמיים. נאנסתי על ידי היוונים והרומאים לא לקיים את אמונתי הדתית, תאבדתי במצדה תחת להסגיר את עצמי לידיו של הלגיון הרומאי, סולקתי מאדמתי למרחקים לאימפריה הבבלית.

בימי הביניים, הייתי בוטאנא ובצרח ישו. האשמתי בצרח ישו. כמעט בכל מדינה באירופה הולכשו עלי עלילות דם. כן, הייתי גם בניורק שבאנגליה כאשר כל יהודי נכלא והועלה באש. הייתי גם בצרפת כאשר רבני הקהילה נרצחו בשריפה בגלל שאמרו "דינו". סולקתי מביתי בספרד בתקופת האינקוויזיציה. הוכאתי ונאנסתי בדינו כמו אבות אבותי בפוגרומים של מזרח אירופה. ב-1939 הייתי על אוניה מלאה בפליטים שברחו מגרמניה ולא קיבלתי חנינה מהנשיא רוזבלט. האשמתי עם הגזים של הנאצים ביחד עם שישה מליון מבני עמי. ב-1948 חגגתי בירושלים. אחרי 2000 שנה מצאתי לי בית, אבל יום אחד לאחר מכן כבר מצאתי את עצמי נלחם באויבים שהקיפו את גבולות ביתי וקראו להשמידני. הייתי שם גם ב-1973 כשהותקפתי ביום כיפור - היום הקדוש ביותר בשנה לעם היהודי.

מאז הייתי לקורבן מלחמת תשיח אין סופיים ברחבי העולם. הייתי קורבן שגבורמניה כאשר ספורטאים ישראלים נרצחו בזמן המשחקים האולימפיים, הייתי גם בשדה התעופה ברומא, יוון ובישראל, כאשר נוסעים תמימים וחפים מפשע נטבחו. לאורך תקופה של 2000 שנה הצדק לא רווח במחוז חפצי. לאחרונה, כאשר בניתי לי את ביתי ביהודה ושומרון, העולם כולו יצא נגדי, אך כאשר טבחו אותי באושוויץ, לאף אחד לא היה זה איכפת!

עדיין אין לי בית, אני לא בטוח בשום מקום בעולם. זכותי לבית, לחלקת אדמה משלי, נדחתה על ידי אויבי. אנשים שאני אפילו לא מכיר, שונאים אותי. הם טוענים שאני שולט בעולם כולו. אם אני אכן שולט בעולם, הכיצד זאת שאני לא נרדם בלילות?

אם נבחר לעצום את עינינו ולהתנתק ממורשתנו, להתרחק מבית תפילתנו ומאנשים שהם אנו, כיצד נוכל אז להאשים מישהו במורשת שנשאיר אחרינו בדורות הבאים?

עלינו לחיות חיים מעורבים. עלינו להתאחד. ההיסטוריה שלידינו וכדינו יקראו וילמדו תיכבת או על ידי מעורבותנו המלאה, או על ידי התעלמותינו המוחלטת. עלינו לקיים לקיים על עתידינו ולא רק להישרד. הבחירה בידינו.

אני מתפלל מדי יום שיישמרוני בריא בכדי להמשיך לעמול למען בני עמי. אני אוהב את שורותיי של המשורר ג'ון רוסלי, אותן אני רואה כרעיון מוביל בחיי שלי. הוא כותב:

"עשו את כל הטוב שביכולתכם
בכל המקומות האפשריים
בכל הזמנים שלכם
לכל האנשים שביכולתכם
לאורך התקופה הארוכה ביותר שתוכלו"

עם העזרה של אלהים ובשביל בני עמי, אני יודע שכך אעשה.

עם ישראל חי.

שלכם,

סם דוזיאל

October 18, 1989

Mr. Sam Domb
Travel Inn Hotels
515 West 42nd Street
New York, New York 10036

Dear Sam:

Please accept my heartfelt thanks for all the time, effort and energy you devoted to making our dinner with the President such an outstanding success. The funds you raised will go a long way in ensuring an aggressive television campaign.

Your strong commitment and the confidence you have demonstrated on behalf of my candidacy means so much to me. I look forward to seeing you at our Victory Party on November 7th.

Best regards.

Sincerely,

Rudy Giuliani

1270 Avenue of the Americas • Suite 700 • New York, N. Y. 10020 • (212) 262-0075
Paid for by Friends of Giuliani, John H. Gross, Treasurer

AL GORE
U.S. Senate

August 8, 1991

Mr. Sam Domb
c/o Travel Inn Hotel
515 West 42nd St.
New York, NY 10036

Dear Sam:

Congratulations on the tremendous job you did as Grand Marshal of the Salute to Israel Parade in New York City!

I have heard about your many accomplishments. I was pleased to learn that you will be meeting with Jonathan Kessler of the National PAC to discuss the important work in which they are involved. NatPAC has been helpful to literally hundreds of friends of Israel in Congress, and has been particularly helpful to me. It's a very worthy organization, and I hope you will support it to the greatest extent possible.

May you continue your many good works on behalf of the State of Israel. Please let me hear from you if I can be of any assistance.

Sincerely,

Al Gore
US Senate

426 C Street, NE   Washington, D.C. 20002   (202) 543-5930   Fax (202) 543-8508
Paid for by Friends of Al Gore

THE WHITE HOUSE

WASHINGTON

February 27, 1991

Dear Mr. Domb:

I was pleased to learn of your terrific letter in the <u>Algemeiner Journal</u>. Thanks so much for your support for what we and the international coalition are trying to achieve through Operation Desert Storm.

Saddam Hussein has sickened the world by indiscriminate attacks that have terrorized and killed innocent people in neighboring countries. My heart goes out to the brave people of Israel, and I have expressed to Prime Minister Shamir my outrage at Iraq's unconscionable actions. I also have told him how much I appreciate his leadership and Israel's restraint during this difficult time.

The brave members of our Armed Forces and the forces of those nations that have joined the coalition to liberate Kuwait are doing an outstanding job. I know that we will accomplish our goals.

Best wishes.

Sincerely,

George Bush

Mr. Sam Domb
88-69 Sancho Street
Hollyswood, New York 11423

בס"ד

ATERET COHANIM

עטרת כהנים

י"ד בטבת תשנ"ג
7 בינואר 1993
מספרנו: עכ/93/1

לכבוד
מר סם דומב

ידידנו היקר!

ברצוננו להודיע לך על המאמצים שהשקעת ועל הקשרים האישיים שהפעלת כדי
שהתושבים היהודים בעיר העתיקה, הנשים והילדים, יזכו לבטחון ולהגנה על חייהם.

דע לך שכל המציל נפש אחת מישראל, כאילו הציל עולם מלא ומי שמציל 600
נפשות מישראל עושה מעשה גדול, ואנחנו מתפללים שכל המעשים הטובים שאתה עושה
למען ירושלים יטיבו עם נשמת רעייתך בעולמות העליונים ותרבו נחת אתה וכל בני
משפחותן ולא תדעו עוד צער.

בברכה,

הרב שלמה אבינר   מתתיהו הכהן דן

An Open Letter To President Clinton
"PUT US ON THE MAP"

Dear Mr. President,

I believe in the greatness of America and the generosity of its people. The United States is committed first to protecting democratic values before exercising its might. Our commitment to individual freedom was established from the beginning of our national existence. The founding fathers borrowed from the experience of the newly established Israelite nation in symbolically representing our nation's values. Benjamin Franklin wanted to incorporate into the great seal of the new constitution the image of Moses raising his staff dividing the Red Sea. Thomas Jefferson chose as the symbol of the young republic the image of the children of Israel struggling through the wilderness led by a cloud during the day and a pillar of fire at night.

Mr. President, our great nation has a rich history and a rich constitutional heritage. Israel is only 50 years old as a state, but has a history spanning thousands of years. As you know, in the past 50 years Israel won five wars, yet never won peace. The road to peace is still very long and bumpy. But we desperately need peace. However, that peace must be good for the entire nation, not just for a narrow political interest. We don't need a peace where one Jew kills another Jew. We do not need a peace that will lead us to the cemetery. We need a peace that will bring hope and not fear. We need a peace that will unite and not divide. As Napoleon once said, the boundaries of a nation are marked by the graves of its soldiers. With the successful campaign of terror committed by the Palestinians, our cemeteries are becoming crowded.

Mr. President, that small piece of land that G-d gave us thousands of years ago belongs to the Jews of Israel and every Jew wherever he is. In every library of the world you will find that Jerusalem is the capital of Israel in every Jewish heart. Some time ago, the British offered the Jews Uganda, the Russians sent the Jews to Siberia and the Nazis sent them to the gas chambers. Where should we go now? Approximately 50 some years ago, the darkest tragedies of humanity occured to the Jewish people. They killed us by the millions, and the world did not care. We must care for ourselves and we must ensure our survival. Mr. President, before you were born, President Roosevelt taught us the lesson that Jewish survival can only be guaranteed by the Jewish nation as was tragically demonstrated by the expulsion of the liner St. Louis from the shores of America. The passengers died in the gas chambers of Auschwitz. We certainly remember those tragedies and learned a significant lesson. America had no compassion for those passengers simply because they were Jews. Our painful past is a lesson for the future. We cannot change our yesterdays, but we can change our tomorrows.

Mr. President, I ask you today to let the people of Israel choose their own destiny. Peace must be loved in the hearts of the people. Murder and suspicion make the people hate the peace process. Palestinian leaders still act as warlords not as heads of state. Thanks to American support we have been able to win wars and overcome tragedies. And now, we feel sufficiently strong to take measured risks to wage a campaign for peace. But that campaign for peace became a campaign of terror. Our children are dying in the streets of our cities. **In Arab schools, children are not taught the value of love and the necessity of peace between Jews and Arabs. In the suburbs of Jerusalem Arab children are taught from maps where Israel does not exist.**

Mr. President as a long time supporter and friend of yours I ask you to put Israel on the map in the Arab schools, and then maybe peace will have a chance to succeed, not only survive.

AM YISRAEL CHAI

Sam Domb

הרב הראשי לישראל
Chief Rabbi Of Israel

בס"ד, ט"ז טבת, תשס"ח
25 דצמבר, 2007

לכבוד
ידידי היקר
סם דומב
<u>ניו יורק</u>

אין מילים בפי להודות לך מעומק ליבי על הכנסת האורחים הנאה שקיימת עבורי בשהותי הקצרה בניו יורק.

טוב ליבך ואצילות הנפש שאלוקים חנן אותך, ונדיבותך הרבה לכל דבר יהודי מעוררת אצל כל אחד תחושה של קירבה לבבית, ידידות והערכה כלפיך.

דירנו הוא דור שעבר סבל רב אבידות רבות אבדו לעמנו על לא עוול בכפם, כל אשמתם היתה על היותם יהודים.

מאידך זכה דורנו לתקומת מדינת ישראל, וזכינו אנו שאתה פליט שואה, הצלחת לשקם עצמך בעשר אצבעותיך והקמת משפחה לתפארת יחד עם רעייתך האהובה שרה ע"ה.

סם ידידי! אני גאה בכל עת להזכירך בפורומים שונים בארץ ובערבי ארה"ב, ובכל עת שמח ליבי להיווכח עד כמה יצרת לעצמך שם טוב ומכובד. שכן אמר כבר החכם מכל אדם "טוב שם משמן טוב" שמן טוב הכוונה לבושם ריחני שהשפעתו מוגבלת למרחק מצומצם, כי רק מי שמתקרב אל הבושם נהנה מריחו. אך שמו הטוב של האדם, הולך ומתפרסם מסוף העולם ועד סופו, לפיכך קבע שלמה המלך כי "טוב שם משמן טוב", ואכן שמך הטוב מתפרסם בכל מקום בגלל הלב הטוב שבקרבך.

ברכותי, שתזכה אי"ה לרוב נחת מכל יוצאי חלציך, ושנפגש יחדיו במהרה בשמחותיהם מתוך בריאות איתנה, אורך ימים ושנים טובות ונעימות אמן כן יהי רצון!

הכותב וחותם באהבה בהערכה ובהוקרה רבה,

יונה מצגר
הרב הראשי לישראל

בית יהב, ירמיהו 80, ירושלים, ת.ד 7525, מיקוד 91360, טל': 02 - 5313191, פקס: 02 - 5377872
Beit Yahav, 80 Yirmiyahu St., Jerusalem P.O.B. 7525, Tel: 02-5313191, Fax: 02-5377872

CHARLES E. SCHUMER
10TH DISTRICT, NEW YORK

WASHINGTON OFFICE
2412 RAYBURN HOUSE OFFICE BUILDING
WASHINGTON, DC 20515
(202) 225-6616
TELEFAX (202) 225-4183

BROOKLYN OFFICE:
1628 KINGS HIGHWAY
BROOKLYN, NY 11229
(718) 965-5400
TELEFAX (718) 998-8256

Congress of the United States
House of Representatives
Washington, DC 20515

September 17, 1991

COMMITTEES:

JUDICIARY
CHAIRMAN
SUBCOMMITTEE ON
CRIME AND CRIMINAL JUSTIC

BANKING, FINANCE
AND URBAN AFFAIRS

INTERIOR AND
INSULAR AFFAIRS

NEW YORK STATE
DEMOCRATIC DELEGATION
TREASURER

WHIP-AT-LARGE

Mr. Sam Domb
515 West 42nd St.
New York, New York 10036

Dear Mr. Domb:

Thank you for contacting my office about the riots in Crown Heights.

I share your deep concern about the blatant displays of anti-Semitism and hatred, and the complete breakdown in the rule of law, that shook our borough and continues to resonate. The many tragedies of this incident will pain us for years to come. Saddest of all is the murder of Yankel Rosenbaum, an Australian Jew who stumbled into the height of the rioting and racial violence. We must never forget these losses.

Furthermore, I hope that the police and its leaders will never forget the important lessons of these tragic days. The police ought to have spared nothing in restoring law and order to the streets of Crown Heights immediately, rather than permitting the rioting to spiral out of control.

I will continue to urge the police to devote extra resources to keeping peace in Crown Heights and in all of Brooklyn, and that crimes motivated by racism and anti-Semitism be swiftly punished.

Thank you again for informing me of your concern. If I can be of further assistance on this or any other matter, please let me know.

Sincerely,

CHARLES SCHUMER
MEMBER OF CONGRESS

CES/ja

JOSEPH I. LIEBERMAN
CONNECTICUT

COMMITTEES:
ENVIRONMENT AND PUBLIC WORKS
GOVERNMENTAL AFFAIRS
SMALL BUSINESS

United States Senate
WASHINGTON, DC 20510

SENATE OFFICE BUILDING
WASHINGTON, DC 20510
(202) 224-4041

STATE OFFICE:
One Commercial Plaza
21st Floor
HARTFORD, CT 06103
203-240-3566
TOLL FREE: 1-800-225-5605

January 30, 1991

Mr. Sam Domb
Main Office
4 West 31st Street
New York, NY 10001

Dear Sam:

What a wonderful open letter you wrote to Secretary of State Baker. Your willingness to show such leadership is truly inspiring to us all.

These are difficult days for both the United States and our great ally, Israel. I pray for peace, as you do, but a peace that will ensure the total destruction of Saddam's ability to wage war and conduct terror throughout the Middle East.

There is much to do, but our course is clear.

Sincerely,

Joseph I. Lieberman

JIL:ml/vh
Enclosure

THE CROWN HEIGHTS
EMERGENCY FUND

January 7, 1992

Mr. Sam Domb
86-69 Sanchow St.,
Holliswood, NY 11423

Dear Sam:

On behalf of our board and the entire Crown Heights community, we would like to convey our deepest feelings of appreciation to you.

Your efforts at being in the forefront on issues facing all Jews has set an example that serves as a role model for us all. The expediency and devotion that you displayed during the crisis in Crown Heights cannot be amply described in words.

May the Almighty continue to give you the strength and wisdom which you have demonstratively used as a true leader in Jewish issues. The insight and feeling that you display is of one who is truly dedicated to his people.

On behalf of the Committee,

S.Drimmer

THE CITY OF NEW YORK
OFFICE OF THE MAYOR
NEW YORK, N.Y. 10007

May 22, 1991

Mr. Sam Domb
c/o Travel Inn
515 West 42nd Street
New York, New York 10036

Dear Sam:

I regret that pressing municipal business kept me from spending more time at City Hall on May 16th with you and members of your committee for the Salute to Israel Parade. I am sure you can appreciate the many unexpected events that alter my schedule at the last minute.

I am grateful for the support you have expressed in the last several months, especially following my trip to Israel. Rabbi Marc Schneier was most thoughtful to personally introduce us. I assure you that my commitment to Israel and a united Jerusalem will always remain firm and that I echo your parade theme - "For Zion's sake I will not be silent". I look forward to personally thanking you and your colleagues at the pre-parade breakfast on June 2nd and to leading all New Yorkers up Fifth Avenue as we show our solidarity with Israel in the grandest parade ever.

Sincerely,

David N. Dinkins
MAYOR

PERMANENT MISSION OF THE
H. K. OF JORDAN TO THE UNITED NATIONS
866 UNITED NATIONS PLAZA • SUITE 552
NEW YORK, N.Y. 10017

البعثة الدائمة للمملكة الأردنية الهاشمية
لدى الامم المتحدة
نيويورك

J/8/3827

25 October 1995

Mr. Sam Domb
Travel Inn
515 W 42nd Street
New York, NY 10036

Dear Mr. Domb,

I refer to my telephone conversation with you this morning and wish to confirm the invitation to Jordan which I had the honour to extend to you, upon the instructions of His Majesty King Hussein, as His Majesty's guest.

I am sending you herewith my calling card, hoping that I may hear from you very soon so we may coordinate the timing of your visit and make the necessary arrangements in this regard.

With my very best wishes and warmest regards.

Sincerely,

Hasan Abu-Nimah
Ambassador
Permanent Representative

cc: H.E. Mr. Ayman Majali
Chief of Royal Protocol

ראש הממשלה
PRIME MINISTER

April 7, 1993
Q.PM.020

Dear Sam,

This year's "Salute to Israel Parade" celebrates the forty-fifth anniversary of the establishment of the State of Israel. It was a year of change, a year of reborn faith and hope, a year of struggle against blind terrorism, a year of peace making.

Indeed, we should be proud of ourselves, and of our achievements. Never has the State of Israel met so many challenges in such a short period of time; we have changed our national priorities, we have devoted ourselves to the absorption of almost half a million Jews from the former Soviet Union, who came to Israel in the past years, thousands of Jews rescued from Ethiopia and from other places in the world. We are on a new path of economic growth, and the creation of jobs for hundreds of thousands of young Israelis and new immigrants.

On the other hand, we have not forgotten our humanitarian message: We have contributed our share in Yugoslavia, Somalia and other stricken areas in the world, and we have maintained our high moral standards in our daily struggle against fanaticism, terrorism and intolerance.

The parade symbolizes the deep bond which exists between Israel and the Jewish community of the diaspora. It is this bond that unites us as a people.

As we enter a new era, we take pride in our past achievements and strive toward a better tomorrow. The continued ingathering of our brethren and the prospects for peace present us with opportunities that could only have been dreamed of in the past. With God's help, let us all join in ushering in a period of hope, prosperity and peace.

Best wishes,

Y. Rabin
Yitzhak Rabin

Mr. Sam Domb
Executive Director
Salute to Israel Parade
515 West 42nd Street
New York, NY. 10036

American Zionist Youth Foundation
מצעד הברכות לישראל
SALUTE TO ISRAEL PARADE
SUNDAY, MAY 9, 1993   12:00 NOON   RAIN OR SHINE
FIFTH AVENUE — 57th to 79th STREETS, NEW YORK CITY
OFFICE: 110 EAST 59th STREET, NEW YORK, N.Y. 10022 — TEL: (212) 339-6918
FAX: (212) 755-4781

May 11, 1993

Mr. Sam Domb
230 Central Park South
New York, New York

Dear Sam:

Words are not adequate to express the admiration and gratitude I feel towards you for your courage in holding fast as "Captain of the Ship" and steering us on the right course, not only in calm waters but also through the turbulence which we experienced this year.

I personally feel honored for the opportunity you afforded me in working with you. You are, without question, the most inspiring and committed person I have had the privilege to work with. In helping to overcome objective hardships, you have made my work an actual pleasure. Without your continued inspiration, this project could not survive.

You indeed deserve the biggest yashar ko'ach – and also some vacation – after which I hope we could discuss our plans for next year.

With best wishes,

Ruth Kastner

THE PRESIDENT

Jerusalem, 28th November, 2007

Mr. Sam Domb
515 W. 42 Street
New York, N.Y.10036
U.S.A.

Dear Mr. Domb,

I wish to thank you for your kind invitation to the Gala Opening and Chanukat Habait of the Sara Domb Youth Center.

A youth center where the future generation can gather in order to maintain their identity and become imbued with the values of our tradition and heritage is indeed a very appropriate and worthy memorial.

I regret that my very busy schedule and numerous commitments prevent me from participating in this significant event and I send you and your family my warmest wishes and congratulations.

Yours sincerely,

Shimon Peres

MINISTER OF INDUSTRY & TRADE

March 2nd, 1989.

Jerusalem. _____

No. _____

Sam Domb

515 W42 Street

New York

Dear Sam,

Shalom U'vracha!

 I want to share with you my feelings of deep respect and
appreciation for all you are doing in helping to reclaim and
rebuild Jerusalem, within the Walled City, especially during
these difficult times when our enemies feast their eyes on East
Jerusalem.

 I encourage you to continue to make every effort you can to
redeem every room and every house, within the old city and
without - a mission which Ateret Cohanim has undertaken to
accomplish with utmost devotion and commitment.

פה אי ותודאבן

Best Regards,

Ariel Sharon